Toast to Omaha
A COOKBOOK

PRESENTED BY THE
Junior League of Omaha

The Blackstone Hotel

The Junior League of Omaha is an organization of women committed to promoting voluntarism, developing the potential of women and improving communities through the effective action and leadership of trained volunteers. Its purpose is exclusively educational and charitable. All proceeds from this cookbook will support The Junior League of Omaha's community outreach activities.

All Rights Reserved
©2006 by The Junior League of Omaha

No part of this book may be reproduced, stored in a retrieval system, or transmitted in any form or by any means, electronic, mechanical, photocopying, recording or otherwise without prior consent from The Junior League of Omaha.

First Edition
ISBN 0-9788429-0-1

Printed in the United States of America by Quebecor Books

To order additional books, contact The Junior League of Omaha Attn: Cookbook
608 North 108th Court • Omaha, NE 68154-1761 • (402) 493-8818
www.juniorleagueomaha.org

TABLE OF CONTENTS

APPETIZERS AND BEVERAGES 7

SOUPS AND SALADS 45

VEGETABLES AND SIDE DISHES 81

BRUNCH 99

ENTREES 115

BREADS AND ROLLS 177

DESSERTS 185

COOKIES AND CANDY 207

LOCAL RESOURCE GUIDE 223

MENU SUGGESTIONS 224

STOCKED PANTRY 226

ACKNOWLEDGEMENTS 228

INDEX 230

An **!O!!** denotes an original Omaha recipe.

Cookbook Committee

Chair
Kate Grabill

Vice Chair
Angie Schendt

Jessica Covi

Caitlin Davis

Carol Keller

Pam Krecek

Julie Linquata

Jackie Lund

Barbara Mueksch

Brandi Popovich

Historian
Mary Johnson

Professional Credits

Design
Paula Presents!

Images
Burnice Fiedler Collection

Douglas County Historical Society

Durham Western Heritage Museum

Lou Marcuzzo

Omaha World-Herald

Printing
Quebecor Books

Production
Kristine Gerber
Omaha Books

The Empress Garden Restaurant, 1514 Douglas Street, in 1921. - *From the Burnice Fiedler collection*

OMAHANS LOVE FOOD. From the Reuben sandwich to the Swanson TV dinner to Omaha Steaks, it all started right here. Whether it's sitting down for a family dinner or savoring a delicious meal at one of our legendary restaurants, food is the center of our lives.

To celebrate this rich culinary heritage, The Junior League of Omaha presents *Toast to Omaha*, a cookbook of tried-and-true recipes from the city's best professional and at-home chefs. We pay homage to Omaha's history of iconic restaurants in the section dividers, where rare glimpses into the past are shared through old menus, photographs and personal memories.

Much like the city and its people, this cookbook's recipes are colorful, flavorful and delightful. It's not about being pretentious - it's about great-tasting food with substance. Fresh ingredients are emphasized, especially those grown by local farmers. Agriculture is a mainstay of Nebraska's economy, and there's no better way to support local growers than to give the fruits of their labor center stage on the dinner table.

Many traditional recipes were updated for current tastes and many classics were given a contemporary twist. Tasters sampled each recipe and judged it on taste, uniqueness and ease in preparation. Only the best are represented here.

Try any of these recipes and you'll soon discover Nebraska's Great Plains are anything but.

Calumet Restaurant Annex, 1411 to 1413 Douglas Street, in 1912 - *From the Burnice Fiedler collection*

Testing Committee

Pam Beardslee

Lesley Brandt

Courtney Dunbar

Judy Gilliard

Gail Graeve

Li Gwatkin

Victoria Halgren

Debbie Hart

Jeanie Jones

Tracy Kempkes

Erin Murnan

Karen Nelsen

Christine Nikunen

Sherri Olson

Lisa Owen

Lisa Russell

Deb Schmadeke

The Junior League
of Omaha Presidents

2005-2006
Karen Nelsen

2006-2007
Christine Nikunen

2007-2008
Lisa Russell

The Junior League of Omaha has been instrumental in developing core community-based organizations and agencies including:

- *Douglas County Immunization Task Force*
- *Emmy Gifford Children's Theatre (now The Rose Theater)*
- *Every Woman Matters*
- *Fontenelle Forest Guild*
- *Friends of the Omaha Public Library*
- *General Crook House*
- *Girls Incorporated of Omaha*
- *Joslyn Art Museum Guild*
- *Nebraska Food Bank Network*
- *Nebraska Special Olympics*
- *Omaha Community Foundation*
- *Omaha Symphony Guild*
- *Race for the Cure (now the Nebraska Race for the Cure)*
- *Parent Assistance Line*
- *Women's Shelter*

JUNIOR LEAGUE OF OMAHA

JUNIOR LEAGUE HISTORY

The Junior League of Omaha was founded in 1919 by Harriet Smith Whiting, Rachel Kincade Gallagher and Elizabeth Davis, and was the 26th League created in the United States. The Junior League has been the driving force behind the kinds of initiatives and institutions that make our community a healthier, more vibrant place to live.

The Junior League of Omaha has been the force behind creating and sustaining organizations that address the challenges of women and children, health, education, domestic violence, mental health and physical disabilities.

The very first activities of the Junior League of Omaha were to provide volunteers for the Visiting Nurses Association, the University of Nebraska Hospital dispensary, the Salvation Army, and other charitable organizations. The League also adopted the "Day Nursery" from the Women's Service League, which operated for more than twenty years before being turned over to the Community Chest. The League was instrumental with establishing support for the arts by sponsoring stage productions and fundraising for the Children's Theater and annually produced a play with League members as the cast.

Junior League members know their community well and know how to get things done. They pragmatically assess problems and solutions, motivate volunteers, and create new partnerships in the public and private sectors. Since The Junior League of Omaha's inception in 1919, members have donated **over $1.9 million dollars and more than 1.4 million volunteer hours** to our community.

APPETIZERS and BEVERAGES

Omaha Athletic Club
1714 Douglas Street

The Omaha Athletic Club originated in 1915 when a group of men, including George Brandeis, met to consider a downtown club and social center. The showpiece building at 1714 Douglas Street opened December 14, 1918, in time for the Christmas season. Chef Rinaldo "Reno" Sibilia, a 23-year-old native of Ticino, Italy, was hired and for 49 years he created well-loved international dishes for the 2,000 members and their guests. The turkey au gratin was a member favorite. The Club was forced to close in 1970 due to declining membership.

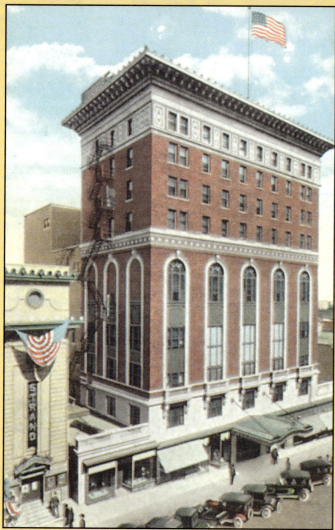

Omaha Athletic Club in 1925

The Omaha Athletic Club bandstand's in 1944. - *From the Bostwick-Frohardt Collection owned by KMTV and on permanent loan to the Durham Western Heritage Museum, Omaha, Nebraska*

"We prided ourselves on making any dish a man wanted... to members this was more like home."
- *Former Omaha Athletic Club chef Rinaldo Sibilia in a 1970 World-Herald article announcing the closing of the Omaha Athletic Club.*

THE COLONY CLUB
19th and Farnam Streets

The Colony Club was a night club and restaurant at 19th and Farnam Streets started by Art Smith. Smith sold the club to Harold "Skee" Fisher and Patrick J. Foley. In 1961, the owners hired Charles Start, a well-known Kansas City designer and decorator, to update the club. The result was the Redhead Lounge with red velvet throughout. The opening brought Joan Crawford to Omaha to add her signature to a wall in the restaurant with celebrity caricatures. The club was destroyed by a fire October 13, 1963. Foley went on to own the Holiday Lounge. - *From the Joe Villella menu collection at the Douglas County Historical Society.*

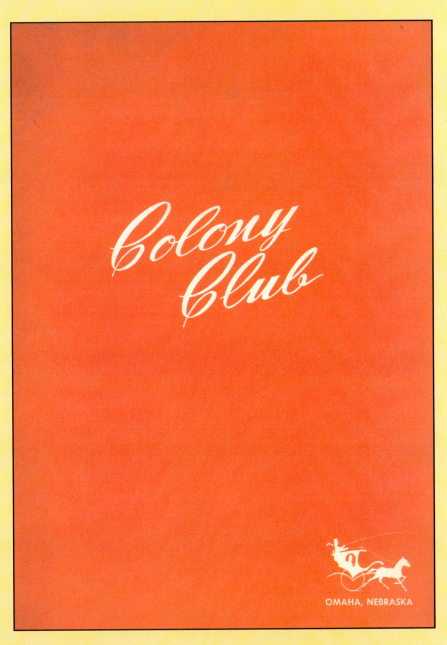

Eggplant Caponata
Serves 6 - 8

1/3 cup olive oil
3 cups eggplant, peeled and cubed
1/3 cup green pepper, chopped
1 onion, chopped
3/4 cup mushrooms, sliced
2 cloves garlic, minced
1/2 cup stuffed green olives, sliced
1/2 teaspoon oregano

1/2 teaspoon basil
1/2 teaspoon thyme
1 1/2 teaspoons sugar
1/2 cup water
1 (6 oz) can tomato paste
2 Tablespoons red wine vinegar
salt and freshly ground black pepper

In a large skillet, heat oil over medium heat. Sauté eggplant, green pepper, onion, mushrooms and garlic, covered, for 10 minutes. Add remaining ingredients and mix well. Season with salt and pepper to taste. Simmer covered until eggplant is tender, about 40 minutes, stirring occasionally. Add water to thin if necessary. Chill and serve with crackers or Melba toast.

This may be made ahead and kept in the refrigerator for several days. Add some feta cheese for flavor, too.

Fernando's Pico de Gallo
Serves 4 - 6

4 - 5 medium to large tomatoes, cored
   and diced
3 green onions, sliced
1 teaspoon fresh cilantro, finely chopped

1 small jalapeño pepper, finely diced
pinch of garlic salt
juice of 1/4 fresh lemon

Combine all ingredients and chill for 2 hours. Serve with tortilla chips or use as a condiment. ¡O!

Black Bean and Corn Salsa
Serves 8

1 (15 oz) can black beans, drained and rinsed
1 (16 oz) bag frozen corn, thawed
1/2 cup cilantro leaves, chopped
1 cup sweet red pepper, finely chopped
3/4 cup green pepper, finely chopped
1/2 cup red onion, chopped
1/2 cup fresh lime juice
1/4 cup vegetable oil
1 1/2 Tablespoons ground cumin
1/2 teaspoon salt
1/8 teaspoon freshly ground black pepper
1/4 teaspoon garlic powder

In a large bowl, combine beans, corn, cilantro, red pepper, green pepper and red onion. Combine the lime juice, oil, cumin, salt, pepper and garlic; pour over corn and bean mixture and toss gently to coat. Cover and chill at least 2 hours or up to overnight. Serve with tortilla chips.

Roasted Red Pepper Dip
Serves 8

1 bunch green onions, sliced
1 (14 oz) jar roasted red peppers or 2 whole red peppers, roasted and skinned
1 Tablespoon fresh lemon juice
1 cup of whipped cream cheese
1/4 teaspoon garlic powder
salt and freshly ground black pepper to taste

In a food processor, chop onions. Add peppers, lemon juice, cream cheese and seasonings and puree mixture. Refrigerate. Serve with toasted French bread, crackers or broccoli florets.

The site of Le Café de Paris at 1228 South 6th Street was initially The Italian Gardens owned by Josephine Marcuzzo. Downtown Omaha executives would come for their great steaks and the city's best spaghetti with meatballs. Their stuffed artichokes and cannoli desserts were also a huge hit.

Le Café de Paris opened in 1970. Since the inception of Distinguished Restaurants of North America in 1993, Le Café de Paris has been recognized with this honor. As the name suggests, Café De Paris is an exceptional French bistro with a menu that does not stray from the classics. Knowledgeable staff go to great lengths to make guest's dining experience one to remember. Dining is European style where a meal is prepared with grace and wines compliment the palate. The dining experience is an adventure, taking 2 - 3 hours. If you want impeccable food, the best wines, and to be pampered, this place is the place to go. *- From the Joe Villella menu collection at the Douglas County Historical Society.*

Stokes Roasted Tomato Salsa
Serves 12

21 roma tomatoes, halved
3 chipotle chiles, dried

1 teaspoon garlic, minced
2 Tablespoons kosher salt

Preheat broiler. Place tomatoes in a roasting pan and roast under the broiler until dark brown. At this point, turn the tomatoes to uniformly roast them on all sides, and when finished, remove from oven to cool to room temperature. Grind chipotles in a spice grinder or coffee grinder used for this purpose, and grind to a fine powder. Set aside. In batches, pulse tomatoes. Place tomatoes in a mixing bowl, mixing in seasonings to taste.

"The key to a successful salsa such as this one lies in the procedures and the final seasoning. Taste as you mix the salsa, and it is done when you agree it is awesome!" - Executive Chef John Ursick

Snappy Kickin' Guacamole
Serves 10 - 12

4 ripe Haas avacados
8 dashes hot sauce
1 1/2 Tablespoons lemon juice
1 1/2 Tablespoons lime juice
1/2 cup red onion or shallot, diced
2 teaspoons garlic, minced
1 teaspoon kosher salt

1 teaspoon ground cumin
1 teaspoon freshly ground black pepper
2 Tablespoons diced green chilies
1 tomato, seeded and diced
1 teaspoon fajita or taco or tex-mex
    seasoning blend
2 Tablespoons cilantro leaves, chopped

Scoop flesh out of avocado halves into large bowl. Season with remaining ingredients. Using hands, fork or a pastry mixer, combine all ingredients. Season with salt and freshly ground pepper to taste. Refrigerate for a couple of hours.

Wonderful as a dip or a condiment!

Avocado Mango Salsa
Serves 12

1 1/4 cups avocado, peeled and chopped
1 cup mango, peeled and chopped
4 teaspoons lime juice
1 Tablespoon cilantro leaves, finely chopped
1/8 teaspoon kosher salt

In a medium bowl, combine avocado, mango, lime juice, cilantro and salt. Toss gently. Let stand 10 minutes. Serve with tortilla chips.

Italian Marinated Cheese
Serves 4

8 ounces cheddar cheese, cut into 1/2-inch cubes
8 ounces cream cheese, cut into 1/2-inch cubes
1/2 cup olive oil
1/2 cup red wine vinegar
2 ounces pimentos, drained
3 Tablespoons basil, chopped
3 Tablespoons parsley, chopped
3 Tablespoons onion, minced
3 cloves garlic, minced
1 teaspoon sugar
1/2 teaspoon salt
1/2 teaspoon freshly ground black pepper

In a bowl, combine cubed cheeses. In a separate bowl, mix oil, vinegar, pimentos, basil, parsley, onion, garlic, sugar, salt and pepper; pour over cheeses. Toss gently to coat. Chill for at least 2 hours or overnight, mixing frequently. Serve with your favorite crackers.

It is easier to cube the cream cheese if it is frozen.

PARBOILING GREEN BEANS

To parboil fresh green beans, snip the ends off, then simmer or steam for 2 - 4 minutes. Immediately plunge the beans in cold water to stop the cooking process. Dry and store in the refrigerator until ready for use.

Creole Dipping Sauce for Crudités
Serves 10 - 12

1/2 cup vegetable oil	3 drops hot sauce
1 garlic clove	1 1/2 teaspoons paprika
1/4 cup green onions, sliced	1 Tablespoon ketchup
1/4 cup celery, chopped	1/4 cup tarragon vinegar
1/2 teaspoon salt	2 Tablespoons horseradish mustard
1/4 teaspoon cayenne pepper	

In a food processor or blender, mix all ingredients on high until the sauce is smooth. Store in the refrigerator for 2 weeks. It is particularly delicious served with parboiled fresh green beans, sugar snap peas and red, yellow and orange bell pepper slices.

Champions Run Hummus
Serves 6 - 8

2 - 3 cups garbanzo beans, drained	salt and freshly ground black pepper
1 garlic clove	3 - 4 parsley sprigs, leaves only
2 Tablespoons lemon juice	1/2 cup olive oil
1/4 cup tahini (sesame seed paste)	

In a food processor, place all ingredients except oil and blend until smooth. While machine is running, slowly add olive oil, adding enough to make the mixture smooth. Chill and serve with pita chips. ¡O!

Parmesan Peppercorn Dip
Serves 12

1 cup plain yogurt
1/2 cup sour cream
1 2/3 cups Parmesan cheese, grated (not
  shredded)
2 Tablespoons black peppercorns,
  cracked
2 green onions, trimmed, thinly sliced,
  both white and green parts

1 Tablespoon Dijon mustard
1/4 cup fresh parsley, cleaned, stems
  removed, chopped
salt to taste
assorted vegetables for dipping

Mix all ingredients to blend, except vegetables. Add more pepper as desired. Chill 3-4 hours before serving. Serve with crudités such as broccoli florets, cauliflower florets, carrot coins, scallion frills (trim ends of of scallion to about 5 inches, then cut finely and place in ice water). Or make a vegetable bouquet.

Caramelized Onion Dip
Serves 6 - 8

4 Tablespoons butter
1/4 cup vegetable oil
3 large Vidalia or sweet onions, sliced
4 cloves garlic, minced
1 Tablespoon Cajun or southwest
  seasoning blend of choice
1 teaspoon kosher salt

1/2 teaspoon freshly ground black pepper
1 teaspoon balsamic vinegar
1 (8 oz) package cream cheese
3/4 cup sour cream
1/4 cup mayonnaise
paprika or cayenne pepper to garnish

In a large skillet, heat butter and oil on medium-high heat. Add onions and sauté for 10 minutes. Reduce the heat to medium low and add garlic and seasonings. Cook, stirring occasionally, for 20 minutes until onions are caramelized. Add vinegar and stir to incorporate. Allow mixture to cool. In a food processor, blend cream cheese, sour cream and mayonnaise. Add mixture to onions and mix well. Adjust seasonings to taste. Garnish with paprika or cayenne. Serve at room temperature with kettle chips, vegetables or baguette slices.

VEGETABLE BOUQUET

Cut off only the green parts of thick green onions and thread a wooden skewer through each. Place sharp end of skewer in a glass vase filled with parsley. Or, use a 1/2 head of cabbage as a base and place in a basket covered with parsley leaves. Cut vegetables into flower shapes and secure to end of skewers to create edible "flowers" such as: a sweet pepper ring with a grape tomato for a center; carrot coins; cauliflower and broccoli florets; radish roses; cucumber slices with cherry tomato slice center; or just be creative and combine your favorites.

Layered Artichoke Pepper Cheese Torte
Serves 8 - 10

2 (8 oz) packages cream cheese, softened
1/4 cup green onion tops, finely sliced
1 (14 oz) can artichoke hearts, drained and finely chopped
1 cup Parmesan cheese, grated

2 cloves garlic, minced
2 Tablespoons olive oil
1 Tablespoon lemon juice
1/2 teaspoon crushed red pepper flakes
3/4 cup roasted red bell peppers, drained and chopped

Blend cream cheese and green onion tops, set aside. In a separate bowl, combine artichoke hearts, Parmesan cheese, garlic, olive oil, lemon juice, pepper flakes and red pepper. Line a 4-cup glass bowl with plastic wrap and spread 1/3 of cream cheese mixture on the bottom. Next, layer with 1/2 of pepper and artichoke mixture. Then add 1/3 of cream cheese mixture on top. Repeat layers with remaining pepper-artichoke mixture and top with remaining cream cheese mixture. Cover and chill at least 2 hours. Invert onto a serving plate and remove plastic wrap. Serve with crackers or bread slices.

Festive Feta Dip
Serves 20

1 cup unsalted butter, softened
3/4 pound feta cheese, crumbled
1 (8 oz) packge cream cheese, softened
2 cloves garlic, chopped
1 shallot, minced

3 Tablespoons dry vermouth, vodka or gin
ground white pepper to taste
1 cup prepared sundried tomato pesto
1/2 cup pine nuts, toasted
3/4 cup prepared basil pesto sauce

In a food processor, combine butter, feta, cream cheese, garlic, shallot, vermouth and white pepper. Process until smooth. Lightly oil a medium dome-shaped mixing bowl and line with plastic wrap. Layer half of the ingredients in the following order: sun dried tomato pesto, pine nuts, basil pesto, and then top with cheese mixture. Repeat layers with remaining ingredients. Chill at least 2 hours. Invert onto a serving plate, remove plastic and serve with crackers.

TOASTING PINE NUTS

Place pine nuts on a baking sheet and toast in a 350 degree oven for about 7 - 10 minutes until they are lightly brown and fragrant.

Six Layer Bombay Cheese Spread
Serves 10

1 (8 oz) package of cream cheese,
   softened
1 cup sharp cheddar cheese, shredded
3/4 teaspoon curry powder
1 (9 oz) jar of Major Grey's Hot Mango
   Chutney

1/3 cup flaked coconut
1/2 cup pecans, toasted and chopped
4 green onions, white parts only, sliced
1/2 cup currants

In a mixing bowl, combine the cream cheese, cheddar and curry. Flatten mixture into a disk on an 11-inch plate or serving dish. Layer the chutney, coconut, pecans, green onions and currants on top. Serve with your favorite crackers.

This may be made ahead and is great the next day.

Peppered Tuna Spread
Serves 10

1 (6 oz) can Albacore tuna, packed in
   water, drained
1 (8 oz) package cream cheese, softened
1/4 teaspoon garlic powder
1/4 teaspoon seasoned salt
1/4 cup green onions, sliced
1/2 jalapeño pepper, minced

1/2 cup celery, diced
1 teaspoon Worcestershire sauce
1/2 cup each red and yellow bell
   peppers, diced (reserving 1/4 cup each
   for garnish)
1/2 cup sour cream
freshly ground black pepper to taste

Place all ingredients in a medium mixing bowl and blend well. Place spread in a serving dish. Garnish with the reserved red and yellow peppers. Serve with assorted crackers.

Jolly Holiday Spread
Serves 10

2 cups pecans, finely chopped
2 cups extra sharp cheddar cheese, finely shredded

1 bunch green onions, chopped
1/2 cup mayonnaise
2 - 3 Tablespoons hot pepper jelly

Mix pecans, cheese, onions and mayonnaise. Press into a serving dish. Spread a thin layer of hot pepper jelly over the top. Serve with wheat crackers.

Colorful Pepper Tomato Salsa
Serves 10

10 roma tomatoes, diced
1 bunch of green onions, sliced
1 green pepper, finely diced
1 hot pepper of choice, minced
1 red pepper, finely diced
1 yellow pepper, finely diced
1 (4 oz) can diced green chiles

2 (4 oz) cans chopped black olives, drained
2 Tablespoons lime juice
1 Tablespoon olive oil
salt and freshly ground black pepper to taste

Combine all ingredients and mix well. Add salt and pepper to taste. Cover and refrigerate overnight. Drain some of the liquid and serve with tortilla chips.

From the Bostwick-Frohardt Collection owned by KMTV and on permanent loan to the Durham Western Heritage Museum, Omaha, Nebraska

The Junior League Day Nursery

During World War 1, women flooded the workforce in order to support not only their families, but their nation, too. The National League of Women's Services had provided child care for working women, but after the war ended, the organization's structure suffered. Day Nurseries were a new idea in the early 1920s. The Junior League of Omaha took over this project in June of 1922.

League members cared for children, ages 18 months to 8 years, and fees were based on a mother's financial hardship. On average, 30 children attended the Day Nursery daily. League members conducted art, sewing, dancing and cooking classes for the children. Provisionals were required to work all service hours at the Nursery! With the need for more room apparent, the JLO purchased a home, at 2240 Landen Court, for $14,000 and spent another $1,000 redecorating the residence.

With additional funds, the League secured a case worker, conducted health screenings, provided house and grounds upkeep and supplied gifts and entertainment for each child. The Day Nursery was a 23-year commitment for the JLO; the longest running project to date.

Smokey Cheese Pear Appetizer

Serves 6

12 large shredded wheat crackers
6 ounces smoked cheese, cut into 12 slices
1 pear, cut into 12 thin slices
2 Tablespoons apricot preserves

Top each cracker with 1 cheese slice, then 1 pear slice then a small dollop of apricot preserves. Serve immediately.

BLT Bites
Serves 14

14 large cherry tomatoes with stems
1/4 teaspoon salt
4 slices bacon, cooked and crumbled
1/4 cup romaine lettuce, shredded
2 Tablespoons green onions, sliced

2 Tablespoons mayonnaise
1/8 teaspoon salt
1/8 teaspoon freshly ground black pepper
2 Tablespoons breadcrumbs

Cut an 1/8-inch slice from the bottom of each tomato with a serrated knife. Gently scoop out pulp and seeds from the cut end with a melon ball cutter or a grapefruit spoon; discard. Sprinkle tomato shells with 1/4 teaspoon of salt and invert on paper towels to drain. In a small bowl, combine bacon, lettuce, green onions, mayonnaise, salt and pepper. Spoon mixture evenly into tomato shells and sprinkle with breadcrumbs.

Marinated Shrimp and Peppers
Serves 8

2/3 cup white wine vinegar
1/4 cup sherry
1 teaspoon thyme
2 teaspoons salt
1 teaspoon sugar
2 teaspoons freshly ground black pepper
2/3 cup olive oil
2 bay leaves

1/2 cup capers, drained
1 red onion, thinly sliced
1 red pepper, sliced in 1/4 inch strips
1 yellow pepper, sliced in 1/4 inch strips
1 orange pepper, sliced in 1/4 inch strips
2 pounds (16-20 per pound), shrimp,
  cooked and peeled

Place all ingredients in a heavy duty freezer bag, except for the shrimp. Shake and refrigerate overnight. Four to five hours before serving, add shrimp and return to the refrigerator. To serve, remove bay leaves from the bag and pour off excess marinade.

Do not add the shrimp to the marinade any earlier than 4 to 5 hours before serving or they will become tough. Green peppers may be substituted.

Vietnamese Shrimp Rolls
Serves 8

1 package spring roll wrappers
1 pound (21 to 25 per pound) shrimp, cooked, peeled and deveined
1 package vermicelli rice noodles, cooked and drained
3 carrots, peeled and shredded (reserve 1/3)
1 bunch cilantro leaves, chopped

SAUCE
1/2 cup rice wine vinegar
1 cup chunky peanut butter
1 Tablespoon sweet red chiles, minced
1 daikon radish, peeled and shredded (white radish)
1/4 cup peanuts, chopped

Assemble each roll separately using the following process: Dip wrapper in warm water to soften. Dry slightly. Place on plate. In the center of the wrapper, place 3 - 4 shrimp. Cover with noodles, sprinkle with carrots and cilantro. Fold wrapper so that the shrimp shows through. Seal with water. Place each completed roll on serving plate, shrimp side up. For the sauce, blend vinegar and peanut butter until smooth. Stir in chiles, reserved carrot and radish. Serve with sauce and garnish with peanuts.

The French Café Shrimp Spring Rolls with Sweet Chile Dipping Sauce
Serves 6

2 cups cabbage, shredded
1/2 cup carrot, shredded
1/4 cup cilantro leaves, chopped
1 teaspoon ginger, grated
2 Tablespoons sesame oil
2 Tablespoons olive oil
juice of one lime
2 Tablespoons honey
2 Tablespoons sesame seeds, toasted
salt and freshly ground black pepper
6 rice paper wrappers
6 (16-20 per pound) cooked shrimp, peeled and cut in half
prepared sweet chile dipping sauce

In a medium mixing bowl, toss cabbage, carrot, cilantro, ginger, oils, lime juice, honey and sesame seeds. Season with salt and pepper, set aside. Working 1 wrapper at a time, place in water to soften. Place wrapper on plate, top with 2 shrimp halves and cover with a small amount of slaw. Roll halfway, fold in sides and finish rolling rest of the way. Repeat with remaining spring rolls. Cut on an angle and serve with remaining slaw and sweet chile dipping sauce. !O!

An Original Ingredient

OMAHA COMMUNITY FOUNDATION

In 1982, The Junior League of Omaha began organizing the Omaha Community Foundation (OCF). At the request of several prominent civic leaders, members on this committee were challenged to secure funds from private sources to build a pool of capital for philanthropic purposes. One month later the Peter Kiewit Foundation contributed $300,000, and the next year, two grants were given to the Children's Crisis Center and Youth Emergency Services. The goal of the OCF was to secure funds for organizations and projects that may be overlooked by traditional philanthropic sources. Today, the OCF is one of 600 community foundations in the United States. Since its inception, the Foundation has distributed over $228 million in grants which support a wide variety of social service programs, the arts and educational projects in Omaha as well as eastern Nebraska.

Salmon Cucumber Toasts
Serves 8

8 ounces cream cheese, softened
1/4 cup lemon juice
1/3 cup chives, chopped
freshly ground black pepper
16 slices thin sandwich bread, toasted

1 English cucumber, sliced into 1/4 inch
   slices
1 pound smoked salmon, divided
fresh dill for garnish

In a small mixing bowl, combine cream cheese, lemon juice, chives and pepper. Spread cheese mixture onto each toast slice and top with a cucumber slice and salmon. Garnish with fresh dill.

Spicy Spinach Spinners
Serves 10

2 (10 oz) packages frozen chopped
   spinach, thawed and squeezed dry
1 cup sour cream
1 (8 oz) package cream cheese, softened
1 cup mayonnaise
2 teaspoons jalapeño pepper, minced
1 Tablespoon garlic, minced
6 green onions, sliced

1/2 cup black olives, chopped
1 (4 oz) can diced green chiles
1/4 teaspoon hot sauce
1 envelope ranch salad dressing mix
1 (8 oz) can water chestnuts, drained
   and chopped
2 teaspoons chili powder
10 large flour tortillas

In a bowl, combine all ingredients except tortillas. Blend well. Spread the spinach mixture evenly on each tortilla. Roll tightly, wrap in plastic and chill at least 1 hour. Cut into bite size pinwheels and serve with salsa.

Classic Crab Fondue

Serves 20

2 (8oz) packages of cream cheese
1 cup sherry
1 cup heavy cream
6 cloves garlic, minced
1 (4 oz) can green chiles, diced

2 Tablespoons Dijon mustard
1/2 teaspoon cayenne pepper
2 cups lump crab meat, picked over and
    flaked

In a sauce pan or double boiler over low heat, melt cream cheese with sherry, adding cream slowly. Add garlic, chiles, mustard and pepper, stirring to blend. Heat for 5 minutes, stirring over low heat for flavors to blend. Fold in crab meat. Serve in a fondue pot or chafing dish.

For dippers, use breads, apples, broccoli or cooked new potato slices.

Buffalo Chicken Dip

Serves 10 - 12

4 boneless, skinless chicken breasts
1 (8 oz) bottle prepared buffalo wing
    sauce
1 (8 oz) package cream cheese, softened

1 cup crumbled blue cheese
1 cup prepared ranch dressing
2 cups cheddar cheese, shredded

Poach chicken breasts and shred. Marinate chicken in wing sauce overnight. Preheat over to 425 degrees. In a 9x13-inch glass pan, layer cream cheese, marinated chicken, blue cheese, ranch dressing and cheddar cheese. Bake for 15 to 20 minutes. Let dish stand a few minutes to let flavors combine before serving. Serve with thick tortilla chips, celery and carrots.

Cha-Cha Cheesy Chicken Enchilada Dip

Serves 10 - 12

1/2 pound chicken, cooked and shredded
1 (4 oz) can diced chiles
1/2 can corn, drained
1/2 cup bell pepper, minced (any color)
2 (8 oz) packages cream cheese,
   softened
1/2 cup sour cream

2/3 cup prepared enchilada sauce
1 1/2 teaspoons hot sauce
1/2 cup colby-jack cheese, shredded
1 Tablespoon lime juice
2 Tablespoons pine nuts

Preheat oven to 350 degrees. In a mixing bowl, combine chicken, chiles, corn and pepper. Set aside. In a food processor, pulse cream cheese, sour cream, enchilada sauce, hot sauce, cheese, and lime juice, until smooth. Fold the cheese mixture into the chicken. Pour into an 8x8-inch baking dish. Top with pine nuts. Bake until browned and bubbling, about 45 minutes. Serve with flour or corn tortilla chips.

SpinArt Dip

Serves 6

1 (13 oz) can artichoke hearts, drained
   and finely chopped
1 (10 oz) package frozen chopped
   spinach, thawed and squeezed dry
1 cup mayonnaise

1 cup Parmesan cheese, grated
2 1/4 cups Monterey Jack cheese,
   shredded and divided
1 Tablespoon Romano cheese, grated
1 Tablespoon pimentos, drained

Preheat oven to 350 degrees. In a bowl, combine artichoke hearts, spinach, mayonnaise, Parmesan cheese, 1 3/4 cups Monterey Jack cheese, Romano cheese and pimentos, stirring until well combined. Transfer artichoke mixture to a 1-quart baking dish and sprinkle with remaining 1/2 cup Monterey Jack cheese. Bake dip until cheese is melted, about 15 minutes. Serve warm with crackers or bread slices.

Dip may be prepared the day ahead and then baked just before serving.

Warm Curried Carrot Dip

Serves 10

2 pounds carrots, peeled
1 (14 1/2 oz) can chicken stock
1/4 teaspoon ground cardamom
2 Tablespoons olive oil
2 cups onion, diced
3 cloves garlic, minced

1 Tablespoon sweet curry powder
1 1/2 teaspoons cumin
1/4 cup cilantro leaves, chopped
1 teaspoon kosher salt
1/2 teaspoon freshly ground black pepper

Cut carrots into 1/2 inch thick slices and place in a saucepan. Cover with water to 1 inch above carrots. Add stock and cardamom and bring to a simmer. Reduce heat and simmer until the carrots are tender, about 20 minutes. Drain, reserving 1 1/2 cups of the liquid. Combine the reserved liquid and carrots and refrigerate overnight. Place carrots and 3/4 cup of the liquid in a food processor and blend until smooth. In a skillet, heat oil over medium-high heat. Add the onions and garlic, sauté about 3 minutes. Add the curry and cumin. Cook until fragrant, about 1 minute. Add the carrot mixture and stir until heated, about 2 minutes. Blend in the cilantro and season with salt and pepper. Serve warm with pita chips.

Brie with Bourbon Walnut Sauce

Serves 6

1/4 cup butter
1 cup dark brown sugar, packed
3/4 cup walnut pieces
1/2 cup pure maple syrup

1/2 teaspoon cinnamon
1/4 cup bourbon whiskey
1 (6 oz) wedge brie cheese, rind
   removed

In a saucepan, melt the butter over medium heat. Stir in brown sugar, walnuts, maple syrup and cinnamon. Bring to a simmer, stirring constantly. Add liquor and simmer 1 - 2 minutes. Place brie on a medium lipped platter and pour warm sauce over cheese. Serve warm with crackers and bread.

PORTABELLO MUSHROOMS

Marinated whole portabellos also make nice vegetarian burgers. Sliced or chopped, they are a great condiment for any meat recipe.

CHIFFONADE

Chiffonade is a French term describing a style of cut. Stack the basil leaves 3 to 4 on top of each other and roll them beginning at the side much like you would a cigar. Roll them as tightly as you can without bruising the leaf. Once rolled, hold tightly and slice them across the "cigar" as finely as you can. They should create nice pinwheels.

Portabello Polynesian

Serves 4

1/2 cup pineapple juice
2 Tablespoons balsamic vinegar
1 Tablespoon fresh ginger, peeled and grated
1 Tablespoon honey
1/2 teaspoon freshly ground black pepper
1/2 teaspoon salt
2 Tablespoons cilantro leaves, chopped
4 large portabello mushrooms, 1-inch slices

In a medium bowl, combine all ingredients, except the mushrooms. Place mushrooms in a baking dish and cover evenly with marinade. Cover and marinate for 1 hour. Grill or sauté in a grill pan, over medium heat, about 5 minutes, turning occasionally.

Tasting Room Bruschetta

Serves 6

10 roma tomatoes, diced
2 teaspoons garlic, minced
1/4 cup red onion, minced
1/4 cup shallot, minced
2 Tablespoons balsamic vinegar
1 teaspoon sugar
8 basil leaves, chiffonade cut
1 teaspoon dried oregano
1/4 cup olive oil
1 1/2 Tablespoons kosher salt
1 teaspoon freshly ground black pepper
1 pinch crushed red pepper flakes
2 baguettes

In a large bowl, combine the tomatoes, garlic, onion, shallot, vinegar, sugar, basil leaves, oregano and olive oil together and taste. Season with salt and peppers. Mixture will hold for 4 - 5 days, but is best served fresh.

"Great variations include blue cheese, pears and walnuts, anchovies and olives, artichokes and goat cheese, or sun dried tomatoes and pine nuts." - Matthew Kellie, The Tasting Room |O!|

Tomato Tapenade Bruschetta

Serves 6

1 cup black olives
2 teaspoons balsamic vinegar
1 teaspoon capers, drained
1 teaspoon olive oil
2 cloves garlic, minced
1 cup red and yellow tomatoes, diced
1/3 cup green onion, sliced

1 Tablespoon olive oil
1 Tablespoon basil, chopped
1/8 teaspoon freshly ground black pepper
1 long baguette
2 Tablespoons olive oil
1/2 cup Parmesan cheese, grated

In a blender or food processor, puree olives, balsamic vinegar, capers, olive oil and garlic. Set aside. Combine the tomatoes, green onion, olive oil, basil and pepper. Gently toss and set aside. Preheat oven to 425 degrees. Slice bread 1/2-inch thick. Brush both sides with olive oil and toast 3 - 4 minutes per side. Spread one side of the bread with olive paste, then top with 2 Tablespoons of tomato mixture and sprinkle with cheese. Return toasts to oven for 2 - 3 additional minutes, until cheese melts. Serve warm.

Tomatillo Triangles

Serves 48

6 tomatillos, peeled and quartered
2 tomatoes, quartered
1 Tablespoon vegetable oil
salt and freshly ground black pepper to taste
12 flour tortillas, cut into quarters (use 6-inch tortillas)
2 Tablespoons diced green chiles
1/2 cup each, mint and cilantro leaves, chopped

2 Tablespoons lime juice
2/3 cup sour cream
1 teaspoon hot sauce
1 teaspoon cumin
1 Tablespoon fajita or southwest seasoning blend, divided
1 pound ground turkey
1 red onion, chopped
4 cups pepper jack cheese, shredded

Preheat oven to 425 degrees. In a roasting pan, toss tomatillos and tomatoes with oil, salt and pepper. Arrange in a single layer. Roast, turning occasionally, for 20 - 25 minutes. Remove from the oven and reduce temperature to 375 degrees. Set the tomato mixture aside, and remove and discard tomato skins when cool. On a greased baking sheet arrange tortillas in a single layer and bake until lightly toasted, 4 or 5 minutes per side. In a food processor, combine tomato mixture, chiles, mint, cilantro, lime juice, sour cream, hot sauce, cumin and half the seasoning blend. Pulse 2 - 3 times until chunky. In a large skillet, sauté turkey and onion in the remaining seasoning. Fold tomatillo mixture into turkey mixture. Spoon onto tortillas and place on a baking sheet. Top with cheese and bake 5 - 6 minutes or until cheese is melted. Garnish with additional cilantro.

HERB BAGUETTES

In a food processor, puree basil stems with a small amount of garlic, crushed red pepper flakes, pinch of salt and 1/4 cup olive oil. Thinly slice the baguettes, lightly brush the bread slices with the herb oil and toast on a hot grill. Top the grilled bread with Tasting Room's Bruschetta and serve.

Roasted Tri-color Pepper Bruschetta
Serves 10

1 each, red, yellow and orange peppers, halved and seeded
1/2 cup red onion, chopped
1/4 cup basil, chopped
2 Tablespoons cilantro leaves, chopped

2 Tablespoons white wine vinegar
1 Tablespoon olive oil
1 1/2 teaspoons sugar
1/4 teaspoon freshly ground black pepper
1 long baguette, cut into 1/2-inch slices

Preheat broiler. On a foil-lined baking sheet, place pepper halves, skin side up, and flatten with hand. Broil 15 minutes until blackened. Place peppers in a zippered plastic bag and seal. Let stand for 12 minutes. Peel cooled peppers and finely chop. In a medium bowl, combine peppers, onion, basil and cilantro. In a small bowl, whisk vinegar, oil, sugar and black pepper. Pour vinegar mixture over bell pepper mixture. Toss gently to coat. Cover and chill for 2 hours. Serve with bread.

Thai-Style Chicken Satay
with Peanut Sauce and Cucumber Relish
Serves 16

8 boneless, skinless, chicken breasts
2 cups plain yogurt
1/2 cup sugar cane or rice wine vinegar
8 cloves garlic, crushed
2 Tablespoons ginger, minced

2 Tablespoons soy sauce
2 Tablespoons Sriracha (Asian chili sauce)
2 Tablespoons honey
1/2 cup peanuts, chopped

Slice chicken into strips, about 4 per breast. In an airtight container, mix yogurt, vinegar, garlic, ginger, soy, Sriracha and honey. Add chicken and toss to coat. Marinate at least 4 hours or overnight in the refrigerator. Soak 32 wooden skewers in water for 30 minutes until ready to use. Drain chicken from marinade and discard marinade. Thread 1 piece of chicken onto each presoaked skewer. Grill or place on a greased baking sheet to broil. Turn skewers over after 3 to 5 minutes when browned. Serve the skewers over a bed of cucumber relish and place peanut sauce in small bowls for each diner. Garnish with peanuts.

PEANUT SAUCE

2 cups chunky peanut butter
2 cans coconut milk
2 limes, juice and zest
2 Tablespoons sugar cane or rice wine vinegar
2 Tablespoons soy sauce
1 Tablespoons Sriracha (Asian chili sauce)

In a saucepan, heat peanut butter, milk and lime juice over low heat, stirring to blend. Add zest, vinegar, soy, and Sriracha. Heat thoroughly.

CUCUMBER RELISH

1 daikon radish, shredded (white radish)
2 carrots, peeled and shredded
1 English cucumber, partially peeled and diced
1/2 cup sugar cane or rice wine vinegar
1 Tablespoon sweet red chiles
2 Tablespoons sugar

In a bowl, mix the radish, carrots and cucumber. In another bowl, whisk together vinegar, chiles and sugar, then pour over the vegetables. Stir to coat. Serve with the Chicken Satay skewers.

Zucchini Oven Crisps
Serves 6

1/2 cup breadcrumbs
1/2 cup Parmesan cheese, grated
1/2 teaspoon seasoned salt
1/4 teaspoon garlic powder
1/2 teaspoon freshly ground black pepper

2 egg whites
2 Tablespoons cornstarch
2 Tablespoons lemon juice
2 large zucchini, sliced into 1/2 inch slices

Preheat oven to 425 degrees. In a deep pie plate, mix breadcrumbs, cheese, salt, garlic and pepper. In a bowl, beat egg whites, cornstarch and lemon juice. Dip zucchini into egg wash, then in cheese mixture, turning to coat. Place on wire rack sprayed with cooking spray and rest for 15 minutes. Place rack on a baking sheet and bake until crisp, about 30 minutes.

Serve with tangy horseradish mustard or a honey mustard sauce.

Sweet and Spicy Chicken Wings
Serves 20

2 Tablespoons sesame oil
3 Tablespoons cilantro leaves, chopped
1 teaspoon ginger, grated
2 Tablespoons garlic, minced and divided
1/2 cup soy sauce
1/2 cup pineapple juice
1 teaspoon crushed red pepper flakes,
    divided
2 Tablespoons green onions, sliced

2 Tablespoons onion, finely chopped
2 1/2 pounds chicken wings
1 cup rice vinegar
3/4 cup sugar
1 Tablespoon chili-garlic sauce
2 Tablespoons mustard
1 teaspoon cornstarch, mixed into 2
    Tablespoons cold water

In a medium bowl, mix the sesame oil, cilantro, ginger, 1 Tablespoon garlic, soy sauce, pineapple juice, 1/2 teaspoon pepper flakes and both onions. Add wings and marinate covered overnight. Preheat oven to 450 degrees. On a large, foil-lined baking sheet, place chicken and bake 30 - 40 minutes, turning as needed. Meanwhile, in a medium saucepan, mix rice vinegar, sugar, chili sauce, 1 Tablespoon garlic, 1/2 teaspoon red pepper flakes and mustard. Heat to a simmer, stirring often, until thickened, about 20 minutes. Thicken with cornstarch mixture if necessary. Transfer chicken to platter and drizzle glaze on to top to serve.

Caramelized Leek and Goat Cheese Crostini

Serves 4

1 baguette, thinly sliced and lightly toasted
1 (4oz) package goat cheese, softened
1 Tablespoon butter
1 cup leeks, separated, rinsed and sliced
   1/4-inch thick, separated and rinsed

1 1/2 teaspoons sugar
salt and freshly ground black pepper to
   taste
thyme for garnish

Spread a thin layer of goat cheese on each baguette. In a skillet, heat butter. Sauté and add leeks, sugar, salt and pepper. Cook over medium heat until caramelized, stirring frequently for 15 to 20 minutes. Top baguettes with caramelized leeks, garnish with thyme and serve immediately.

Asian Chicken Lettuce Wraps
"Larb Gai"

Serves 10 - 12

Another wonderful way to serve this dish is to have lettuce cups stacked up, like chairs. Guests self-serve larb into lettuce cups. Top with peanuts, cilantro and cucumbers.

1 head lettuce
2 Tablespoons rice powder
1/4 cup each cilantro and mint leaves,
   chopped
3 green onions, sliced
1 shallot, sliced
1/2 teaspoon crushed red pepper flakes
1 Tablespoon ginger, grated
1/2 teaspoon cayenne pepper
2 teaspoons chili garlic paste
2 teaspoons sesame oil

1 1/2 pounds boneless, skinless, chicken
   breast, poached and shredded
3 Tablespoons lime juice
2 Tablespoons fish sauce
2 Tablespoons brown sugar

GARNISH
1/3 cup dry roasted peanuts, chopped
cilantro and mint leaves, chopped
cucumber, peeled, sliced thin

Remove 10 - 12 whole leaves from lettuce. In a small bowl, mix rice powder, cilantro, mint, green onions, shallot, red pepper, cayenne, ginger and chili garlic paste. In a skillet, heat sesame oil over medium heat. Add chicken, lime juice, fish sauce and sugar, stir to heat. Remove skillet from heat and mix in mint mixture. Stir to combine. Spoon mixture into center of lettuce leaf. Garnish with peanuts, additional chopped cilantro and sliced cucumber. Fold lettuce around chicken and enjoy!

Rice powder is available in Asian markets (rice flour) or may be made by roasting raw rice in a dry skillet until brown, stirring constantly, then pulverized with mortar and pestle, or ground in a spice mill, clean coffee grinder or pepper mill. Garlic chili paste is also readily available, often in supermarkets.

Manchego Cheese
and Smoked Walnut Stuffed Dates

Serves 4

12 whole dates
2 ounces walnut halves
3 ounces manchego cheese, crumbled

1/4 cup bourbon wood chips, soaked in
    water
1/2 cup balsamic vinegar

Remove the pits of the dates by either slicing down the side lengthwise or carefully using your fingers to open the side of the date and remove the pit. The goal is to keep the natural shape of the date intact. Set them aside. Place the soaked wood chips in a disposable pan and set on the grill. Heat grill to medium, until smoke forms. Lay a piece of foil on the grill and place walnuts on the foil in a single layer. Cover and smoke for about 8 minutes, then remove walnuts and allow to cool. Finely chop the walnuts and combine with the cheese. Stuff about 1/2 an ounce into each date. Press the seam lightly together to seal and arrange on a platter. Drizzle dates with balsamic vinegar. Serve with grapes and assorted cheeses.

Blue Mussels

Serves 4

1 Tablespoon olive oil
1 teaspoon garlic, minced
1 shallot, minced
1 pound blue mussels
1/3 cup Momokawa Pearl sake

1/2 cup heavy cream
1/2 cup ripe tomato, diced
1/4 cup green onion, sliced
1 Tablespoon butter
1 long baguette, sliced and toasted

In a 10-inch skillet, heat olive oil until almost smoking. Quickly sauté garlic and shallot, add mussels and gently cook for 1 to 2 minutes. Deglaze pan with sake and reduce by half. Add cream and reduce until thickened. Add tomato, green onion and butter; swirl pan until butter is incorporated. Discard any mussels that are not fully opened. Serve with toasted baguette or over pasta.

This recipe is served as an appetizer at Blue Sushi Sake Grill but certainly could be served as an entree. If Momokawa Sake isn't available, any sake will work. |O!|

Catering Creations Jalapeño and Shrimp Stuffed Tomatoes

Serves 8 - 10

1/2 cup cream cheese, softened
1/2 cup jalapeño or Monterey Jack
   cheese, shredded
1 cup cooked shrimp, peeled and rough
   chopped
2 Tablespoons breadcrumbs
2 Tablespoons Parmesan cheese, grated
1/2 cup green onions, sliced

2 Tablespoons cilantro leaves, chopped
1 lime, zest and juice
1/4 teaspoon cumin
1/4 teaspoon chili powder
salt and freshly ground black pepper to
   taste
10 roma tomatoes, cut in half lengthwise
   and seeds removed

Preheat oven to 400 degrees. In a medium bowl, place cheeses, shrimp, breadcrumbs, Parmesan cheese, green onions, cilantro, lime zest and juice and seasonings. Mix well with a hand mixer. Taste mixture and season with salt and pepper. Place tomato halves on baking sheet with the sliced side facing up. Lightly season tomatoes with salt and pepper. Fill tomato halves with approximately 2 - 3 Tablespoons of mixture and bake for 10 - 15 minutes. Serve warm. ¡O!¡

Curried Crab Salad Crostini

Serves 15

1 cup mayonnaise
1/2 cup onion, grated
1 cup cheddar cheese, shredded
1/2 teaspoon hot sauce

1/2 teaspoon curry powder
1 cup crab meat, picked over and flaked
2 long bread baguettes, sliced 1/2-inch
   thick

In a medium bowl, combine mayonnaise, onion, cheese, hot sauce, curry and crab meat. This may be made one day in advance and placed in refrigerator. To serve, spread mixture on bread rounds and broil until golden brown. Serve warm.

Mini Eggrolls with Zowie Dipping Sauce

Serves 20

1 1/2 pounds mild ground pork sausage
    or ground pork
2/3 cup Sioux Z Wow Marinade
1 pound bag of coleslaw mix, finely
    shredded
1 60-count package won ton wrappers
1 large egg white, slightly beaten

1 Tablespoon water
vegetable oil for frying

ZOWIE DIPPING SAUCE
1 cup sour cream
1/4 cup grainy mustard
1/2 cup Sioux Z Wow Marinade

In a large skillet, cook sausage over medium-high heat until browned. Add Sioux Z Wow and simmer until thickened, 10 - 15 minutes. Cool completely. In a large bowl, combine sausage and coleslaw and chill overnight. Assemble using directions on the won ton wrappers and seal by brushing with egg mixture. Each egg roll will need about 1 heaping teaspoon of filling. To make sauce, in a bowl whisk together sour cream, mustard, and Sioux Z Wow. Set aside. In a Dutch oven, heat oil about 1 - 2 inches deep, to 350 degrees. Using a slotted spoon, working in batches, fry for about a minute a side. Drain on paper towels. Serve hot or at room temperature with sauce.

Catering Creations Stuffed Mushrooms

Serves 10 - 12

1 pound ground Italian sausage, cooked,
    drained and crumbled
1 pound cream cheese, softened
2 Tablespoons garlic powder
1 Tablespoon onion powder
1 cup Parmesan cheese

1/2 cup breadcrumbs
2 Tablespoons fresh basil, chopped
salt and freshly ground black pepper to
    taste
20 - 35 large mushroom caps

In a medium bowl combine sausage, cream cheese, garlic powder, onion powder, Parmesan, breadcrumbs and basil. Taste mixture and season with salt and pepper. Preheat the oven to 400 degrees. Pull the stems out of mushrooms and fill the caps with 2 - 3 Tablespoons of the mixture. Place on a baking sheet and bake for 20 minutes. Serve warm. !O!

Sioux Z Wow marinade is a unique, sweet, savory, and salty sauce...all at the same time. It may be ordered online or purchased locally at PHG, see resource guide.

Scottish Eggs

Serves 12

1 1/2 pounds ground sausage
2 Tablespoons fresh sage, chopped
1 teaspoon freshly ground black pepper
1/2 teaspoon salt
3 eggs, beaten
2 cups fine breadcrumbs

1/4 cup fresh chives, minced
1/4 cup flour
1 dozen eggs, hard-boiled and peeled
vegetable oil
stone-ground mustard

In a bowl, blend sausage, sage, pepper and salt. Divide the meat mixture into 12 equal parts. Place beaten eggs in a small bowl. Mix breadcrumbs and chives in another bowl. On a lipped-edge plate, place flour. Roll each egg first in flour to coat all sides and then mold the sausage mixture around each egg. Dip each egg in the beaten egg mixture and roll in breadcrumbs to coat. In a large skillet heat about 3 - 4 inches deep of oil to 350 degrees. Place eggs in the oil and brown until the sausage is golden. Remove with a slotted spoon and drain on paper towels placed on a wire rack. Chill until ready to serve. Slice each egg and place on appetizer plates with mustard garnish for each guest.

Crunchy Pork Bites

Serves 15

1 pound ground pork
1/2 teaspoon cinnamon
1/2 teaspoon freshly ground black pepper
    and salt
1/2 cup apples, peeled, cored and
    shredded

1/4 cup breadcrumbs, rye preferred
1/4 cup walnuts, toasted and finely
    chopped
2 Tablespoons water
1/2 cup apple jelly

In a medium bowl, mix pork with cinnamon, pepper and salt. Add apple, breadcrumbs and walnuts. Mix well. Form into 1-inch balls. In a large skillet, brown bites in batches over medium heat. Pour off excess fat and add water. Return all bites to the skillet and continue to cook over low heat for about 15 minutes. Place in a preheated chafing dish and stir in apple jelly to melt. Serve hot with toothpicks.

Smokey Chipotle Meatballs

Serves 20

1 chipotle chile in adobo sauce, chopped
2 shallots, minced
1/2 cup cilantro leaves, chopped
1/3 cup oatmeal
1/4 cup breadcrumbs
1 cup tomato sauce, divided
1 Tablespoon parsley, chopped
1 teaspoon kosher salt
1 teaspoon cumin
1 teaspoon oregano

1 teaspoon basil
1 teaspoon freshly ground black pepper
2 cloves garlic, minced
2 egg whites, lightly beaten
1 Tablespoon liquid smoke
1 1/2 pounds ground turkey
1 Tablespoon mustard
1 Tablespoon brown sugar
1 Tablespoon white wine vinegar

Preheat oven to 350 degrees. In a large bowl, combine chile, shallots, cilantro, oatmeal, breadcrumbs, 1/2 cup tomato sauce, parsley, salt, cumin, oregano, basil, pepper, garlic, egg whites, liquid smoke and turkey. Mix thoroughly. Shape meat mixture into 1-inch meatballs. Place meatballs into a greased 9x13-inch baking dish. Bake for 30 - 40 minutes, turning occasionally. To prepare the baste, combine the remaining 1/2 cup tomato sauce with mustard, brown sugar and vinegar. Pour over meatballs. .

Mini Maytag Blue Cheese Burgers

Serves 8

1 pound ground sirloin
salt and freshly ground black pepper
8 small dinner rolls, sliced in half

olive oil spray
5 ounces Maytag blue cheese, crumbled

Divide sirloin into eight small patties. Season with salt and freshly ground black pepper and grill over medium heat until desired doneness is achieved. Spray insides of dinner rolls with olive oil and toast them on the grill. Place burgers on the buns and sprinkle with Maytag blue cheese.

Mini Grilled Cheese and Tomato Sandwiches
Serves 20

1/2 - 1 cup butter, softened
1 loaf cocktail bread, sourdough or wheat
1/3 cup Parmesan cheese, grated
1/3 cup grainy mustard
1/3 cup mayonnaise
1 pound American cheese, sliced and quartered
6 roma tomatoes, sliced

Spread butter generously on 1 side of each slice of bread. Place Parmesan cheese in a pie plate. In batches, press the bread butter side down into the cheese. On a baking sheet, place half the slices, cheese side down. Spread mustard and mayonnaise on plain side. Top with American cheese and tomato slices. Top sandwich with remaining bread slices, making sure cheese side is on top. Heat a large skillet or grill sandwiches over medium heat until browned and cheese is starting to melt, 2 - 3 minutes. Turn and grill for another 2 - 3 minutes, until browned.

This is an easily modified recipe. Since the bread slices are big enough to manage, this translates nicely for mini Monte Cristos, Croque Monsieurs, Patty Melts or even Reubens.

Sailing the Seven Seas

These Junior League women took part in the Junior League Cruise Ball at the Fontenelle Hotel in October 1936. Costumed to represent steamships are left to right: Kathryn Hosford as the George Washington; Mrs. John Byrne as the Bremen; Harriet Kelly, the President Coolidge; Jean Dudley Gallagher as the Ile de France and Mrs. Hearne Christopher as the Empress of Russia. - *Reprinted with permission from the Omaha World-Herald*

36

Won Ton Cups
Serves 20 - 30

1 60-count package won ton wrappers   *1 cup sesame oil*

Preheat oven to 350 degrees. Place mini muffin tins turned upside down on baking sheets. Separate won ton wrappers and lightly brush each side with sesame oil. Press each wrapper around the bottom of a tin. Bake 10-12 minutes or until golden brown and crunchy. Cool on racks and store in airtight containers or zipped bags with paper towels to absorb excess oil. When ready to use, fill cups with desired filling.

AHI TUNA FILLING

1/2 cup mayonnaise, homemade
  preferred
1 lime, juice and zest
Sriracha sauce
1 (6 oz) piece Ahi tuna, sushi grade,
  diced
salt and freshly ground black pepper
cilantro leaves, chopped

Blend mayonnaise, lime juice, zest, and Sriracha. Fold tuna into mayonnaise mixture and season to taste. Chill for 1 - 2 hours, do not make ahead. Garnish with cilantro.

SMOKED SEAFOOD FILLING

1/4 cup mayonnaise, homemade
  preferred
salt and freshly ground black pepper to
  taste
1 cup smoked seafood: salmon, trout or
  scallops, flaked
fresh herbs for garnish

Blend mayonnaise with salt and pepper. Fold in the seafood chosen. Chill 1 - 2 hours before use. Garnish with fresh herbs.

CRAB-CARROT FILLING

1/2 cup mayonnaise, homemade
  preferred
1 lime, juice and zest
1/2 teaspoon hot sauce
1 cup crab meat, picked over and flaked
1/4 cup carrots, peeled and shredded
salt and freshly ground black pepper
orange slices

Mix mayonnaise, lime juice, zest and hot sauce. Fold in crab meat and carrots. Season to taste. Chill 1 - 2 hours before use. Garnish with a tiny slice of orange.

THE CAVE
506 South 16th Street

A 1938 photograph of The Cave Bar, a popular meeting place in the basement of the old Hill Hotel at 506 South 16th Street. - *From the Bostwick-Frohardt Collection owned by KMTV and on permanent loan to the Durham Western Heritage Museum, Omaha, Nebraska*

The Forty Niner Bar
49th and Dodge Streets

The Forty Niner Bar at 49th and Dodge Streets in 1945. - *From the William Wentworth collection at the Douglas County Historical Society*

Cranberry Cooler
Serves 10

32 ounces cranberry juice
8 ounces orange juice
4 ounces lemon juice

32 ounces ginger ale
10 orange slices

In a 3-quart pitcher, mix cranberry juice, orange juice, lemon juice and ginger ale. Pour into tall glasses filled with ice. Garnish with orange slices. If making ahead of time, pour in the ginger ale just before serving.

Raspberry Lemonade
Serves 8

6 lemons
2 limes
1 cup sugar

6 cups water
1 cup fresh raspberries
lemon and lime slices for garnish

In a 2-quart pitcher combine the juice from the lemons (about 1 1/2 cups) and from the limes (1/3 cup) with the sugar and the water. Stir to dissolve. Add the raspberries, cover and chill overnight. Serve over ice and garnish with lemon and lime slices.

Pineapple Tea
Serves 20

1/4 cup unsweetened instant tea
2 cups sugar
4 cups boiling water

8 cups pineapple juice
3 cups cold water
1 cup lemon juice

In a large container, combine tea and sugar. Add boiling water, stirring to dissolve. Then add pineapple juice, cold water and lemon juice. Transfer to a pitcher and chill.

Watermelon Lemonade with Kiwi Splash

Serves 6

2 kiwi fruit, peeled and quartered
1 1/2 teaspoons sugar
4 cups seedless watermelon, cubed

1 (12 oz) can frozen lemonade
*   concentrate*
2 cups water

Place kiwi fruit and sugar in a blender. Cover and blend on medium speed until smooth. Pour mixture into another container and freeze 1 to 2 hours, until firm. Place watermelon in the blender; cover and blend on medium speed until smooth. Place frozen lemonade and water in a large pitcher. Add watermelon mixture and mix well. Pour the watermelon lemonade into glasses over ice. Spoon a dollop of frozen kiwi fruit mixture on top. Serve immediately.

Scooter's Junior League Morning Rush

Serves 1

1 ounce chocolate sauce
1/2 ounce vanilla flavoring syrup
1/2 ounce hazelnut flavoring syrup

2 ounces chilled espresso
6 ounces milk

Shake all ingredients with ice to chill. Serve over ice. |O!|

Beer Margaritas

Serves 4 - 6

1 (6 oz) can frozen limeade concentrate
6 ounces beer
6 ounces tequila

ice
lime wedges

Combine limeade, beer, tequila and ice in a blender. Blend to desired consistency. Serve with lime wedges.

An Original  *Ingredient*

The Omaha Symphony Guild

By the late 1950's, the Omaha Symphony had "fallen on hard times," according to Jean Day, Past President, 1946-48. Several Symphony Board members approached the Junior League to start a fundraising arm for the Symphony. In 1957, under the direction, guidance and volunteer efforts of JLO members, The Omaha Symphony Guild was created. The purpose of the Guild was to promote growth and awareness of the Symphony through "pyramiding luncheons or coffees" with 20 key women contributing $1.00 for their Guild membership. The JLO would also put on a promotional and money-raising event - The Viennese Ball. Today, the Omaha Symphony Guild is still a powerful force. They established a strong following in the community for their Designer Showhouse and the Debutante Ball has provided record incomes.

Chocolate Martini
Serves 1

chocolate syrup
1 ounce Frangelico hazelnut liqueur
1 ounce vanilla vodka
cocoa or chocolate kiss

Drizzle chocolate syrup around the rim of a very cold martini glass. Shake Frangelico and vanilla vodka in a martini shaker with ice. Gently pour into the prepared glass, straining ice. Shake cocoa over the top or garnish with a chocolate kiss.

For a pretty presentation, melt 2 ounces of white chocolate in the microwave in a wide, shallow dish. Dip the rim of a chilled martini glass in the melted chocolate.

Hpnotiq Breeze Martini
Serves 1

1 1/2 ounces Hpnotiq liqueur
1/2 ounce Malibu rum
splash of pineapple juice
maraschino cherries and lime twists for garnish

Shake all ingredients in a martini shaker with ice. Strain into a cold martini glass and garnish with a maraschino cherry or twisted lime.

Cosmopolitan
Serves 2 - 3

6 ounces lemon vodka
2 ounces triple sec
10 ounces cranberry juice
squeeze of lime
lime slices

Chill martini glasses. Pour vodka, triple sec, cranberry juice and a squeeze of lime into a shaker and add ice. Shake until frost forms on the outside of the shaker. Serve in martini glasses with slices of lime.

Maui's Best Caramel Apple Martini

Serves 1

2 ounces apple schnapps
2 ounces apple vodka

1 ounce butterscotch schnapps
2 ounces pear or white grape juice

Shake the apple schnapps, apple vodka, butterscotch schnapps and juice with ice. Strain into a chilled martini glass. Serve immediately.

Midnight Coffee Express

Serves 2

2 ounces vanilla vodka
2 ounces Kahlua coffee liqueur
2 ounces Frangelico hazelnut liqueur

2 ounces Bailey's Irish Creme
2 ounces espresso, chilled
chocolate sprinkles

Into a martini shaker, pour equal parts of the liqueurs, expresso and ice. Shake vigorously until frothy. Pour into chilled martini glasses and add chocolate sprinkles.

Mango Splash

Serves 4

4 ripe mangoes or 1 (20 oz) jar mangoes
1/3 cup triple sec
3 Tablespoons fresh lime juice

3 Tablespoons sugar
2 bottles sparkling white wine, chilled
lime or orange wedges, for garnish

If fresh, remove mango flesh from pit and skin. Place mango in a food processor or blender and puree. Add triple sec, lime juice and sugar and pulse until blended. Pour 1 - 2 Tablespoons into a tall glass, top with sparkling wine and garnish with lime or orange wedges.

The mango puree may be kept in the refrigerator for up to 8 hours. A great alternative to a mimosa.

Vodka Slushies
Serves 10 - 15

9 cups water
2 cups sugar
2 cups vodka
1 (12 oz) can frozen lemonade
  concentrate

1 (12 oz) can frozen orange juice
  concentrate
1 liter lemon-lime soda

In a medium saucepan, combine the water and sugar, and boil for 15 minutes. Cool for 30 minutes. Mix in vodka, lemonade and orange juice and freeze. Defrost to a slush and add soda to taste.

Rum Coolers
Serves 8 - 10

1 (6 oz) can frozen limeade concentrate
3/4 cup rum
2 liters lemon-lime soda

24 frozen raspberries
lime wedges

In a pitcher, combine limeade, rum and soda. Stir until limeade dissolves. Pour over ice. Garnish with frozen raspberries and lime wedges.

White Sangria
Serves 6

1/2 cup peach schnapps
1/2 cup cognac
1/4 cup white sugar
4 oranges, sliced into rounds

2 mangoes, peeled and sliced
4 (750 mL) bottles dry white wine
1 liter ginger ale, chilled

In a large pitcher or jar, combine the peach schnapps, cognac, sugar, oranges, mangoes and wine. Chill for at least 4 hours. When ready to serve, pour fruit mixture into a large punch bowl and add the ginger ale.

Add any summer fruit, melons are especially good.

SOUPS and SALADS

BRANDEIS
16th and Douglas Streets

Diners enjoy lunch in 1936 at J.L. Brandeis. - *From the Bostwick-Frohardt Collection owned by KMTV and on permanent loan to the Durham Western Heritage Museum*

"The Pompeian Room is so unusual that it has excited favorable comments from every traveler through Omaha who has visited the store. A lofty ceiling gives her an appearance of height that is truly commanding. In this room light luncheon is served and candies and refreshments may be obtained." - *Charles Koethen, Down Through The Years, privately printed by the Brandeis Stores, 1916*

A 1915 postcard from the J.L. Brandeis Pompeian Room - *From the collections of the Omaha Public Library*

Harkert House

Walter E. Harkert opened a five-stool hamburger joint at 24th and L Streets in 1925, serving hamburgers, coffee and pop. The place became a success, and in the subsequent years Harkert opened 21 Harkert Houses from Des Moines to Denver. Hamburgers sold for 5 cents or six for a quarter. Customers also came for the homemade pies and the homemade soups including chili, chicken noodle and bean. - *From the William Wentworth collection at the Douglas County Historical Society*

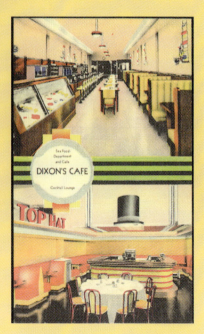

Dixon's Cafe
16th and Jackson Streets

Dixon's Cafe opened in 1914 immediately south of 16th and Jackson Streets before moving to 18th and Farnam Streets. It was a hot spot for business people who came for their steaks and seafood. *- From the Burnice Fiedler Collection*

Taxi's Cabbage and Bleu Cheese Soup
Serves 2 quarts

1/4 cup butter
1 onion, chopped
1 bay leaf
1 head cabbage, cored and shredded
1/2 Tablespoon caraway seeds
3 1/2 cups chicken stock

1/4 pound bleu cheese, crumbled
2 cups heavy cream
white pepper to taste
1/2 Tablespoon dry sherry
bleu cheese crumbles

In a large Dutch oven, melt butter over medium heat. Add onion and bay leaf. Cook until onions are translucent, stirring occasionally for 15 minutes. Add cabbage and caraway to onions and cook cabbage until it wilts, stirring occasionally, about 5 minutes. Add chicken stock and simmer 15 minutes to blend flavors. May be made ahead, cover and refrigerate. Reheat before continuing. Remove bay leaf. Add cheese and stir well until melted. Stir in cream and heat through. Do not boil. Season with pepper and sherry. To serve, top with more bleu cheese and serve with crusty French bread. !O!

Vivace Tomato Bisque
Serves 8

3 tomatoes, quartered
2 shallots, quartered
8 garlic cloves, peeled
1/2 red bell pepper, seeded
1/2 jalapeño pepper, seeded
olive oil

1 1/2 cups whole milk
1 cup cream
1 cup vegetable stock
1 1/2 Tablespoons dill, chopped
2 Tablespoons basil, chopped
salt and freshly ground black pepper

Preheat oven to 425 degrees. In a large mixing bowl, place the tomatoes, shallots, garlic and peppers. Toss with just enough olive oil to coat. Transfer vegetables to a sheet pan and roast in the upper third of the oven for 45 minutes, stirring occasionally. Remove the vegetables from the oven and cool. Remove the skins from the tomatoes and peppers. In a stock pot, add the vegetables, milk, cream, and stock. Heat to a simmer and cook uncovered for 15 - 20 minutes. Using an immersion or stick blender, puree until the soup is completely smooth. Next add fresh herbs and season to taste. !O!

Autumn Butternut Squash Soup

Serves 8

5 Tablespoons butter
2 1/2 pounds butternut squash, peeled,
  seeded and cubed
1 onion, diced
1 pear, peeled and diced

1/4 teaspoon cinnamon
1 pinch nutmeg
1/4 cup sugar
5 cups vegetable stock
1/2 cup heavy cream

In a large saucepan melt butter until bubbly. Add squash, onion and pear. Sauté until softened, about 15 minutes, stirring occasionally. Add spices, sugar and stock. Simmer 15 - 20 minutes. Puree with an immersion or a stick blender until smooth. Reheat and simmer on low and whisk in cream. Heat through but do not boil.

Garnish with parsley, chives or croutons. A sweet and savory fall favorite.

Curried Pumpkin Soup

Serves 4 - 5

2 Tablespoons butter
1/2 cup onion, finely chopped
1/2 pound mushrooms, finely chopped
2 Tablespoons flour
1 teaspoon curry powder
3 cups chicken stock

1 (15 oz) can pumpkin
1 (15 oz) can evaporated milk
1 Tablespoon honey
1/2 teaspoon salt
1/4 teaspoon nutmeg
1/2 teaspoon freshly ground black pepper

In a large saucepan, melt butter over medium heat. Add onions, stirring often until translucent and soft. Add mushrooms and sauté another 5 minutes. Stir in the flour and curry. Add stock and gradually and bring to a simmer. Cook until the liquid begins to thicken, stirring occasionally. Stir in the pumpkin, milk, honey and seasonings. Add additional curry to taste.

Makes a nice first course for a fall dinner or a mid-day meal. Serve with crusty bread and a green salad.

Asparagus Mushroom Chowder

Serves 6 - 8

6 Tablespoons butter
3 cups mushrooms, sliced
3 leeks, sliced, rinsed and dried
1 (10 oz) package cut asparagus,
   thawed
3 Tablespoons flour
1/2 teaspoon salt

dash of freshly ground black pepper
2 cups chicken stock
2 cups half and half
1 (12 oz) can white whole kernel corn,
   drained
1 Tablespoon pimentos, chopped
dash of crushed saffron

In a large saucepan, melt butter. Sauté mushrooms, leeks and asparagus until tender but not browned, about 10 minutes. Stir in flour, salt and pepper. Add stock and half and half. Cook and stir until mixture is thickened. Stir in the corn, pimentos and saffron. Heat through but do not boil. Season to taste.

Caramelized Sweet Onion Soup
with Goat Cheese Croutons

Serves 10

1 Tablespoon olive oil
2 Tablespoons butter
2 pounds sweet onions, sliced
2 Tablespoons sugar
2 Tablespoons thyme, chopped
3 cloves garlic, minced
2 bay leaves

1 teaspoon salt
1/2 teaspoon freshly ground black pepper
1 1/2 cups sweet vermouth, divided
1/2 cup sherry
10 cups beef stock
1/2 cup Parmesan cheese, grated
sour cream

In a stock pot melt oil and butter over medium heat. Add onions and sugar, stirring frequently for 10 minutes. Add thyme, garlic, bay leaves, salt and pepper. Stir occasionally until caramelized, about 40 minutes. Add 1/2 cup vermouth and sherry, stirring occasionally until absorbed, about 15 minutes. Add remaining vermouth, stock and cheese. Heat to a simmer, partially covered, for 20 minutes. Remove bay leaves. Serve in individual bowls and top with a dollop of sour cream and goat cheese croutons.

This recipe is very easy and absolutely delicious. Heats up beautifully and freezes well.

GOAT CHEESE CROUTONS

1 long baguette, sliced 1/2-inch pieces
olive oil
salt and freshly ground black pepper
6 ounces goat cheese, softened

Preheat oven to 375 degrees. Brush olive oil on each baguette slice, sprinkle lightly with salt and pepper. Bake until lightly brown, about 5 minutes. Cool. When ready to serve the soup, spread each crouton with goat cheese and broil for 1 - 2 minutes until bubbly. Serve in the soup or on the side.

Croutons may be made 1 - 2 days in advance.

Lobster Corn Chowder

Serves 4

3 (6 oz) lobster tails
1 quart half and half
4 Tablespoons butter
3 potatoes, peeled and diced
1 onion, diced

2 shallots, diced
2 cups fresh corn
1/4 teaspoon cayenne pepper
salt and freshly ground black pepper to
    taste

In a covered pot, boil lobster for 10 minutes. Drain. Remove meat and cut into pieces. Place lobster shells and half and half into a saucepan. Heat and simmer for 5 minutes. Set aside. In a large pot, melt butter and add the potatoes, onions, shallots and corn. Sauté over medium heat until the onion is translucent. Strain the lobster cream to remove any shell pieces and pour over the vegetables. Simmer slowly until the potatoes are tender, 10 - 12 minutes. Stir in the reserved lobster meat and cayenne pepper. Add salt and pepper to taste. Heat until meat is warmed through and serve.

Tortellini Spinach Soup

Serves 6

2 Tablespoons butter
6 cloves garlic, minced
1/2 cup onion, chopped
4 cups chicken stock
2 cups water
1 (9 oz) package cheese tortellini
1 (14 1/2 oz) can diced tomatoes with

    liquid
1 (10 oz) bag spinach
8 basil leaves, sliced
1 egg
1/2 cup Parmesan cheese, grated
salt and freshly ground black pepper to
    taste

In a large saucepan, melt butter. Sauté garlic and onion. Add stock and water. Bring to a boil, add tortellini and reduce heat and simmer 5 minutes. Add tomatoes and cook 4 minutes. Add spinach and basil, cook 1 - 2 minutes. In a small mixing bowl, whisk egg, Parmesan, salt and pepper. Slowly drizzle into soup and cook 2 minutes.

An excellent first course for a classic Italian dinner.

Mulligatawny Soup

Serves 6

1/4 cup butter	1 teaspoon salt
1/2 cup onions, diced	1/4 teaspoon freshly ground black pepper
1 1/4 cups carrots, sliced	1/4 teaspoon thyme
2 stalks celery, sliced	1/4 teaspoon ground cloves
1 1/2 Tablespoons flour	1/4 teaspoon ground ginger
1 Tablespoon curry powder	1/4 teaspoon ground cumin
4 cups chicken stock	1 Tablespoon lemon juice
1/4 cup tart apples, diced	dash of cayenne pepper
1 cup cooked rice	1/2 cup heavy cream
1 cup chicken, cooked and cubed	

In a large saucepan, melt the butter. Sauté the onions, carrots and celery for 5 minutes. Stir in the flour and curry. Cook for 3 minutes. Add stock and simmer for 20 minutes. Stir in apples, rice, chicken and seasonings. Cook for 10 minutes. Stir in cream, just before serving.

Mulligatawny is a soup from Southern India and translated means pepper water.

Smoked Chicken Chipotle Chowder

Serves 8

1/2 cup vegetable oil	1 (14 1/2 oz) can petite-diced tomatoes
3 onions, diced	2 cups corn
2 russet potatos, peeled and cubed	1 cup Monterey Jack cheese, shredded
3 cloves garlic, minced	1 Tablespoon cilantro leaves, chopped
1/4 cup flour	1 chipotle chile in adobo sauce, minced
3 cups chicken stock, divided	1 pound smoked chicken breast, cubed
2 cups heavy cream	salt and freshly ground black pepper

In a 6-quart stock pot, heat oil over medium heat. Cook onions until softened. Add potatoes and garlic. Cook 1 minute. Stir in flour, reduce heat to medium-low, and cook 2 minutes while continuously stirring. Add 2 cups stock and cream; bring to a simmer. Add tomatoes, corn, cheese, cilantro, chipotle and chicken. Simmer, stirring occasionally. Add remaining cup of stock to achieve desired consistency. Simmer for 30 minutes. Season with salt and pepper. Garnish with cilantro.

This soup is a perennial favorite and always gets rave reviews. Do not substitute the heavy cream. Also use powdered chipotle chile (in the spice aisle) instead of opening a whole can for just one chile. The smoked chicken is the secret ingredient.

White Cheddar Chicken Chili

Serves 8 - 10

2 pounds whole chicken
2 cups chicken stock, reserved
3 (14 1/2 oz) cans great white northern
   beans, drained
1 (14 1/2 oz) can Mexican-style
   tomatoes
1 onion, chopped

1 (4 oz) can diced green chiles
1/2 teaspoon salt
2 teaspoons ground cumin
1 1/2 teaspoon cayenne pepper
1 teaspoon oregano
3 cups Monterey Jack cheese, shredded
1 cup sour cream

In a slow cooker, cook chicken on low for 8 hours. Remove chicken, and reserve two cups of chicken stock. Debone chicken and shred meat. In a stock pot, combine chicken, beans, tomatoes, onions, chiles, spices and stock. Cook on medium heat for 1 hour. Ladle into soup bowls, sprinkle with cheese and a dollop of sour cream.

Ideal for a cold winter's night!

Avgolemono
Greek Chicken and Rice Soup

Serves 8 - 10

8 cups chicken stock
1/2 cup plus 1 Tablespoon lemon juice
1/2 cup carrots, shredded
1/2 cup celery, chopped
1/2 cup onions, chopped
6 Tablespoons concentrated chicken soup
   base
freshly ground white pepper

1/4 cup butter, softened
1/4 cup flour
8 egg yolks
2 cups long grain rice, cooked
2 cups chicken, seasoned, cooked and
   cubed
8 lemon slices for garnish

In a Dutch oven, combine stock, lemon juice, carrots, celery, onion, soup base and pepper and bring to a boil. Reduce heat, cover partially and simmer until vegetables are tender, about 20 minutes. In a bowl, blend butter and flour until smooth. Using the back of a fork, scrape butter mixture into hot soup a little at a time, stirring well after each addition. Simmer 10 minutes, stirring frequently. In a large bowl, beat egg yolks with an electric mixer on high speed until light and lemon colored. Reduce speed and slowly mix in two ladles of the hot soup. Return mixture to the Dutch oven and cook until thoroughly heated. Stir in rice and chicken and garnish with lemon slices.

A light and lemony Greek treat.

ROUX

Roux is a slowly cooked mixture of flour and fat. Cooked over low heat, it is used to thicken soups and sauces.

Game Day Gumbo
Serves 12

1 pound bone-in chicken breast	3 bay leaves
1 1/2 pounds andouille sausage, sliced	1/8 teaspoon ground cloves
7 Tablespoons flour	1/4 teaspoon cayenne pepper
6 Tablespoons oil	1/4 teaspoon crushed red pepper flakes
2 onions, chopped	1/2 teaspoon basil
1 bell pepper, chopped	1/8 teaspoon allspice
1 cup celery, chopped	1 teaspoon salt
3 cloves garlic, minced	1 teaspoon freshly ground black pepper
1/2 teaspoon thyme	

In a large stock pot, cover chicken breasts with water. Bring to a boil, reduce heat and simmer for 1 hour. Remove chicken from stock. Cool. Then debone chicken and shred meat. Discard skin and bones. Strain broth and reserve. Add additional broth, if needed, to make 2 1/2 quarts. In a large stock pot, brown sausage. Remove sausage. To make a roux, add flour and oil to the sausage drippings. Stir constantly for 15 to 25 minutes until roux is a medium to dark-brown color. Add chopped onions, bell peppers and celery to roux. Sauté until limp, adding stock if necessary. Add chicken stock, garlic, thyme, bay leaves, cloves, cayenne, pepper flakes, basil and allspice. Simmer for 40 minutes. Add chopped chicken and sausage; continue to simmer. Remove from heat. Let gumbo rest 10 - 15 minutes. Serve over rice. Garnish gumbo with sliced green onions and Louisiana-Style hot sauce. Add salt and pepper to taste.

Spice up your tailgate party with this classic Southern dish.

M's Pub Cream of Caramelized Onion and Apple Soup with Brie
Serves 12

2 quarts plus 2 cups chicken stock	1/2 cup white wine
2 cups heavy cream	1/2 cup flour
1/2 cup butter, divided	8 1/2 ounces Brie cheese, rind removed
2 onions, sliced	and diced
2 Tablespoons garlic, minced	salt and white pepper
2 1/2 green apples, peeled, cored and sliced	

In a large stock pot, heat chicken stock and cream. In a sauté pan, cook the onions in 2 Tablespoons of butter until caramelized, set aside. Sauté garlic, apples and wine in 2 Tablespoons of butter until apples soften. Add 1/4 of the caramelized onions to the apple mixture and puree in a blender. Add the remaining onions to the puree and sprinkle with a little flour. Add two ladles of the hot liquid to the puree mix and stir until thick. Repeat the process until flour is gone. Transfer the thickened onion and apple mixture back into the stock pot. Reduce heat to low and add the Brie cheese stirring until incorporated. Season with salt and white pepper. !O!

Chicken Tortilla Soup

Serves 6

2 skinless chicken breasts, poached and
   cubed
1 (12 oz) can chicken stock
1 (10 3/4 oz) can tomato puree
1 (10 oz) can Mexican-style tomatoes
1 (15 oz) can corn, drained
1 (15 oz) can chili beans
1 1/2 cups water
1 onion, chopped

2 cloves garlic, minced
2 Tablespoons oil
1/2 teaspoon chili powder
2 1/4 teaspoons hot sauce
2 teaspoons Worcestershire sauce
sour cream
cheddar cheese, shredded
tortilla chips, crumbled

In a large stock pot, combine chicken, stock, tomato puree, tomatoes, corn,
chili beans and water. In a skillet, sauté onion and garlic in oil for 2 - 3
minutes. Add to the chicken mixture. Add chili powder, hot sauce and
Worcestershire sauce. Simmer 20 - 30 minutes. Top each serving with sour
cream, shredded cheese and crumbled tortilla chips.

Italian Sausage Vegetable Soup

Serves 5

1 pound spicy Italian sausage
2 cloves garlic, minced
2 (14 oz) cans beef stock
2 (14 1/2 oz) cans Italian-style tomatoes
1/2 pound carrots, sliced into coins
salt and freshly ground black pepper

1 (14 1/2 oz) can great white northern
   beans, undrained
2 zucchini, cubed
2 (10 oz) bags washed spinach
1 Tablespoon oregano, chopped
1 Tablespoon basil, chopped
1/2 Tablespoon thyme leaves, chopped

In a skillet, brown sausage over medium heat. Add garlic and cook until
fragrant. Transfer sausage and garlic into a saucepan and stir in stock, tomatoes
and carrots. Season with salt and pepper. Reduce heat and simmer for 15
minutes. Stir in beans and zucchini. Cover and cook 15 minutes. Add spinach
and herbs. Cover and cook just until the greens wilt.

An Original Ingredient

GENERAL CROOK HOUSE

This Italianate style house was constructed in 1879 for General George Crook. The General was a celebrated Civil War hero and a defender of Ponca Chief Standing Bear. In 1976, The Junior League of Omaha contributed $41,000 to refurbish the home to its original condition. Kimball Lauritzen, past president, 1982, said, "It was an important project because there was nothing else like it in this area." After completion of the renovation, visitors were able to tour the home, sit on original furnishings and page through books from a century ago. By 1979, in conjunction with the Douglas County Historical Society, the JLO purchased a historic marker for the site and it remains a popular tourist attraction today.

Ham and Cheese Chowder
Serves 4

2 cups potatoes, diced
1/2 cup celery, chopped
1/2 cup carrots, chopped
1/4 cup onion, chopped
2 cups water
salt and freshly ground black pepper
1/4 cup butter
1/4 cup flour
1 cup milk
1 (15 oz) can evaporated milk
1 cup cheddar cheese, shredded
1 cup ham, diced
hot sauce
bacon, cooked and crumbled

In a large stockpot, combine potatoes, celery, carrots, onion and water. Season to taste with salt and pepper. Cook until tender. Do not drain water. In a small saucepan, combine butter, flour, milk and evaporated milk. Heat until thickened over medium heat. Add cheese and warm until melted. Add cheese mixture to the soup. Stir in the ham. If soup is too thick, add more milk. Garnish with hot sauce and bacon crumbles.

Herb Bean Soup
Serves 8

2 cups dried pinto beans
1 large meaty ham bone
1 quart chicken stock
1 (22 oz) can tomato juice
2 cups water
3 onions, chopped
3 cloves garlic, minced
1/4 cup parsley, finely chopped
1/2 cup green pepper, chopped
2 Tablespoons brown sugar
1 Tablespoon chili powder
1 bay leaf
2 teaspoons oregano
1/2 teaspoon rosemary
1/2 teaspoon thyme
1/4 teaspoon marjoram
1/2 teaspoon sweet basil
salt and freshly ground black pepper to taste
hot sauce
1 cup sherry

In a large stock pot, soak beans overnight in enough water to cover. Drain. Add to the beans, all other ingredients, except the sherry. Simmer 3 1/2 hours. Remove the ham bone and discard. Add the sherry. Simmer 30 minutes.

Wonderful served with a thick slice of Black Bread, page 184

Savory Vegetable Hamburger Soup

Serves: 12

2 teaspoons olive oil
1 onion, finely chopped
1 shallot, diced
1 teaspoon beef roast seasoning blend
1 teaspoon pizza seasoning blend
1/2 teaspoon crushed red pepper flakes
1/2 teaspoon celery seed
salt and freshly ground black pepper
1 teaspoon garlic, minced
1 pound ground beef
1/2 Tablespoon Worcestershire sauce
1/2 Tablespoon balsamic vinegar
1 teaspoon steak sauce

1 (14 1/2 oz) can of diced tomatoes
1 (8 oz) can tomato sauce
1 (14 1/2 oz) can chicken stock
1 (14 1/2 oz) can beef stock
1/2 cup carrots, diced
1/2 cup green beans
1/2 cup celery, diced
1 cup potatoes, cubed
1/2 cup corn
2 bay leaves
1 cup Parmesan cheese, grated and
    divided

In a stock pot, heat oil over medium heat. Add onion and shallot. Sauté until translucent, about 3 - 5 minutes. Combine all dry seasonings and garlic into a small bowl. Add to onions and stir until fragrant, 1 minute. Add ground meat, and brown. Add Worcestershire, vinegar and steak sauce, cook 2 minutes. Add remaining ingredients, except cheese. Bring to just a boil, then reduce heat and simmer for 30 minutes. Add 1/2 cup of cheese. Stir. Remove bay leaves, ladle into bowls, and top with remaining cheese.

Many spice companies create beef or steak seasoning blends. Look for prime rib, beef roast, or brisket-type mixes in your grocery aisle. See our resource guide. This dish is great reheated. It may be necessary to add broth to thin.

Bistro Steak Soup

Serves 6 - 8

1/2 cup butter
1 cup flour
8 cups water
2 cups ground beef
1 cup onion, chopped
1 cup carrot, chopped
1 cup celery, chopped
2 cups frozen mixed vegetables

1 cup tomatoes, diced
2 Tablespoons beef concentrate (see
    note)
1/2 Tablespoon freshly ground black
    pepper
1 Tablespoon Italian seasoning blend
1 teaspoon salt

In a large stock pot, melt butter and whisk in flour to make a smooth paste, a roux. Cook slowly until browned in color. Stir in water. In a separate pan, sauté beef and drain. Add beef to soup pot. Stir in onions, carrots, celery and mixed vegetables. Add tomatoes, beef concentrate, pepper, Italian seasoning and salt, to taste. Bring just to a boil, reduce heat and simmer until vegetables are done.

Beef concentrate is located with the spices and is also called beef base.

Cold Cucumber Soup with Almonds, Tomatoes and Chives

Serves 5 - 7

3 cucumbers, peeled and seeded
3 cloves garlic, minced
3 cups chicken stock, divided
3 cups sour cream or plain yogurt
3 Tablespoons white vinegar

2 teaspoons salt
1/3 cup slivered almonds, toasted
1 tomato, chopped
3 Tablespoons chives, chopped

In blender, combine cucumber with garlic and 1 cup of stock. Puree until smooth. In a large pot, combine remaining stock, sour cream or yogurt, vinegar and salt. Fold in pureed cucumbers. Chill at least 1 hour. Garnish chilled soup with toasted almonds, chopped tomatoes and chopped chives.

A nice, cool and fresh summer dish. Perfect for a garden party or bridal shower. For toasted almonds, melt 1 Tablespoon butter in a small skillet over medium heat. Add almonds, stirring constantly, until almonds are slightly browned.

Cool Cantaloupe Soup

Serves 6

1 cantaloupe, peeled, seeded and cubed
2 cups orange juice, divided
1 Tablespoon lime juice

1 Tablespoon honey
1/4 teaspoon cinnamon
mint leaves, for garnish

In a food processor, place cantaloupe and 1/2 cup orange juice. Process until smooth. Transfer the mixture into a large bowl and stir in the lime juice, honey, cinnamon and remaining orange juice. Cover and chill for at least 1 hour. Garnish with mint leaves.

Honeydew melon may be substituted or used in combination for variety in flavor.

Upstream Brewing Company Smoked Gouda Beer Soup

Serves 6 - 8

1/2 pound bacon, diced
1/2 cup onion, diced
1 1/2 Tablespoons garlic, minced
1 cup corn
1/2 cup red bell pepper, diced
1/2 cup green bell pepper, diced
2 (12 oz) bottles Upstream Brewing Company's Gold Coast Blonde Ale
2 cups chicken stock
2 cups red potatoes, diced
4 cups heavy cream
1 1/2 pounds smoked Gouda cheese, shredded
3 Tablespoons cornstarch
2 teaspoons Old Bay seafood seasoning
1 Tablespoon Worcestershire sauce
1 Tablespoon thyme, chopped
1/2 teaspoon kosher salt
1/2 teaspoon freshly ground black pepper
1/4 teaspoon cayenne pepper

In a large stock pot, fry bacon until crisp over medium heat. Remove bacon bits, reserving half of the drippings in the pan. Drain bacon on paper towels and set aside. To the remaining bacon drippings, add onions and sauté until transparent, stirring to ensure even cooking. Add the garlic to the pan and cook with the onions, stirring for 3 minutes until no color remains. Stir in corn and peppers, cooking for 5 minutes and then deglaze the pan with beer. Add stock and bring mixture to a simmer and then add potatoes, stirring to incorporate well. Cover and simmer for 10-15 minutes until the potatoes are cooked.

At this point, either reduce the heat to low or place soup in a double boiler. While stirring constantly, slowly add the cream. Toss the cheese with the cornstarch and add to the soup in small batches, stirring to melt the cheese. Do not overheat. Slowly heat the soup to melt the cheese. This will be a thick soup. If the soup is too thick, slowly add more beer. Next add the seafood seasoning, Worcestershire, thyme, salt and peppers. Taste and adjust seasonings to your preference. To serve, garnish with reserved bacon. Other serving suggestions are topping with croutons or fresh thyme sprigs.

Award-winning recipe from Upstream Brewing Company. If Upstream's Gold Coast Blonde Ale isn't readily available, try another light ale. |O!|

SIDEWALK CAFE

A menu from the Sidewalk Cafe in Omaha's Regency Court. - *From the Joe Villella menu collection at the Douglas County Historical Society*

Planning The 1935 Follies

Arthur Seelig, left, and Wesley Totten, both of New York, meet with Junior League members Mrs. H. Malcom Baldrige, seated, and Mrs. Loring Elliott, standing to the left, and Mrs. Bernard Wickham, standing to the right, to discuss plans for the 1935 Follies at the Central High School Auditorium. Junior Leagues across the country partnered with Cargill Company to produce Follies-style shows in the 1920s and 30s to raise money.

The Cargill Company would send an advance team to Omaha to scout locations, audition League members and produce the show from their pool of choreographers and linguists. After two weeks of intense rehearsal, the Junior League cast would put on the Follies. Revenue grew from netting a reported $3,000 in 1920 to around $17,000 in the final years. - *Reprinted with permission from the Omaha World-Herald*

Spring Greens and Mango Salad

Serves 6

DRESSING
2 Tablespoons red onion, grated
1/4 cup lime juice
1 Tablespoon rice vinegar
1 Tablespoon soy sauce
1 Tablespoon olive oil
2 teaspoons honey
1/4 teaspoon ginger, grated
3/4 teaspoon Dijon mustard
1/2 teaspoon horseradish
salt and freshly ground black pepper

SALAD
2 (10 oz) packages spring green mix
1/2 cup pecans, toasted
1 mango, cubed

For the dressing, whisk all ingredients together. Season to taste with salt and pepper. Place lettuce in a large bowl, add nuts and mango. Toss with dressing.

Zesty Cobb Salad

Serves 10

DRESSING
1 1/2 cups buttermilk
1/4 cup sour cream
2 Tablespoons mayonnaise
2 teaspoons Worcestershire sauce
2 teaspoons salt
1 teaspoon hot sauce
5 Tablespoons red wine vinegar
5 Tablespoons lemon juice
2 1/2 Tablespoons Dijon mustard
2 teaspoons fish sauce
1 shallot, minced
1 teaspoon tarragon
2 teaspoons sugar

SALAD
10 cups romaine lettuce hearts, chopped
1/2 pound bacon, cooked and crumbled
2 cups chicken, cooked and cubed
2 avocados, diced
1 (5 oz) package blue cheese, crumbled
1 cup tomato, diced
3/4 cup pecans, toasted and chopped
2 hard boiled eggs, chopped
chives, for garnish

The Cobb Salad originated at the famous Brown Derby, a Hollywood celebrity hotspot. The traditional presentation is to arrange each salad ingredient in rows on top of a bed of lettuce, served with the dressing on the side. This recipe is a time-saving and updated twist on the original.

For dressing, whisk together all ingredients. Chill for 2 hours. In a large salad bowl, arrange lettuce, bacon, chicken, avocados, blue cheese, tomato, pecans and eggs. Add dressing to taste. Toss well, until all elements are well coated. Garnish with chopped chives. Serve with crusty bread.

This amazing dressing works well on other salads as a Ranch substitute.

Scrumptious Cornbread Salad

Serves 6

1 loaf prepared cornbread, left out for
   several hours or one day
1 red onion, diced
1/2 pound bacon, cooked and crumbled
1 tomato, diced
2 jalapeño s, seeded and minced

1 cup cheddar cheese, shredded
3/4 cup celery, diced
1/2 cup corn
1 1/2 teaspoons freshly ground black
   pepper
1 cup mayonnaise

In a large bowl, crumble cornbread into bite size chunks and toss with remaining ingredients, except mayonnaise. Gently fold in mayonnaise. Chill for 1 hour and serve.

This unique salad is extremely easy to prepare. The flavors and textures will bring your guests back for a second helping and the recipe!

Omaha Country Club Grilled Chicken with Vegetable and Goat Cheese Tart

Serves 6

2 whole boneless, skinless chicken
   breasts, about 2 pounds
18 zucchini slices, sliced lengthwise,
   1/4-inch thick
1 eggplant, peeled and cut into 6,
   1/4-inch slices
1/4 cup olive oil
salt and freshly ground black pepper, to
   taste
6 tomatoes, sliced 1/4-inch thick
6 slices goat cheese, 1/8-inch thick
6 cups spring mix salad
1/2 cup grated Parmesan cheese, for
   garnish

BALSAMIC VINAIGRETTE
1 Tablespoon Dijon mustard
1 clove garlic, minced
salt and freshly ground black pepper, to
   taste
1/4 cup balsamic vinegar
3/4 cup olive oil

Preheat the grill. Slice each chicken breast into 3 pieces, 6 pieces total, and flatten with a smooth mallet. Lightly brush the chicken, zucchini and eggplant with olive oil. Season with salt and pepper, to taste. Place chicken, zucchini and eggplant on a hot grill and cook about 10 minutes until browned.
For the vinaigrette, in a small bowl, whisk together the mustard and garlic. Season with salt and pepper, to taste. Add vinegar and whisk, slowly pour in the oil while whisking to blend and thicken. Set aside.

Preheat oven to 350 degrees. Spray 6 non-stick stack cylinders with vegetable oil and place them on a baking sheet. Layer ingredients in the following order: 3 slices of zucchini, 1 slice tomato, 1 slice goat cheese and 1 slice of eggplant. Top with grilled chicken. Press down gently then bake for 10 minutes. To serve, slide a spatula under each cylinder and transfer to a serving plate and unmold. Toss spring mix with dressing and arrange around each chicken stack. Garnish with Parmesan cheese. |O!|

Omaha Country Club's (OCC) Executive Chef Lionel Havé has tantalized the senses of OCC members, their families and their guests for almost 20 years. Born and trained in France, Chef Lionel began his cooking career at the young age of 15. After a series of moves, Chef Lionel landed in Omaha in 1975 and began working at the French Café. He continued to work in a number of different hotels and restaurants in Dallas and Cincinnati before returning to Omaha in 1987 as the Executive Chef at the Omaha Country Club.

Mandarin Spinach Salad

Serves 4

DRESSING
1/4 cup olive oil
2 Tablespoons balsamic vinegar
1 1/2 teaspoons Dijon mustard
1/2 teaspoon salt
1/2 teaspoon freshly ground black pepper

SALAD
1 (16 oz) package spinach leaves
1 (15 oz) can mandarin oranges, drained
1/2 cup olives, sliced
1/2 cup red onion, sliced
1/4 cup feta cheese, crumbled
1/4 cup almonds, sliced and toasted

For the dressing, in a small bowl, combine all dressing ingredients. Whisk until blended.

In a large serving bowl, combine spinach, oranges, olives and onion. Pour dressing over salad and toss evenly to coat. Top with feta cheese and almonds.

Add some crunch with your favorite walnuts, candied pecans or almond slivers.

Fresh Tuna Salad with Avocado

Serves 4

1/2 cup olive oil
1 Tablespoon fennel seeds
1 Tablespoon black peppercorns
1 (12 oz) tuna steak, cut 1-inch thick
salt
1/2 cup mayonnaise, plus 2 Tablespoons
2 anchovy fillets, minced
2 Tablespoons capers, drained and chopped

1 clove garlic, minced
2 Tablespoons lemon juice, divided
2 celery ribs, sliced, 1-inch thick
1 red onion, diced
1/3 cup black olives, chopped
4 Haas avocados, peeled, pitted and sliced
pea shoots or alfalfa sprouts, for garnish

In a medium saucepan, bring olive oil, fennel seeds and peppercorns to a simmer over medium heat. Season tuna with salt and add to the saucepan. Simmer the tuna steak over low heat, turning once, until barely pink in the center, about 15 minutes. Transfer to a plate and remove the fennel and peppercorns. Strain and reserve the oil.

Meanwhile, in a large bowl, blend the mayonnaise with the anchovies, capers, garlic and 1 Tablespoon of the lemon juice. Stir the celery, onion and olives into the dressing. Using a fork, break the tuna into 1-inch pieces and fold into the dressing. Season with salt. Place the avocado slices on a serving plate and drizzle with the reserved spice-infused oil and remaining 1 Tablespoon of lemon juice. Spoon the tuna salad onto the avocados. Top with pea shoots or alfalfa sprouts.

For individual servings, halve and pit the avocados, do not peel. Drizzle flesh with the oil and lemon juice and mound the tuna salad into the avocado boats. Garnish as above.

Royal Deli Salad and Dressing

Serves 4

DRESSING
3/4 cup vegetable oil
1/4 cup tarragon vinegar
1/4 teaspoon freshly ground black pepper
1/2 teaspoon salt
1/4 teaspoon garlic powder
1/2 teaspoon oregano

SALAD
3 hard rolls or bread sticks
3 tomatoes, diced
1 head lettuce, chopped
1 onion, diced
1 1/2 cups Provolone cheese, shredded
1 1/2 cups cheddar cheese, shredded
1/4 pound ham, thinly sliced into strips
1/4 pound salami, thinly sliced into strips
1/4 pound turkey, thinly sliced into strips

For the dressing, whisk together all ingredients in a small bowl. Chill for 1 - 2 days. In a large bowl, pull apart bread into walnut-sized pieces. Toss with tomatoes, lettuce, onion, cheeses and meats. Toss with dressing.

Spring Strawberry Spinach Salad

Serves 6

DRESSING
1/2 cup sugar
2 Tablespoons sesame seeds
1 Tablespoon poppy seeds
1 1/2 teaspoons onion, minced
1/4 teaspoon Worcestershire sauce
1/4 teaspoon paprika
1/2 cup raspberry vinegar
1/4 cup vegetable oil

SALAD
1 pound fresh spinach, washed
1 pint fresh strawberries, sliced
1/2 cup almonds, sliced and toasted

In a blender or food processor, blend all dressing ingredients, except the oil. While running, slowly add oil and mix until thickened. Refrigerate. When ready to serve, in a large bowl, place spinach and strawberries. Toss with dressing and garnish with almonds.

For a different taste, substitute raspberries for the strawberries.

Steak House Salad

Serves 6

1 pound sirloin steak
garlic salt and freshly ground black
   pepper
1 Tablespoon butter
1 cup chopped English walnuts
4 cups baby salad greens
1 pear, cored and sliced
1/4 cup blue cheese

DRESSING
1/3 cup balsamic vinegar
1 1/2 Tablespoons fresh herbs, chopped
   (oregano, basil, rosemary)
1 Tablespoon green onion, sliced
salt and freshly ground black pepper
pinch of sugar
1/2 cup olive oil

Preheat broiler to high. Generously season meat with garlic salt and pepper. Using a broiler pan, add 1/2 inch of water to the bottom. Place the seasoned steak on top and broil 15-20 minutes, turning once to desired doneness.

In a small sauté pan, melt the butter over low heat and add the walnuts, stirring to coat. Cook and stir until the nuts become fragrant and toasted, about 6 minutes. Arrange salad greens in a serving bowl. Arrange pear on the lettuce. Add walnuts. Slice steak on the diagonal and add to salad.

To make the dressing, in a small jar, combine the vinegar, herbs, onion, salt, pepper and sugar. Shake vigorously. Add oil and two ice cubes, shake again and remove the remaining ice. Toss the salad with the vinaigrette and top with blue cheese.

This dish may be served on individual salad plates, arranging all ingredients and drizzling dressing over the top or tossed together in a large salad bowl.

Summer Salad

Serves 4

DRESSING
1/3 cup lemon juice
1/2 cup sugar
1 teaspoon Dijon mustard
1 Tablespoon poppy seeds
2 Tablespoons green onion, sliced
salt and freshly ground black pepper, to
   taste
1/3 cup olive oil

1 (16 oz) bag lettuce
1/2 cup golden raisins
1 cup Swiss cheese, shredded
2 apples, peeled and cubed
1 pear, peeled and cubed
1 cup cashew pieces

In a small bowl, whisk dressing ingredients except oil. Slowly whisk in oil. Chill. In a large bowl, arrange lettuce and top with remaining ingredients. Add dressing and toss.

SEASONED CROUTONS

1 loaf Ciabatta or 1 long baguette
1/2 cup butter
4 teaspoons Cajun seasoning blend

Preheat oven to 350 degrees. In a small bowl, mix butter with seasoning. Cut bread into 1-inch cubes. Place bread in a large bowl or zippered bag, and toss with seasoned butter. Spread cubes onto a baking sheet, in a single layer, and bake until crisp, about 15 minutes.

Roman Caesar Salad with Seasoned Croutons
Serves 8

DRESSING
5 tablespoons cider vinegar
2 Tablespoons garlic, minced
2 1/2 Tablespoons lemon juice
2 Tablespoons Worcestershire sauce
1 1/2 teaspoons freshly ground black
   pepper
1 1/2 teaspoons anchovy paste
1 teaspoon salt
1 teaspoon sugar
1/4 teaspoon dry mustard
1/4 teaspoon onion powder
1/4 teaspoon hot sauce
3 Tablespoons egg substitute
3/4 cup olive oil
1 cup Parmesan cheese, grated

SALAD
12 cups romaine lettuce hearts, chopped
seasoned croutons (see note)
1/2 cup Parmesan cheese, shaved curls

In a food processor, combine vinegar, garlic, lemon juice, Worcestershire, pepper, anchovy paste, salt, sugar, mustard onion and hot sauce and blend. Add egg substitute and process for 1 minute. With the machine running, slowly pour in olive oil. Add the cheese and pulse to blend. Season to taste. Refrigerate. In a large bowl, place lettuce and croutons. Toss with dressing and garnish with shaved cheese curls.

Tuscan Tortellini Salad
Serves 6

2 (9 oz) packages cheese tortellini pasta
1/2 cup balsamic vinegar
3 cloves garlic, minced
1/2 cup basil, chopped
1/4 cup olive oil

1 teaspoon kosher salt
1/2 teaspoon freshly ground black pepper
2 pints grape tomatoes, halved
1/2 cup herbed feta cheese, crumbled

Cook tortellini according to package directions. Drain and cool. In a small bowl, whisk together vinegar, garlic, basil and oil. Season with salt and pepper. In a large bowl, combine pasta, with tomatoes and cheese. Add dressing and toss.

Crunchy Chicken Wild Rice Salad

Serves 4

1 (6 oz) package long grain and wild rice
  mix (yield 3 cups)
2 Tablespoons lemon juice
3 cups chicken, cooked and shredded
3 green onions, sliced
1/2 red pepper, diced
12 pea pods, cut into 1-inch pieces
2 ripe avocados, chopped just before
  serving
1 cup pecan halves, toasted

DRESSING
1 clove garlic, minced
1 teaspoon Dijon mustard
1/2 teaspoon salt
1 teaspoon lemon pepper
1/4 teaspoon sugar
1/4 cup rice wine vinegar
1/4 cup vegetable oil

Prepare rice according to package directions. Meanwhile, in a small bowl, drizzle lemon juice over chicken. For the dressing, in a small bowl, whisk together all ingredients except the oil. Slowly add oil and blend. In a covered bowl, mix rice, chicken, onions, peppers and peas. Toss with dressing, cover and chill at least 2 hours. To serve, toss with avocados and pecans.

Greek Village Salad

Serves 6

DRESSING
2 Tablespoons red wine vinegar
2 Tablespoons balsamic vinegar
2 Tablespoons lemon juice
pinch sugar
pinch garlic powder
1/3 cup olive oil

SALAD
2 heads romaine lettuce, chopped
1 cucumber, peeled, seeded and sliced
1 clove garlic, minced
3 tomatoes, cut into wedges
1 bunch green onions, sliced
1/2 cup fresh dill, minced
1/2 cup mint leaves, minced
1 Tablespoon oregano
2 Tablespoons capers, drained
3/4 cup herbed feta cheese, crumbled
3/4 cup kalamata olives, pitted and
  drained

For dressing, in a small bowl, combine vinegars, lemon juice, sugar and garlic. Whisk in oil. In a large bowl, toss together lettuce, cucumber, garlic, tomatoes, onions, herbs and capers. Toss salad with dressing. Garnish with cheese and olives.

JOE TESS PLACE
5424 South 24th Street

Joe Tess Place, is a South Omaha mainstay offering some of the freshest, tastiest fried fish sandwiches in town. The carp and catfish served here are farmed in Minnesota and trucked to Omaha, where they are kept in large tanks in the basement. Betty R. Langenfeld of Omaha likes this coleslaw recipe because it reminds her of the slaw she enjoys at the Joe Tess Place restaurant in Omaha. She submitted this recipe to the Omaha World-Herald's Let's Swap recipe column in 2000.

COLESLAW
1 cup sour cream
1 teaspoon dry mustard
4 Tablespoons sugar
1/4 cup cider vinegar
1 teaspoon celery seed
1/2 teaspoon salt
4 cups cabbage, finely shredded
1/4 cup carrots, finely shredded

Mix sour cream with dry mustard, sugar, vinegar, celery seed and salt. Toss with cabbage and carrots, mixing well. Serve cold. Serves six. !O!

Hunter's Wild Rice Chicken Salad

Serves 6

3 cups wild rice
2 (6 oz) jars marinated artichoke hearts, halved
1 green pepper, diced
1 bunch green onions, sliced
1 cup red grapes, halved
4 whole boneless chicken breasts, cooked and diced
1 (10 oz) bag frozen peas
1 cup almond slivers, toasted

DRESSING
1 1/3 cups vegetable oil
1/2 cup white vinegar
1/4 cup Parmesan cheese, grated
1 Tablespoon sugar
2 teaspoons salt
1 teaspoon celery salt
1/2 teaspoon white pepper
1/2 teaspoon dry mustard
1/4 teaspoon paprika
1 clove garlic, minced

Cook wild rice in a large stock pot in 8 cups of salted water for 45 minutes or until tender. Drain excess liquid. Meanwhile, in a blender combine all dressing ingredients and puree until smooth. Drain the artichoke hearts and add artichoke marinade to the dressing. Blend well. When rice is cooked, add artichokes, peppers, onions, grapes and chicken. Toss with half of the dressing. Chill. To serve, toss with peas and almonds and additional dressing.

Sliced fresh pea pods and asparagus are spectacular additions in the summer months. Substitute cashews, walnuts or pecans for the slivered almonds.

Crispy Asian Salad

Serves 8

1/2 cup butter
2 Tablespoons sesame seeds
2 packages chicken flavored ramen noodles, broken into pieces
1/2 cup sliced almonds
2 Tablespoons sugar
2 pounds bok choy or Napa cabbage, stalk and leaves chopped
5 green onions, sliced
1 (6 oz) can water chestnuts, drained and chopped
1 (6 oz) can pineapple tidbits, drained
2 cups chicken, grilled and cubed

DRESSING
1/4 cup rice wine vinegar
1/2 cup sugar
2 Tablespoons soy sauce
1 seasoning pack from ramen noodles
1/2 cup canola oil

In a large skillet, melt butter over medium heat. Brown sesame seeds, noodles, almonds and sugar, about 5 minutes. Remove from heat and cool to room temperature. In a small bowl, combine vinegar, sugar, soy sauce and seasoning. Slowly whisk in oil. In a large covered bowl, place cabbage, onions, water chestnuts, pineapple and chicken. Toss with dressing and chill. To serve, toss chilled salad with crispy mixture.

Tomato-Basil Couscous Salad

Serves 6

2 1/4 cups chicken stock
1 (10 oz) package couscous
1 cup green onions, sliced
1 cup roma tomatoes, seeded and diced
1/3 cup fresh basil, sliced
1 pint cherry tomatoes, halved

DRESSING
1/4 cup balsamic vinegar
1/4 teaspoon crushed red pepper flakes
2 cloves garlic, minced
1/8 teaspoon salt
1/8 teaspoon freshly ground black pepper
1/2 cup olive oil

In a small saucepan, simmer stock over medium high heat. Add couscous, remove from heat and stir. Cover and let stand for 5 minutes. Transfer couscous to large serving bowl and fluff with a fork. Cool for 1 hour.

Meanwhile, in a small bowl, combine vinegar, pepper flakes, garlic, salt and pepper. Whisk in oil. Chill. To the cooled couscous add onions, roma tomatoes and basil. Toss with dressing and garnish with cherry tomato halves.

Tasty Chicken and Tabbouleh Salad with Avocado

Serves 4

1 cup tabbouleh
1 1/2 pounds boneless, skinless chicken
  breasts
1 Tablespoon olive oil
salt and freshly ground black pepper
1/2 cup white wine
1 (14 oz) bag spring mix salad
2 Haas avocados, cubed
12 grape tomatoes, halved
1 cucumber, peeled, seeded and diced
1 fennel bulb, cored and sliced

DRESSING
1/2 cup fresh orange juice
1/2 cup basil leaves, sliced
5 Tablespoon lemon juice
2 large green onions, sliced
1/4 cup olive oil
salt and freshly ground black pepper

Preheat oven to 350 degrees. In a metal bowl, cover tabbouleh with 1 cup boiling water. Stir, cover and place in the refrigerator for 30 minutes. In a baking dish, place chicken breasts, drizzle with olive oil and season with salt and pepper. Add wine and bake for 20 minutes. Cool chicken and slice 1/2-inch thick. To make dressing, in a small bowl, combine orange juice, basil, lemon juice and onions. Whisk in oil and season. In a large bowl, layer the spring mix, tabbouleh, chicken, avocados, tomatoes, cucumber and fennel. Toss with vinaigrette dressing.

Time saving tip: The tabbouleh, chicken and vinaigrette may be made ahead. Toss the salad just before serving.

Asian Stir-Fried Chicken Slaw
Serves 4

1/4 cup chicken stock
1/4 teaspoon crushed red pepper flakes
1 pound, boneless, skinless chicken
    breasts, cut into thin strips
3 Tablespoons sesame oil, divided
1 Tablespoon soy sauce
1 clove garlic, minced
2 Tablespoons rice wine vinegar
1 Tablespoon fish sauce

2 teaspoons lime juice
2 teaspoons sugar
1 (16 oz) bag cole slaw
1/4 cup basil, sliced
1/4 cup red onion, sliced
2 Tablespoon green onions, sliced
1/4 cup celery, sliced
1/2 cup slivered almonds, toasted
1 lime, cut into wedges

In a covered bowl, combine stock and red pepper flakes. Stir, add chicken and toss to coat. Cover and place in refrigerator. Marinate 3 hours or overnight. In a large skillet, heat 1 Tablespoon sesame oil over medium-high heat. Drain chicken from marinade and cook thoroughly, 5 - 7 minutes, stirring. Discard marinade. For the dressing, in small bowl, combine soy sauce, garlic, vinegar, fish sauce, lime juice and sugar. Whisk in remaining 2 Tablespoons sesame oil. In a large serving bowl, combine slaw, basil, onions and celery. Add chicken and toss with dressing. Garnish with nuts and lime wedges.

Thai Pork Spring Salad
Serves 6

DRESSING
2 Tablespoons fish sauce
1 Tablespoon sesame seeds, toasted
1 Tablespoon sugar
1 Tablespoon ginger, minced
1/2 teaspoon crushed red pepper flakes
1 teaspoon salt
3 Tablespoons lemon juice
1/3 cup vegetable oil

2 (10 oz) packages spring mix salad
2 cups pork loin, roasted and shredded
2 cups sweet bell peppers, julienned
2 cups celery, sliced
1 cup red onion, sliced
2 cucumbers, peeled, seeded and sliced
1/2 cup cilantro leaves, chopped
1 (8 oz) can mandarin oranges, drained
1/4 cup dry roasted peanuts, chopped

In a small bowl, combine dressing all ingredients, except oil. Whisk in oil. In a large serving bowl, place, lettuce, pork, peppers, celery, onion, cucumber, cilantro, and oranges. Toss with dressing and garnish with peanuts.

Great recipe for leftover pork or chicken.

Kaleidoscope Chicken Salad

Serves 6

2 Tablespoons olive oil, divided
3 cloves garlic, minced
1 sweet onion, sliced
1 red bell pepper, sliced
1 green bell pepper, sliced
2 pounds, boneless, skinless chicken
   breasts, sliced
salt and freshly ground black pepper
2 (10 oz) bags baby salad greens
1 cucumber, peeled, seeded and chopped
1 cup grape tomatoes, halved
1 avocado, cubed
1/2 cup pepper jack cheese, shredded

DRESSING
1/4 cup balsamic vinegar
1 clove garlic, minced
pinch of sugar
1/2 cup olive oil
salt and freshly ground black pepper

In a large sauté pan, heat 1 Tablespoon oil on medium heat. Add garlic, onion and peppers. Cook until vegetables are softened, 8 - 10 minutes. In another sauté pan, heat 1 Tablespoon oil on medium heat, add chicken and season with salt and pepper. Place lettuce, cucumber, tomatoes and avocado on a platter. Top lettuce with warm vegetables and chicken. Sprinkle with cheese and drizzle with dressing.

For a spectacular salad presentation, serve on individual plates.

Peanuty Asian Noodle Salad

Serves 4

12 ounces angel hair pasta
1 large bell pepper, julienned
1 cup carrots, julienned
1/2 cup green onions, sliced
1/4 cup sesame seeds, toasted
1 (8 oz) can water chestnuts, drained
   and chopped
cilantro, peanuts and sesame seeds,
   for garnish

DRESSING
1/4 cup chunky peanut butter
2 teaspoons chili-garlic sauce
1/4 cup cilantro leaves, chopped
1/4 cup dry roasted peanuts
1/4 cup vegetable stock
3 Tablespoons rice wine vinegar
3 Tablespoons soy sauce
1 1/2 Tablespoons sugar
1 clove garlic, minced
1 Tablespoon ginger, minced
2 Tablespoons sesame oil

In a large pot, cook pasta according to package directions. Drain and set aside. In a food processor, combine peanut butter with chili-garlic sauce. Add remaining dressing ingredients and pulse until well blended, scraping down the sides occasionally. In a large bowl, place noodles, peppers, carrots, onions, sesame seeds and water chestnuts. Toss with dressing to coat noodles and garnish as desired.

For extra heat, add a dried chile, chill for 4 hours then remove chile and serve cold. Add shredded cooked chicken or pork for a main course dish.

Fruit Spinach Salad

Serves 4

DRESSING
1/4 cup honey
2 Tablespoons lemon juice
1/2 teaspoon poppy seeds

1 cup cantaloupe, cubed
1 cup honeydew melon, cubed
1 cup fresh pineapple, cubed
1 (10 oz) package spinach leaves
1 cup green or red grapes, halved
1/2 cup mint leaves, chopped
1/4 cup almond slices, toasted

In a small mixing bowl, whisk together honey, lemon juice and poppy seeds. In a large serving bowl, toss fruit, spinach and mint with the dressing. Sprinkle with almond slices.

Blackstone Hotel Caesar Salad, Maitre d'Governor

Serves 2 - 4

1 teaspoon salt
1 clove garlic
2 teaspoons Dijon mustard
1/2 teaspoon freshly ground black pepper
1 lemon, juice and zest
2 Tablespoons tarragon vinegar
6 Tablespoons oil

2 heads romaine lettuce, chopped
1/2 cup Parmesan cheese, grated
1 egg, coddled
1 cup croutons
1 avocado, cut into 6 slices
2 anchovy fillets, drained
freshly ground black pepper

Sprinkle a wooden salad bowl with salt and rub it well with garlic. Discard the garlic. Add the mustard, pepper, lemon juice, zest and vinegar to the bowl, stirring with a wooden spoon. Gradually add the oil, stirring rapidly with a fork. Add the romaine and cheese. Lightly beat the coddled egg and pour it over the greens. Toss greens with the dressing. Top with croutons, avocado slices and anchovies. Add more freshly ground black pepper to taste.

This salad was made tableside at the Blackstone Hotel for a dramatic presentation. |O!|

CODDLED EGG

To coddle an egg, dip a whole egg in its shell into simmering water for 1 minute. Remove and beat egg. Coddled egg may be omitted from the recipe.

Chicken Chutney Pasta Salad

Serves 4 - 6

DRESSING
2 Tablespoons orange juice
1 teaspoon curry powder
3/4 cup mayonnaise
6 Tablespoons prepared chutney

1 (12 oz) package penne pasta
2 cups chicken, cooked and cubed
1 celery rib, sliced
1 green onion, sliced
1 red apple, cored and chopped
1/2 cup golden raisins
2 Tablespoons cilantro leaves, chopped
lettuce, for garnish

Cook pasta according to package directions. Drain and set aside. In a medium bowl, make dressing by stirring together orange juice and curry powder to dissolve curry. Blend in mayonnaise and add chutney to combine. In a large bowl, mix pasta with chicken, celery, onion, apple, raisins and cilantro. Toss with dressing. On a large platter, place lettuce and mound salad in the center.

Savory Chilled Chicken Salad

Serves 8

DRESSING
1 1/2 cups mayonnaise
1 1/2 cups sour cream
3 Tablespoons fresh lemon juice
1/2 teaspoon salt
1 teaspoon celery seed

1/2 teaspoon lemon pepper
2 cups celery, diced
1 cup bell pepper, diced
1 cup mushrooms, sliced
6 cups chicken breast, cooked and cubed
3/4 cup pecan halves, toasted

In a small bowl, whisk together dressing ingredients. In a mixing bowl, toss celery, pepper, mushrooms and chicken. Fold dressing to coat. Cover and chill overnight. Toss with pecans before serving.

Tastes best if made 1 day before serving it! Great by itself or served on fresh croissants.

Macadamia Nut Chicken Salad

Serves 4

DRESSING
1 teaspoon salt
1 teaspoon freshly ground black pepper
1/3 cup rice wine vinegar
1/2 cup sugar
1/2 cup vegetable oil

1 (10 oz) bag lettuce
1 roasted chicken, boned and diced
1 bunch green onions, sliced
1 (6.5 oz) jar macadamia nuts, halved
1/2 cup sesame seeds, toasted
1 small can chow mein noodles

To make the dressing, in a small bowl whisk salt, pepper, vinegar and sugar. Slowly add in oil to blend. In a large serving bowl, place lettuce, chicken, onions, nuts, sesame seeds and noodles. Toss and serve with dressing on the side.

Exotic Butter Lettuce Salad

Serves 4

DRESSING
1/4 cup lime juice
1 Tablespoon honey
1/2 teaspoon salt
1/2 teaspoon freshly ground black pepper
1/2 cup olive oil

1 head butter lettuce, torn
3/4 cup jicama, peeled and julienned
1 (11 oz) can mandarin oranges,
  drained
1 avocado, pitted, peeled and sliced

To make the dressing, in a small bowl whisk together lime juice, honey, salt and pepper. Slowly add oil to thicken. In a large serving bowl, place lettuce. jicama and oranges. Toss salad with dressing and garnish with avocado slices.

Southwest Salsa Salad
Serves 6

DRESSING
1/4 cup lime juice
1/4 teaspoon cumin
salt and freshly ground black pepper to taste
1/4 cup vegetable oil

SALAD
1 (10 oz) package salad greens
1 (15 oz) can of corn, drained
1 (15 oz) can black beans, rinsed and drained
2 cups chicken, cooked and cubed
1/2 cup tomatoes, diced
1/2 cup prepared salsa
1/3 cup cilantro leaves, chopped
1/2 cup pepper jack cheese, shredded
1 cup fried tortilla strips, for garnish
1 avocado, sliced, for garnish

For dressing, in a small bowl, whisk lime juice with seasonings. Slowly whisk in oil. In serving bowl, place lettuce, corn, beans, chicken, tomatoes, salsa, cilantro and cheese. Toss with dressing and garnish by fanning avocado slices on top and sprinkling with tortilla strips.

Quick Carrot Slaw
Serves 6

DRESSING
2 Tablespoons cider vinegar
1/4 cup lemon juice
1/2 teaspoon salt
1/4 teaspoon paprika
1/4 teaspoon cumin
1/4 teaspoon cayenne
2 Tablespoons olive oil

3 cups carrots, shredded
1/2 cup currants
1/2 cup cilantro leaves, chopped

To make dressing, in a small bowl whisk vinegar, lemon juice and seasonings. Slowly add oil. In a covered bowl, place carrots, currants and cilantro. Toss with dressing. Cover and refrigerate at least 2 hours before serving.

Great for potlucks and picnics!

An Original Ingredient

VOLUNTEERS INTERVENING FOR EQUITY (VIE)

In 1977, The Association of Junior Leagues International appointed the JLO as one of 10 sites to develop a paralegal model; testing the theory that older retired citizens could be valuable volunteers in solving community problems. Senior volunteers were trained as Benefits Counselors and 12 "counseling" sites were established; tackling such issues as health insurance, misleading sales tactics and elderly consumer fraud. JLO volunteers carefully researched these complaints and waged a battle with the legislature. The result: the passage of L.B. 877, a law that sets guidelines and standards for supplemental health insurance policies.

Today, VIE continues to be an advocate for elderly rights and privileges, conducting community workshops and counseling programs.

Creamy Spinach Salad
Serves 4

DRESSING
1 cup mayonnaise
3/4 teaspoon Italian herb seasoning
1/2 teaspoon garlic powder
1/4 teaspoon sugar
1/2 cup olive oil
1/4 cup red wine vinegar
2 Tablespoons half and half

1 large bag fresh spinach
2 slices red onion, separated into rings
4 bacon slices, cooked and crumbled
1 egg, hard-boiled (sliced into rings)

For dressing, in a blender mix mayonnaise, seasonings and sugar. Blend and with machine running gradually add oil alternating with vinegar in a slow, steady stream, followed by half and half. In a serving bowl, place spinach and onion rings, tossing with dressing. Garnish with bacon and egg slices.

Sweet Potato Salad
Serves 6

2 3/4 pounds sweet potatoes, peeled and cubed
1 1/2 pounds russet potatoes, peeled and cubed
1/4 cup olive oil
4 slices bacon, chopped
1 shallot, minced
1 teaspoon cayenne pepper
1 teaspoon salt
freshly ground black pepper

DRESSING
1 Tablespoon lemon juice
1 teaspoon hot sauce
1 Tablespoon sesame seeds, toasted
1 Tablespoon parsley, chopped
1/4 cup olive oil
salt and freshly ground black pepper to taste
1 Tablespoon sesame seeds, toasted, for garnish
1 Tablespoon parsley, chopped, for garnish

Preheat oven to 375 degrees. In a large bowl, toss potatoes with 1/4 cup olive oil. Add bacon, shallot and seasonings. In two lightly oiled 9x13-inch pans, divide potato mixture. Bake 30 - 40 minutes until tender, stirring every 10 minutes. Remove from oven and cool 20 minutes.

To make dressing, in a small bowl, whisk together lemon juice, hot sauce, sesame seeds and parsley. Slowly add in olive oil and then season with salt and pepper. In a large serving bowl, place potatoes and toss with dressing. To garnish, sprinkle with sesame seeds and parsley. Serve chilled or at room temperature.

Ranch Potato Salad

Serves 8

RANCH DRESSING
1/2 cup buttermilk
1/2 cup sour cream
1/2 cup mayonnaise
1 Tablespoon cider vinegar
2 teaspoons ranch dressing mix
2 Tablespoons mustard
1 teaspoon dill weed
1 teaspoon celery seed
1 teaspoon salt
1 teaspoon freshly ground black pepper

SALAD
4 pounds russet potatoes, scrubbed
4 eggs, hard-boiled and chopped
4 green onions, sliced
1 shallot, minced
6 bacon slices, cooked and crumbled
1/2 cup sliced almonds, toasted
1/2 cup roasted red peppers, diced
3 celery ribs, sliced
1/4 cup chives, chopped, for garnish

In a large stock pot, place potatoes and add water to cover. Cook on medium heat until tender but still firm, about 30 minutes. Meanwhile make dressing. In a food processor blend all dressing ingredients until smooth. Scrape down sides as needed. Drain and cool potatoes. Peel potatoes (if desired) and dice the potatoes.

In a covered bowl place potatoes, eggs, onions, shallot, bacon, nuts, peppers and celery. Toss with dressing. Cover and refrigerate for at least 2 hours. To serve, garnish with chives.

Marinated Citrus-Mushroom Salad

Serves 6

MARINADE
1/4 cup rice wine vinegar
2 Tablespoons sugar
2 Tablespoons lime juice
1 Tablespoon soy sauce
1/2 teaspoon crushed red pepper flakes
1/2 teaspoon salt
1 teaspoon freshly ground black pepper
3 cloves garlic, minced

2 teaspoons orange zest, grated
2 teaspoons lime zest, grated
2 teaspoons sesame oil
1 teaspoon olive oil
1 1/2 pounds mushrooms, cleaned and halved
1/4 cup cilantro leaves, chopped

In a small saucepan, combine vinegar, sugar, lime juice, soy sauce, red pepper, salt, black pepper and garlic. Bring to a simmer and cook, stirring, for 1 - 2 minutes until sugar dissolves. Remove from heat. Carefully stir in zests and oils. In a large covered bowl, place mushrooms and toss with hot marinade. Cover and refrigerate overnight. To serve, toss with cilantro and drain excess marinade.

Fiesta Slaw

Serves 6

2 cups green cabbage, shredded
2 cups red cabbage, shredded
1/2 cup black olives, drained and sliced
1 cup tomatoes, chopped
1 (15 oz) can black beans, rinsed and
    drained
1/2 cup cilantro leaves, chopped
1/4 cup lime juice

1 Tablespoon jalapeño pepper, seeded
    and chopped
1 teaspoon garlic, minced
3/4 teaspoon cumin
1/2 cup red onion, chopped
1/2 cup corn
1 avocado, sliced

In a large mixing bowl, combine all ingredients and toss. Cover and chill until ready to serve.

Adjust jalapeño to taste.

Hilltop House Roquefort Dressing

Serves 8

1 (8 oz) package cream cheese, softened
2/3 cup half and half
2 teaspoons Worcestershire sauce
2 teaspoons lemon juice
1/2 teaspoon salt
1/2 heaping teaspoon garlic salt

1/2 heaping teaspoon white pepper
2 Tablespoons onion, grated
2 dashes hot sauce
5 ounces Roquefort cheese, crumbled
1 cup mayonnaise

In a medium bowl, mix cream cheese, half and half, Worcestershire, lemon juice, seasonings, onions and hot sauce until creamy. Stir in Roquefort cheese. Add mayonnaise and thin with additional half and half if needed. !O!

Hilltop House Russian Dressing
Serves 8

1/2 cup sugar
1 cup olive oil
1/2 cup malt vinegar
1/3 cup chili sauce

1 teaspoon Worcestershire sauce
1 teaspoon salt
1/2 onion

In a food processor, place all ingredients, except the onion, and blend well. In the bottom of a glass jar, place the onion, intact. Pour the dressing over the onion. Cover and chill until ready to serve.

Once complete, this jar of homemade salad dressing makes a great hostess or "welcome to the neighborhood" gift. Dress up the jar with a ribbon and sticker identifying the ingredients. |O!|

Sewing at the Hattie B. Munroe Center now known as the Monroe-Meyer Center

Provisional Junior League members (left to right) Harriet Gordon, Cornelia Cary and Louise Reynolds help girls learn how to sew at the Hattie B. Munroe home in November 1940. - *Reprinted with permission from the Omaha World-Herald*

Mad Hats

Mrs. William Sample and Mr. and Mrs. Arthur Weaver are all smiles wearing their creations for the Mad Hatter's Ball at the Blackstone Hotel, May 3, 1947. - *Reprinted with permission from the Omaha World-Herald*

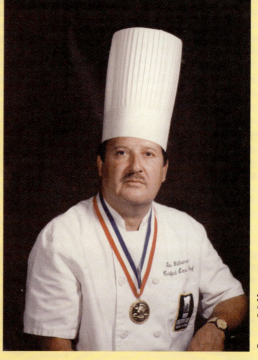

Luis Villamonte

If you would like to try making your own Thunderbird Salad Dressing Mary Ann Cooley of Omaha sent this recipe to Omaha World-Herald's Let's Swap column in August 1996. She received the recipe from Barrett's Barley Corn at 4322 Leavenworth Street.

Thunderbird Salad Dressing

1 1/4 quarts mayonnaise
1/4 cup wine vinegar
1/2 cup vegetable oil
1 ounce lemon juice
1/4 cup Worcestershire sauce
1/2 teaspoon ground celery seed
1/2 teaspoon garlic powder
1/4 teaspoon white pepper
1/4 teaspoon dry mustard
1 teaspoon Accent (monosodium glutamate)
1/4 cup horseradish
1/4 teaspoon ground rosemary
1/4 teaspoon ground oregano

Mix ingredients in order listed for 15 minutes with an electric mixer on low speed. Refrigerate. Makes 2 quarts.

The classic Thunderbird Salad is a must at private clubs, restaurants and for caterers in the Omaha area and beyond. Luis is credited with bringing the salad and the dressing to Omaha while he was a chef at Happy Hollow Club. His son Steve has bottled the dressing under the name Villamonte's Cuisine Original Classic Thunderbird Salad Dressing. It is available at HyVee Stores.

According to Villamonte, to make 4 servings of traditional Thunderbird Salad, start with 4 cups of packed chopped iceberg or romaine lettuce. Add the following ingredients to 3 ounces of Villamonte's Cuisine Original Classic Thunderbird Salad Dressing: 2 Tablespoons real bacon bits, 1/2 cup diced tomatoes, 1/2 cup mozzarella cheese, 2 Tablespoons chives and 1 Tablespoon blue cheese crumbles. Top with diced avocado and homestyle croutons.

VEGETABLES and SIDE DISHES

Asparagus-Prosciutto Rolls
Serves 6

DRESSING
1 Tablespoon red wine vinegar
1/2 Tablespoon Dijon mustard
1 clove garlic, minced
1/4 cup olive oil
1 Tablespoon fresh chives, minced
salt and freshly ground black pepper to
    taste

3 slices prosciutto, cut in half
3 Tablespoons cream cheese or goat
    cheese, softened
18 stalks asparagus, blanched
parsley for garnish

In a small bowl, whisk vinegar, mustard and garlic. Whisk in oil to thicken. Stir in the chives and season. Spread each piece of prosciutto with 1/2 Tablespoon of cheese. Place 3 stalks of asparagus on top. Roll prosciutto to seal. Place on a serving platter and drizzle with vinaigrette. Serve at room temperature.

For a change, try this vinaigrette in the recipe.

RASPBERRY VINAIGRETTE
1/4 cup raspberry vinegar
3/4 cup vegetable oil
2 Tablespoons honey

In a medium bowl, whisk vinegar with oil until thickened. Whisk in honey and serve.

Roasted Asparagus with Wild Mushrooms
Serves 4

1 pound asparagus, ends trimmed
2 teaspoons olive oil
salt and freshly ground black pepper
3 Tablespoons butter
1 shallot, minced

12 ounces wild mushrooms, cleaned and
    sliced
1/2 cup dry white wine
1 Tablespoon Italian parsley, minced
1 teaspoon tarragon, minced

Preheat oven to 475 degrees. On a rimmed baking sheet, arrange asparagus and drizzle oil over asparagus. Sprinkle generously with salt and pepper. Roast about 10 minutes until tender. In a large skillet, melt butter over medium heat. Add shallot and sauté for 1 minute. Add mushrooms and sauté about 5 minutes to brown. Cover mushrooms and cook until tender, about 3 minutes. Add wine and cook uncovered 2 minutes. Stir in herbs and season with salt and pepper to taste. On a serving platter place asparagus and top with mushrooms.

The French Café
Nebraska Sweet Corn Puree
Serves 8

2 Tablespoons oil
1/4 sweet onion, diced
6 ears sweet corn, cleaned
1 cup milk
2 cups cream
salt and freshly black ground pepper, to taste
2 ounces goat cheese
2 Tablespoons green chiles, diced
1 tortilla, cut into strips and fried in vegetable oil

In a large stock pot, sauté onions in oil until soft, about 3 minutes. Reduce heat and add corn. To pot add milk and cream, cover and simmer for 30 minutes. Remove from heat, remove corn from pot and cut the corn from the ears. Return cut corn to the pot with liquid and simmer for 30 minutes, until reduced. Working in small batches, puree in food processor. Season to taste. Garnish with goat cheese, chiles and tortilla strips. |O!|

South of the Border
Grilled Corn on the Cob
Serves 6

1/4 cup mayonnaise
1 Tablespoon lime juice
3 Tablespoons Parmesan cheese, grated
1/2 teaspoon chili powder
1/4 teaspoon crushed red pepper flakes
1/2 teaspoon cumin
1 pinch salt
6 ears corn, cleaned

Prepare grill or preheat oven to 450 degrees. In a small bowl, combine mayonnaise, lime juice, cheese, chili powder, red pepper flakes, cumin and salt. Grill or roast corn for 20 - 30 minutes, turning often, until tender. Remove corn from heat and immediately cover with mayonnaise mixture, covering ears entirely. Serve hot.

THE FRENCH CAFÉ
1017 Howard Street

Opened in 1969, The French Café has become an Omaha icon for its romantic atmosphere and excellent food and service. Owner Tony Abbott's ability to 'pay attention' and 'reinvent the wheel from time to time' makes this French restaurant, in Omaha's Old Market, the place to come for a memorable dining experience. - Menu from The French Café owners Tony and Valerie Abbott

Roasted Green Beans
Serves 8

1 1/2 pounds green beans, trimmed and
   cut into 2-inch pieces
3 Tablespoons olive oil
4 cloves garlic, minced
1 1/2 Tablespoons thyme, minced
2 teaspoons lemon pepper seasoning

1 teaspoon salt
2 teaspoons anchovy paste
2 teaspoons balsamic vinegar
1 Tablespoon lemon juice
1 teaspoon lemon zest
1/2 cup slivered almonds, toasted

Preheat oven to 450 degrees. In a large mixing bowl, toss green beans with oil, garlic, thyme, lemon pepper and salt. On a baking sheet, spread the beans in a single layer and roast, stirring occasionally, for 12 - 15 minutes until tender. Meanwhile in a small bowl, mix anchovy paste, vinegar and lemon juice and zest. In a large serving bowl, place roasted beans and while still warm toss with anchovy mixture and almonds. Serve hot or at room temperature.

Experiment with herbs. This works well with rosemary, oregano, mint and basil. Substitute cauliflower, zucchini, broccoli, asparagus or mushrooms for green beans. Substitute shallots or green onions for a change.

Brussels Sprouts with Peppered Bacon
Serves 6

1/2 pound peppered bacon, cooked and
   diced
bacon drippings
2 shallots, minced
2 pounds Brussels sprouts, halved
2 Tablespoons thyme, chopped

1 teaspoon salt
1 teaspoon freshly ground black pepper
1 Tablespoon balsamic vinegar
2 teaspoons sugar
1/3 cup chicken stock

In a large skillet, heat bacon drippings and sauté shallots for 2 minutes over medium heat. Add Brussels sprouts, thyme, salt, pepper, vinegar and sugar. Sauté 5 minutes, stirring often. Add stock and simmer over high heat covered for 8 - 10 minutes until tender. Add more stock, if needed. Place in serving bowl and toss with bacon.

Herb Roasted Cauliflower
Serves 6

3 Tablespoons olive oil
2 Tablespoons balsamic vinegar
2 Tablespoons thyme, chopped
2 Tablespoons rosemary, stems removed
  and chopped
1 teaspoon salt
1 teaspoon freshly ground black pepper

1 teaspoon Dijon mustard
1/2 teaspoon garlic powder
1 head cauliflower, cored and cut into
  bite-size florets
2 Tablespoons Italian-style breadcrumbs
2 Tablespoons Parmesan cheese, grated

Preheat oven to 450 degrees. In a large bowl, whisk oil, vinegar, herbs, salt, pepper, mustard and garlic. Add cauliflower, bread crumbs and cheese. Toss to coat. In a lipped baking pan, spread cauliflower in a single layer and roast, turning occasionally, for 15 - 20 minutes, until tender and browned. Serve hot or at room temperature.

Experiment with different vinegars, herbs and spices.

Mediterranean Green Beans
Serves 6

2 Tablespoons olive oil
1 red onion, diced
2 cloves garlic, minced
1 teaspoon lemon pepper
1 Tablespoon Greek or Italian seasoning
  blend

1/2 teaspoon salt
2 cups tomatoes, diced
2 Tablespoons balsamic or red wine
  vinegar
1 pound green beans, trimmed
1/2 cup feta cheese, crumbled

In a skillet, heat oil over medium heat. Sauté onion, stirring occasionally for 5 minutes. Add garlic, lemon pepper, Greek or Italian seasoning and salt. Stir and cook 2 minutes. Add tomatoes and vinegar. Cover and simmer for 10 minutes, stirring occasionally. Add green beans and simmer uncovered, stirring frequently, until beans are tender and sauce has thickened, about 15 minutes. Place in a serving dish and top with cheese.

Italian seasoning is usually comprised of oregano, basil, marjoram, thyme and rosemary. Greek seasoning is usually comprised of oregano, garlic, lemon, pepper and marjoram. If you have fresh herbs available, chop about 3 Tablespoons of combination of your choice of herbs. Mint, cilantro or parsley also work well.

An Original  *Ingredient*

The Emmy Gifford Children's Theatre (Omaha Junior Theatre / The Rose)

The Omaha Junior Theatre was created in 1949 under the direction of League member Emmy Gifford and volunteers from the JLO, whom after an adventurous trip to New York City, were committed to bringing children's theater to Omaha. Over the next 25 years, JLO volunteers worked with amateur artists to construct props and detailed costumes creating elaborate productions. A permanent home was established in 1974 and thousands of Omaha youth visited The Emmy Gifford Children's Theatre located at 35th and Center Streets. In 1993, the theater moved in a new direction and to a new home - The Rose Blumkin Performing Arts Center. Today, the Omaha Theatre Company, housed at The Rose, reaches over 700,000 people each year in Omaha and on national tours. It is a nationally recognized "premier" professional children's theater.

Parmesan Crusted Cauliflower
Serves 6

2 egg whites
2 Tablespoons cornstarch
2 Tablespoons lemon juice
1/2 teaspoon salt
1/2 teaspoon freshly ground black pepper
2/3 cup Parmesan cheese, grated
2/3 cup seasoned breadcrumbs

2 teaspoons seasoning of choice (Southwest, Cajun, or herbs of choice)
2 Tablespoons butter
1 head cauliflower, cored and cut into bite-size florets

In a small bowl, mix egg whites, cornstarch, lemon juice, salt and pepper. In a deep pie plate, mix cheese, breadcrumbs and seasonings. Working in batches, dip cauliflower in egg mixture and then place in cheese mixture, turning to coat. Place cauliflower on a wire rack to rest for 15 minutes. In a large skillet, melt butter over medium high heat. In batches, sauté cauliflower, browning on all sides, about 5 - 6 minutes. Return all cauliflower to the pan, cover and simmer, stirring occasionally for 7 minutes until tender. Place in a serving dish.

This is also a great brunch item or an appetizer, garnished with parsley, cilantro or watercress. Use toothpicks and accompany with a spicy mustard.

Sautéed Kale with Sun-Dried Tomatoes
Serves 6

1 bunch kale, stems removed and torn into bite-size pieces
2 Tablespoons olive oil
2 cloves garlic, sliced

3 Tablespoons olive oil packed sun-dried tomatoes, julienned
coarse salt and freshly ground black pepper to taste

In a pan, set a steamer basket over simmering water. Add kale, cover, and steam until tender, about 10 minutes. In a skillet, heat oil over medium heat. Add garlic and cook, stirring until tender, about 3 minutes. To skillet, add steamed and drained kale and tomatoes. Toss to combine and season. Cover skillet and continue cooking, stirring occasionally, for 5 minutes.

Chilled Herb Asparagus

Serves 10

2 1/2 pounds asparagus. trimmed
1 cup onion, diced
1 cup red wine vinegar
1/2 cup water
2 teaspoons sugar
1 teaspoon oregano

1 teaspoon tarragon
1 teaspoon dry mustard
1 teaspoon Worcestershire sauce
1/2 teaspoon salt
1/4 teaspoon freshly ground black pepper

In a large saucepan, heat water, add asparagus and simmer for 5 minutes until still crisp. In a colander, drain asparagus and shock with cold water for 3 minutes until cooled. In a 9x13-inch glass baking dish place asparagus. In a medium mixing bowl, whisk together onion, vinegar, water, sugar, herbs, mustard, Worcestershire sauce, salt and pepper. Pour mixture over asparagus. Cover dish with foil and refrigerate for 2 to 8 hours. To serve, remove asparagus from the marinade mixture and arrange on a chilled serving platter. Discard marinade.

Fresh Herbed Potato Cakes

Serves 6

2 russet potatoes, baked and insides
    completely removed. Discard skins.
1 egg, beaten
1/4 cup flour
1/2 teaspoon baking powder
1/2 cup breadcrumbs
2 Tablespoons chives, chopped
2 Tablespoons rosemary, chopped

1/4 teaspoon kosher salt
1/4 teaspoon freshly ground black pepper
2 teaspoons Dijon mustard
2 Tablespoons Parmesan cheese, grated
1/2 cup heavy cream, as needed
1/2 cup seasoned bread crumbs
1/2 cup butter, divided

In a large bowl, place potatoes, egg, flour, baking powder, breadcrumbs, herbs, seasonings, mustard and cheese. Use a pastry cutter or a potato masher to blend. If mixture is too stiff, add cream 1 tablespoon at a time. In a pie plate, place seasoned breadcrumbs. Form potato mixture into balls, about 1/3 cup size. Press balls into patties and dredge in breadcrumbs on both sides. In a large skillet, melt butter over medium heat and sauté patties in batches until browned, about 3 - 4 minutes each side. Add more butter if needed. Do not overcook. Serve immediately or at room temperature.

Sweet Potatoes in Orange Cups

Serves 6

3 navel oranges, halved
2 (15 oz) cans sweet potatoes
1/2 cup heavy cream

1/2 teaspoon salt
1 Tablespoon brown sugar, packed
2 cups miniature marshmallows

Preheat oven to 350 degrees. Working over a bowl, from oranges remove all pulp, membrane and juice using a grapefruit knife. Discard membrane. In a 9x13-inch glass baking dish, arrange the orange cups. In a medium bowl, mash sweet potatoes and add cream, salt and brown sugar to blend. Stir in reserved orange pulp and juices and blend well. Fill orange cups with mixture, top with marshmallows pressed into the potatoes. Bake for 20 minutes until heated through and oranges and marshmallows are browned.

Sugar and Spice Sweet Potatoes

Serves 8 - 10

3 pounds sweet potatoes, whole
3/4 cup brown sugar, packed
3 Tablespoons butter
1 teaspoon cinnamon

1/2 teaspoon nutmeg
1/4 teaspoon salt
1/2 cup half and half
2 Tablespoons brown sugar, packed

Preheat oven to 400 degrees. Grease a 1 1/2 quart casserole dish. In a large stock pot of salted water, cook sweet potatoes on medium-high heat until done. Peel sweet potatoes. In a large bowl, mash potatoes and stir in brown sugar, butter, cinnamon, nutmeg, salt and half and half. Blend well. Place in a casserole dish and sprinkle with brown sugar. Bake for 30 minutes.

Colorful Curried Potatoes
Serves 6

1/4 cup vegetable oil
1 onion, sliced
1 1/2 teaspoons mustard seeds
1 teaspoon salt
1/2 teaspoon garlic powder
1/2 teaspoon crushed red pepper flakes

1 1/2 Tablespoons curry powder
2 cups tomatoes, diced
2 1/2 pounds russet potatoes, cooked, peeled and cubed
1 Tablespoon cilantro leaves, chopped

In a large skillet, heat oil over medium heat. Add onions and sauté until softened, about 5 minutes. In a small mixing bowl, mix mustard seed, salt, garlic, pepper and curry. Add to onions and stir constantly for 1 - 2 minutes. Add tomatoes and potatoes and cook covered for 10 minutes. Transfer mixture to serving dish and garnish with cilantro.

This is a wonderful vegetarian side to serve with any Indian main dish.

Louie Cantoni's started at 16th and Leavenworth Streets and moved to 19th and Leavenworth. It was a popular lunch place for downtown businessmen and judges. *- From Lou Marcuzzo*

Overnight Mashed Potato Casserole
Serves 10 - 12

8 russet potatoes, boiled and peeled
1/4 cup hot milk
6 ounces cream cheese, softened
1 cup sour cream
2 Tablespoons butter

2 teaspoons onion salt
1/2 teaspoon salt
1/4 teaspoon freshly ground black pepper
paprika
butter

In a large bowl, place potatoes and add hot milk and mash until creamy. Blend in cream cheese, sour cream, butter, salts and pepper. In a 2-quart greased casserole dish, spread potatoes evenly. Sprinkle with paprika and dot with butter. Cover and refrigerate overnight. Thirty minutes before baking, remove potatoes from refrigerator. Preheat oven to 350 degrees. Bake casserole 30 - 40 minutes until browned.

POTATOES O'BRIEN

According to a 1970 Omaha World-Herald article, Potatoes O'Brien was invented at Omaha's old Henshaw Hotel, 1511 Farnam Street, in 1913 by their Italian chef, Pete Nicolini. They were named after the hotel owner at the time, Thomas J. O'Brien. According to Rinaldo "Reno" Sibilia, who worked with Nicolini before becoming the chef at the Omaha Athletic Club, a popular entrée at the Henshaw was a small steak served with Minute O'Brien Potatoes.

Hasselback Potatoes
Serves 4 - 6

6 russet potatoes
1/2 cup butter, melted
salt and freshly ground black pepper to taste

1/4 cup Parmesan cheese, grated
2 Tablespoons breadcrumbs
paprika

Preheat over to 375 degrees. Rinse and pat dry potatoes. Cut slits into the potato crosswise three-fourths of the way through spacing each slit about 1/8-inch apart. Cut slits across the entire length of each potato. Place potatoes in a greased baking dish. Drizzle with half of melted butter and season with salt and pepper. Bake for 30 minutes, brushing occasionally with remaining half of butter. In a small bowl, mix cheese and breadcrumbs. Sprinkle cheese mixture and paprika on top of the potatoes. Bake potatoes until tender, about another 20 - 30 minutes.

Bravo Potatoes
Serves 6

2 Tablespoons olive oil
1 1/2 pounds russet potatoes, peeled and cubed
1 (14 oz) can diced tomatoes, drained
5 cloves garlic, sliced
1/2 teaspoon cumin
1/2 teaspoon sugar

1/2 teaspoon crushed red pepper flakes
1/2 teaspoon hot sauce
salt to taste
lemon juice
cilantro leaves, chopped
coarse salt

In a large skillet, heat oil over medium-high heat. Add potatoes and cook until browned about 10 minutes, turning occasionally. In a food processor, place tomatoes, garlic, cumin, sugar, pepper and hot sauce. Pulse a few times to blend but do not puree. Add salt to taste. Add tomatoes to browned potatoes reduce heat to medium and cook 6 - 8 minutes, until potatoes are tender, stirring occasionally. Place in a serving dish. Garnish with lemon juice, cilantro, and coarse salt. Serve warm or at room temperature.

Layered Mashed Potatoes and Mushrooms

Serves 10

12 ounces mushrooms
1/2 cup butter, divided
1 1/4 cups onion, minced
3 Tablespoons thyme, chopped and
  divided
2 teaspoons salt, divided
2 teaspoons freshly ground black pepper,
  divided

4 cloves garlic, minced
1/2 cup sherry
1 1/4 cups milk, divided
1 Tablespoon flour
3 1/2 pounds potatoes, peeled and cubed
1 egg, lightly beaten
1 (8 oz) package cream cheese
1/2 cup breadcrumbs

Preheat oven to 350 degrees. In a food processor, finely chop mushrooms. In a large skillet, melt 1 Tablespoon butter over medium heat. Add onion and cook for 3 minutes, stirring frequently. Add 2 Tablespoons thyme, 1 teaspoon salt, 1 teaspoon pepper and garlic. Cook for 5 minutes, stirring occasionally. Add sherry and simmer for 3 minutes. Whisk in 1/2 cup milk and the flour. Continue to simmer for 1 minute to thicken. Set aside. Bring a large pot of salted water to a boil, add potatoes and cook for 15 minutes until tender. Drain potatoes and return to pot. Add remaining 3/4 cup milk, 3 Tablespoons butter, 1 teaspoon salt, 1 teaspoon pepper, 1 Tablespoon thyme, egg and cream cheese. Mash potato mixture and blend well. In a greased 9x13-inch baking dish, spread half of the potato mixture. Top with mushroom mixture and cover with remaining potatoes. Sprinkle with breadcrumbs. Cover with foil and bake until heated, about 25 minutes.

Baked Potatoes on the Grill

Serves 6

6 russet potatoes, scrubbed
6 Tablespoons butter
6 cloves garlic, minced
6 Tablespoons Parmesan cheese, grated

1 teaspoon freshly ground black pepper
2 Tablespoons fresh herbs, chopped
  (chives, rosemary, oregano)
6 Tablespoons butter

Heat grill to medium high. Cut heavy duty aluminum foil into 12 squares, each more than double the size of potatoes. Melt 6 Tablespoons butter and divide among each set of 2 pieces of foil. Slice potatoes 1/2-inch thick. Fan the potato slices on each foil pack, covering 1/2 of the next slice. Sprinkle potato slices evenly with garlic, cheese, pepper and herbs. Place butter evenly over potatoes. Wrap foil packets tightly to seal. Place on hot grill for about 20 minutes. Cool slightly before opening.

Grilled Red Onions
Serves 6

3 red onions, peeled and halved
1/2 cup balsamic vinegar
1/4 cup olive oil
2 Tablespoons Dijon mustard

1 1/2 teaspoons freshly ground black
    pepper
1/2 teaspoon course salt
1 bunch basil leaves, cleaned and
    chiffonade cut

In a large glass baking dish, place onions cut side up. In a small bowl, whisk together vinegar, oil, mustard, pepper and salt. Pour marinade over onions slowly to absorb. Heat grill to medium hot. Place onions in a grill basket, cook 20 - 25 minutes turning every 5 minutes until tender and caramelized. Place on a serving platter and garnish with basil. Serve warm or at room temperature.

Baked Sweet Potato Fries
Serves 4

1 egg, beaten
2 Tablespoons water
2/3 cup breadcrumbs
1/4 cup Parmesan cheese, grated
1/2 teaspoon cayenne pepper

1/2 teaspoon garlic powder
2 sweet potatoes, cut in 1-inch wedges,
    crinkle cut in 1/2-inch pieces, or cut
    into 1/2-inch coins
1 Tablespoon olive oil

Preheat oven to 450 degrees. In a small bowl whisk egg and water. In a zippered plastic bag, toss breadcrumbs, cheese, pepper and garlic. Dip potatoes into egg mixture, then breadcrumbs, tossing to coat. Arrange on a greased baking sheet in a single layer. Drizzle lightly with oil. Bake for 25 - 30 minutes, turning halfway through baking process. Serve warm.

Carrot Ring

Serves 10

1 cup butter, softened
1/2 cup brown sugar, packed
1 egg, beaten
1 Tablespoon water
1 1/2 cups flour
2 cups carrots, grated
1/2 teaspoon baking soda

1 teaspoon baking powder
1/2 teaspoon nutmeg
1/2 teaspoon salt
1/2 teaspoon cinnamon
2 cups frozen peas, thawed
2 Tablespoons butter
mint sprig

In a small bowl, cream butter and brown sugar. Stir in egg, water and flour to blend. Add carrots, baking soda, baking powder, nutmeg, salt and cinnamon. Mix well like a cake batter. In a greased 9-inch ring mold, place batter and push down. Cover and refrigerate overnight. Thirty minutes before baking, remove from refrigerator and preheat oven to 350 degrees. Bake for 50 - 60 minutes. Meanwhile heat peas with butter. Remove ring from oven and invert onto a round tray and unmold. Place a bowl in the center of the ring for the peas. Garnish with mint.

Use this instead of stuffing or potatoes with a turkey dinner and it is wonderful. This recipe came from Junior League member, Suzy Barker.

• •

Roasted Vidalia Onion Tarts

Serves 12

6 Vidalia or other sweet onions
6 Tablespoons unsalted butter
1/3 cup unsalted butter, melted
1/3 cup turbinado or other fine white sugar

1 package puff pastry sheets
1 egg yolk
1 Tablespoon water

Preheat oven to 350 degrees. In foil squares, place each onion with skin intact except for the very top sliced off. Place 1 Tablespoon butter on top of each onion. Wrap tightly in foil and place in a baking pan. Bake until soft about 45 - 60 minutes. Squeeze with a hot pad to check doneness. Using molds or ramekins to fit each onion half, brush each mold with melted butter and dust with sugar. When the onions are soft, use gloves to unwrap the foil and remove the onion skins. Cut the top and bottom roots off, discarding. Cut each onion in half and place in prepared molds. Increase heat to 400 degrees. Cut puff pastry in 12 rounds to overlap the edge of the molds. Cover onions with puff pastry and seal tightly. In a small bowl, beat egg yolk with 1 Tablespoon water. Brush each puff pastry top with egg wash. Place ramekins on a baking sheet and bake 15 - 20 minutes until pastry is golden brown and puffed. Serve hot or warm.

Spinach Artichoke Supreme

Serves 6

2 (10 oz) packages frozen spinach, thawed and drained
1 (8 oz) package cream cheese, softened
1/2 cup butter, melted and divided

salt and freshly ground black pepper to taste
1/2 pound artichoke hearts, canned or frozen and halved
1 cup seasoned croutons

Preheat oven to 350 degrees. In a medium bowl, mix spinach, cream cheese and 1/4 cup of the melted butter. Season mixture to taste. Pour mixture into a greased 1-quart dish. Arrange artichokes on top. In a small bowl, toss croutons with 1/4 cup melted butter and sprinkle over casserole. Bake for 20 - 30 minutes or until brown.

Marinated Asparagus

Serves 6

1 cup vegetable oil
1/2 cup white wine vinegar
2 cloves garlic, crushed
1 1/2 teaspoons salt
1 teaspoon freshly ground black pepper

1 (15 oz) can hearts of palm, sliced
3 pounds asparagus, trimmed and steamed
1 pint cherry tomatoes, halved

In a small bowl, whisk oil, vinegar, garlic, salt and pepper. In a glass baking dish, place hearts of palm, asparagus and tomatoes. Drizzle marinade over vegetables. Cover and refrigerate for 1 - 2 hours.

Baked Bean Medley
Serves 10 - 12

1 1/2 pounds ground beef
1 onion, chopped
1 teaspoon salt
1/4 cup barbeque sauce
1/4 cup ketchup
1/3 cup brown sugar, packed
1 Tablespoon chili powder
1 Tablespoon honey mustard

2 Tablespoons molasses
1 teaspoon salt
1 teaspoon freshly ground black pepper
1 (15 1/2 oz) can kidney beans, drained
1 (16 oz) can butter beans, drained
1 (16 oz) can pork and beans
1 (16 oz) can pinto beans, drained
1/2 pound bacon, cooked and crumbled

In a large skillet over medium heat, place ground beef, onion and salt. Cook until meat is browned and drain excess fat. Preheat over to 350 degrees. In a large bowl, combine barbeque sauce, ketchup, brown sugar, chili powder, mustard, molasses, salt and pepper. To the bowl, add beans and meat mixture. Place in a greased 2 1/2 quart casserole dish. Bake for 1 hour. To serve, sprinkle with bacon.

Good as a side or main dish.

Mushroom Pilaf
Serves 10

1 cup butter
2 1/2 cups long grain rice
1/2 cup onion, diced
1 cup celery, diced
1 pound mushrooms, sliced
3 cups chicken stock

1/2 cup sherry
1 teaspoon thyme
1/4 teaspoon freshly ground black pepper
1 teaspoon salt
1/2 cup parsley leaves, minced

In a large skillet melt butter and add rice, stirring to coat. To skillet, add onion, celery and mushrooms, and sauté, stirring constantly. In a saucepan heat stock, sherry, thyme, pepper and salt. Bring just to a boil and add to rice mixture. Heat partially covered and cook until liquid is absorbed and rice is tender. To serve, fluff with a fork and fold in parsley.

Husker Harvest

Serves 8

3 cups corn, cooked
3 green onions, sliced
2 tomatoes, diced
3/4 cup unpeeled cucumber, diced
1/4 cup onion, diced
1/4 cup sour cream
2 Tablespoons mayonnaise

1 Tablespoon white vinegar
1 teaspoon sugar
1/2 teaspoon salt
1/4 teaspoon celery seed
1/4 teaspoon dill weed
1/4 teaspoon dry mustard
dill sprigs

In a large bowl, combine corn, green onions, tomatoes, cucumbers and onion. Toss well. In a small bowl, combine sour cream, mayonnaise, vinegar, sugar, salt, celery seed, dill weed and dry mustard. Pour mixture over vegetables and toss to coat. Cover and refrigerate several hours or overnight. To serve, garnish with fresh dill sprigs.

Chicken Fried Rice Skillet

Serves 4

1/4 cup oyster sauce
2 Tablespoons soy sauce
2 Tablespoons peanut oil, divided
1 shallot, minced
3 cloves garlic, minced
1/2 cup frozen peas, thawed

1 (8 oz) can water chestnuts, drained
  and chopped
1 cup chicken, cooked and shredded
6 cups cooked white rice, cooled
2 eggs, beaten
1/2 cup green onions, sliced

In a small bowl, whisk oyster sauce and soy sauce. Set aside. Heat a large skillet over medium-high heat and add 1 1/2 Tablespoons of oil. Sauté shallot and garlic for 1 minute. To skillet, add peas, water chestnuts and chicken, stirring constantly for 1 minute. Add rice and reserved sauce, breaking up the rice clumps, and cook until heated, about 3 minutes. Reduce heat, and move ingredients to one side of skillet. Add 1/2 Tablespoon of oil to empty side of pan and add eggs. Cook without stirring until they just begin to set, then scramble and cook thoroughly. Then mix eggs with the rice mixture. Add green onions and cook to heat. Serve hot.

This is a great master recipe. Experiment with vegetables, like bean sprouts, corn, shitake mushrooms, carrots, or peppers and meats.

Zucchini Boats

Serves 10

6 zucchini
1 cup cheddar cheese, shredded
3/4 cup small-curd cottage cheese
2 eggs, beaten
1 Tablespoon mustard
1 Tablespoon chives, minced

1 1/2 Tablespoons thyme, chopped
1/2 teaspoon freshly ground black pepper
1/2 teaspoon cumin
1/2 teaspoon salt
paprika

Preheat oven to 400 degrees. Puncture zucchini with a fork, and place on a plate. Microwave for 3 - 4 minutes until slightly tender. Let cool. Trim ends and cut each zucchini in half, lengthwise. Remove pulp to create a canoe shape. Dry pulp and transfer to food processor. Add to the food processor cheddar cheese, cottage cheese, egg, mustard, chives, thyme, pepper, cumin and salt. Process to combine. Place zucchini boats in a greased baking pan. Fill with cheese mixture and sprinkle with paprika. Bake for 35 - 45 minutes, until puffed and golden brown. Serve warm.

Flatiron Cafe Shitake Crab and Havarti Gratin

Serves 4

1/2 cup butter
1 Tablespoon garlic, minced
3 pounds shitake mushrooms, cleaned, destemmed and sliced
1 teaspoon salt

1/2 teaspoon freshly ground black pepper
1 pound crab meat (lump or blue), picked over and flaked
8 ounces Havarti cheese, thinly sliced

In a large sauté pan, melt butter over medium heat and add garlic and cook 1 minute. Add mushrooms and cook until soft and tender, about 5 minutes stirring occasionally. Season with salt and pepper and cool. Preheat oven to 400 degrees. Toss the cooled mushroom mixture with the crabmeat and place in a casserole dish. Top with Havarti cheese and bake for 25 minutes until brown and bubbly. Finish under the broiler if necessary to get the top browned. |O!|

Merry-Go-Round Restaurant and Hosman's Drive Inn
Turner Boulevard and Farnam Streets

The Merry-Go-Round restaurant and Hosman's Drive Inn at Turner Boulevard and Farnam Streets in 1940. - *From the Bostwick-Frohardt Collection owned by KMTV and on permanent loan to the Durham Western Heritage Museum, Omaha, Nebraska*

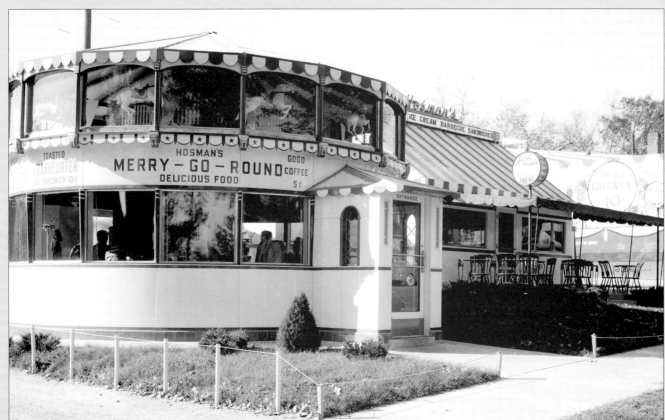

BRUNCH

Kaufmann's Pastry Shoppe
3920 Farnam Street

German-trained baker Henry Kaufmann opened Kaufmann's Pastry Shoppe at 3920 Farnam Street in 1944 after working at Ortman's Bakery and Louis Sommers' Grocery. From the beginning, Kaufmann's products sold literally like hot cakes. The shop made wedding cakes and supplied bread and rolls to area restaurants, but otherwise all merchandise was sold over-the-counter beginning with hot donuts and breakfast rolls when the doors opened at 7 a.m. Monday through Saturday. Also at the counter were Kaufmann's European-style breads and cakes, "richer than you'll find in Germany," according to the baker. Kaufmann retired and sold the bakery in 1979 and it later closed. - *Reprinted with permission from the Omaha World-Herald*

Northrup Jones
1617 Farnam Street

Exterior of the Farnam Building September 29, 1930. Northrup Jones is in the lower right store front. A.D. Northrup and Wilbur A. Jones started the store in 1916 providing coffee, rolls and fancy pastries for many downtown workers. - *From the Bostwick-Frohardt Collection owned by KMTV and on permanent loan to the Durham Western Heritage Museum, Omaha, Nebraska*

Northrup Jones Date Nut Drop Cookies

1 1/2 cups sugar
1 cup butter, softened
3 eggs, beaten
1 teaspoon baking soda
2 Tablespoons hot coffee
3 cups cake flour

1 teaspoon cinnamon
1/2 teaspoon nutmeg
1/2 teaspoon ground cloves
1 pound dates, cut into quarters
1 1/2 cups nuts, chopped
2 Tablespoons molasses

Preheat oven to 350 degrees. In a bowl, cream sugar and butter until well blended. Add the eggs. Dissolve baking soda in hot coffee and add to mixture. Combine the flour and spices, sifting if needed. Add 1/2 of the flour mixture to the wet ingredients. Next add the dates and nuts and mix well. Add the molasses and the remaining flour mixture. Mix to blend. On a greased cookie sheet drop dough by teaspoonfuls. Bake for 9 minutes or until browned. Cool on a wire rack.

Mother's Coffee Cake

Serves 10

1/2 cup butter, softened	1 cup sour cream
1 cup sugar	1/2 cup brown sugar, packed
2 eggs	1/2 cup flour
1 teaspoon vanilla	2 teaspoons cinnamon
2 cups flour	1/4 cup butter, softened
1 teaspoon baking soda	1/2 cup sliced almonds
1 teaspoon baking powder	1 Tablespoon powdered sugar

Preheat oven to 350 degrees. In a large bowl, cream together butter and sugar. Add eggs and vanilla. Mix well. In a separate bowl, mix flour, baking soda and baking powder. Combine dry mixture into wet ingredients. Add sour cream and beat thoroughly. For the topping, in a separate bowl, mix together brown sugar, flour, cinnamon and butter. Add sliced almonds. Into a greased and floured fluted tube pan, pour half the cake batter. Sprinkle with half of the topping. Add remaining batter and sprinkle with the remainder of topping. Bake for 40 minutes. Just before serving, sprinkle with powdered sugar.

Place a paper lace doily on top of the coffee cake and then sprinkle the powdered sugar for an extra special touch.

Pecan, Caramel and Sour Cream Coffee Cake

Serves 10 - 12

2 cups butter, softened and divided	1/2 teaspoon baking soda
1 1/2 cups sugar	1 cup sour cream
2 eggs	2 cups brown sugar, packed and divided
1 teaspoon vanilla	2 teaspoons cinnamon
2 cups flour	2 cups chopped pecans, divided
1 teaspoon baking powder	6 Tablespoons milk

Preheat oven to 350 degrees. In a large bowl, cream together 1 1/2 cups butter and sugar. Add eggs and vanilla. In another bowl, combine flour, baking powder and baking soda. Alternate adding the sour cream and flour mixture into the butter mixture. Mix until well blended. For the filling, combine 1 cup brown sugar, cinnamon and 1 cup pecans. Grease and flour a 9x13-inch baking dish. Pour half of the batter into the pan and spread evenly. Pour half of the filling over the batter. Repeat each layer. Bake 35 minutes. For the topping, in a medium saucepan melt 1/2 cup butter and add milk, 1 cup brown sugar and 1 cup pecans. Stir for 3 - 4 minutes over medium heat. Pour caramel mixture over the top of the baked cake. Broil cake, until caramel topping bubbles, about 3 - 5 minutes. Let cake cool completely before cutting into squares.

Cake may be prepared 1 day ahead. Keep covered and store in refrigerator.

Apple Pecan Spice Cake

Serves 10 - 12

2 1/2 cups sugar
2 teaspoons baking soda
2 teaspoons pumpkin pie spice
1 1/4 teaspoons salt
3/4 cup vegetable oil
3 eggs, slightly beaten

2 teaspoons vanilla
4 large Granny Smith apples, peeled, quartered and sliced into 1/4-inch pieces
1 1/2 cups chopped pecans
3 cups flour

Preheat oven to 300 degrees. Grease a 9x13-inch baking dish, lightly sprinkle sugar on the bottom of the pan. In a large bowl, sift together sugar, soda, pumpkin pie spice and salt. Whisk in oil, eggs and vanilla until smooth. Add apples and pecans to batter and stir until well coated. Whisk in flour until just combined. Spread batter evenly in baking dish. Bake for 1 3/4 hours, until tester comes out clean. Cool completely and cut into squares.

Use 2 loaf pans, if desired. Great warmed up and served with vanilla ice cream or rum caramel sauce. Although it seems like a long bake time, be sure not to remove cake from the oven too soon.

Blackstone Hotel Crumb Coffee Cake

Serves 8

1 1/2 cups flour
1 Tablespoon baking powder
1/2 teaspoon salt
3/4 cup sugar
1/2 cup butter
1 egg, well-beaten
1/2 cup milk

1 teaspoon vanilla
4 Tablespoons butter, melted
2 Tablespoons cinnamon
2 Tablespoons flour
1 cup brown sugar, packed
1 cup pecans, chopped

Preheat oven to 375 degrees. Grease an 8-inch square baking pan. In a large bowl, combine flour, baking powder, salt and sugar. Cut in butter with a fork until fine, do not use mixer. Blend in well-beaten egg and milk by hand. Add vanilla and beat just enough to mix well. In a separate bowl, mix together the melted butter, cinnamon, flour, brown sugar and pecans with a spatula. Spread half of the batter in the greased pan, and then sprinkle half of the cinnamon and nut mixture on top. Spread remaining batter on top of the cinnamon and nut mixture, and then top with the remaining cinnamon mixture. Bake for 40 - 45 minutes. |O!|

An Original Ingredient

CHILD SAVING INSTITUTE/ CHILDREN'S CRISIS CENTER

The JLO has a long tradition of supporting and caring for Omaha youth. In 1975, the JLO developed the Parent Assistance Line with Family Service of Omaha-Council Bluffs. Beginning in 1980, the JLO would pledge nearly $30,000 over a three-year period toward the creation and implementation of the Children's Crisis Center. This center provided 24-hour respite care for children 12 and under, whose families were experiencing a crisis. JLO volunteers designed courses to teach parenting and coping skills, developed and organized children activities during stays and planned weekly menus. League members worked directly with staff to provide child care and acted as family advocates. In 1985, the JLO assisted in the merger of the Children's Crisis Center, Parent Assistance Line and Child Saving Institute (CSI). Currently, CSI has two emergency shelters, caring for children under the age of 19 and provides individual service plans to ensure a child's safe environment.

Magi Bread
Serves 8-10

1/2 cup butter, softened
1 cup sugar
2 eggs, beaten
1 teaspoon vanilla
2 cups flour
1 teaspoon baking soda
dash of salt
1 cup bananas, mashed
1 cup coconut flakes
1 cup maraschino cherries, quartered
1/2 cup dates, chopped
1 cup mandarin oranges, cut each slice in half
1 cup chocolate chips
2/3 cup sliced almonds, divided
1/2 cup powdered sugar

Preheat oven to 350 degrees. In a large bowl, cream together butter and sugar. Add eggs and vanilla and beat until fluffy. In a separate bowl, combine the flour, baking soda and salt, add to the creamed mixture and beat until well-blended. Fold in mashed bananas, coconut, fruits, chips and 1/2 cup almonds. Pour into 2 greased and sugar-dusted 8-inch loaf pans and sprinkle remaining almonds over the top. Bake for 60 minutes or until the tester comes out clean. Dust with powdered sugar. Cool for 10 minutes before removing from the pans to wire racks. Cool completely before slicing.

Fruitcake done right! May also drizzle top with a powdered sugar icing.

Blueberry-Lemon Scones
Serves 8

2 cups flour
1 Tablespoon baking powder
1/2 teaspoon baking soda
1/4 teaspoon salt
2 Tablespoons sugar
1 Tablespoon lemon zest
1/2 cup butter
2/3 cup buttermilk
3/4 cup dried blueberries
1 Tablespoon milk
1 Tablespoon sugar

Preheat oven to 400. In a large bowl, combine flour, baking powder, baking soda, salt, sugar and lemon zest. Cut in the butter with a pastry blender until crumbly. Add buttermilk and blueberries. Stir until moistened. Turn dough out onto a floured surface and knead 5 - 6 times. Pat into an 8-inch circle. Cut into 8 wedges and place 1 inch apart on a greased baking sheet. Brush with milk and sprinkle with sugar. Bake for 15 minutes.

Replace lemon zest and blueberries with grated orange peel and dried cranberries for a holiday touch.

Sweet Almond Cake

Serves 8

3/4 cup butter
1 1/2 cups sugar
2 eggs
1 1/2 cups flour

pinch salt
1 teaspoon almond extract
sliced almonds and sugar for topping

Preheat oven to 350 degrees. In a saucepan, melt the butter and add the sugar. Stir in the eggs, flour, salt, almond extract and mix well. Line a 10-inch skillet with foil and grease. Pour batter and cover with sliced almonds and sugar. Bake for 30 - 40 minutes.

This cake is delicious served at brunch, with coffee or tea, or as a dessert. Guests always request the recipe.

Crème Brûlée French Toast

Serves 6

1/2 cup unsalted butter
1 cup brown sugar, packed
2 Tablespoons light corn syrup
6 (1-inch thick) slices French bread
5 eggs

1 1/2 cups half and half
1 teaspoon vanilla
1 teaspoon Grand Marnier liqueur
1/4 teaspoon salt
powdered sugar

In a small saucepan, melt butter. Add brown sugar and corn syrup, stirring until sugar is dissolved. Pour into a 9x13-inch pan. Remove crust from bread and arrange bread in the pan in a single layer. In small bowl, whisk together eggs, half and half, vanilla, orange brandy and salt. Pour over bread. Cover and chill overnight. Preheat oven to 350 degrees. Bring pan to room temperature and bake uncovered for 35 - 40 minutes. To serve, invert pan onto a serving platter and sprinkle with powdered sugar.

Stuffed Orange French Toast
Serves 8

4 eggs
1 cup milk
1/2 teaspoon cinnamon
1 teaspoon vanilla
8 ounces cream cheese, softened
16 slices French bread or egg Challah
1 cup marmalade, or other fruit preserve

ORANGE BUTTER
1 pound powdered sugar
8 ounces cream cheese
1 cup butter
1 (6 oz) can frozen orange juice, thawed

Preheat griddle. In a bowl, whisk together eggs, milk, cinnamon and vanilla. Spread softened cream cheese on 1 side of the French bread. Spread marmalade over the cream cheese. Sandwich with another slice of bread. Dip into egg mixture. Cook on a griddle until brown on both sides. Sprinkle with powdered sugar and serve with orange butter.

To make the orange butter beat together powdered sugar, cream cheese, butter and orange juice. Orange butter may be frozen until ready to use.

Always a hit with overnight guests. Orange butter recipe may be halved and there will still be more than enough for 1 loaf.

Skier's French Toast
Serves 4 - 5

1/2 cup butter
2 Tablespoons white corn syrup
1 cup brown sugar
1 loaf Texas toast or French bread
5 eggs

1 cup evaporated milk, scant
1 teaspoon vanilla
1/2 teaspoon salt
powdered sugar

In a medium saucepan, combine butter, syrup and brown sugar. Boil for 1 minute then pour into a buttered 9x13-inch pan. Slice bread into 1-inch thick slices. Crowd bread slices on top of the caramel sauce. Beat together eggs, milk, vanilla and salt. Pour over the bread. Cover and refrigerate overnight. Preheat oven to 350 degrees and bake 45 minutes. Invert the pan on a platter and cut into squares, sift powdered sugar on top and serve.

No need for syrup with this rich morning treat.

Cheesy Dill Zucchini Bake

Serves 8

4 Tablespoons butter, divided
1 teaspoon olive oil
2 shallots, minced
2 cloves garlic, minced
2 pounds zucchini, peeled, shredded and
   wrung dry
1 teaspoon salt
1 teaspoon freshly ground black pepper
3 Tablespoons dill, chopped
1/2 teaspoon crushed red pepper flakes

1 1/2 cups colby-jack cheese, shredded
1 cup cottage cheese
4 eggs
1 cup butter crackers, finely crushed
1/2 cup Parmesan cheese, grated

Preheat oven to 350 degrees. Over medium heat, in a skillet, melt 2 Tablespoons of the butter and oil over medium heat. Add shallots and garlic, sauté for 3 minutes. Add zucchini, season with salt, pepper, dill and red pepper. Cook, stirring occasionally, until vegetables are softened, about 3 - 5 minutes, and lightly browned. Drain any excess liquid. Remove from heat, add colby-jack cheese, blend well, and set aside. In a food processor, blend cottage cheese and eggs until smooth. Combine with zucchini mixture. Fold in crackers. Pour into a buttered 8x8-inch baking dish. Melt remaining 2 Tablespoons butter and pour evenly over the top. Sprinkle with cheese. Bake until lightly browned and set, about 45 - 55 minutes. Let sit for 10 minutes. Cut into squares.

Wild Rice Chicken Casserole

Serves 8 - 10

1 (10 oz) package, long grain and wild
   rice
2 Tablespoons butter
1/2 pound fresh mushrooms, sliced
1/4 cup butter
1/4 cup flour
1/2 teaspoon salt
freshly ground black pepper
1/2 teaspoon dry mustard

1 cup chicken stock
1/2 cup half and half
1 cup cheddar cheese, shredded
2 Tablespoons white wine
2 (10 oz) packages frozen chopped
   broccoli, thawed and drained
4 chicken breasts, seasoned, cooked and
   cubed
Parmesan cheese, grated

Cook rice according to package directions and set aside. Preheat oven to 325 degrees. Sauté mushrooms in 2 Tablespoons of butter and set aside. In a large saucepan, melt 1/4 cup butter and blend in flour, salt, pepper and mustard. Stir in chicken stock and half and half. Cook over medium heat until mixture thickens and bubbles. Add cheese and stir until cheese melts. Stir in wine and remove from heat. In a 9x13-inch pan, layer rice, broccoli, chicken and mushrooms. Pour sauce over all. Sprinkle with Parmesan. Bake for 30 - 40 minutes until top is browned.

Casserole may be assembled up to 24 hours in advance and stored, covered, in the refrigerator. Artichoke hearts are also a nice addition to this dish.

Bacon, Mushroom and Egg Breakfast Bake

Serves 8

4 cups day-old bread, cubed
2 cups cheddar cheese, shredded
10 eggs
2 cups milk
1/2 teaspoon salt
1/4 teaspoon freshly ground black pepper

1 teaspoon dry mustard
1/2 teaspoon onion salt
1 pound bacon, cooked and crumbled
1/2 cup mushrooms, chopped
1/2 cup tomatoes, chopped
1 cup colby-jack cheese, shredded

Lightly spray a 9x13-inch baking dish with cooking spray. Arrange bread cubes evenly on the bottom of the dish. Sprinkle with 2 cups cheddar cheese. In a large bowl, whisk together eggs, milk, salt, pepper, mustard and onion salt. Pour mixture evenly over cheese and bread. Sprinkle top with bacon, mushrooms and tomatoes. Cover and chill overnight. Preheat oven to 350 degrees. Bake casserole, covered with foil, for 60 minutes. Uncover and sprinkle with colby-jack cheese and bake an additional 15 minutes or until brown.

Must be made 1 day ahead as it needs to chill overnight.

Chicken Cheese Strudel in Puff Pastry

Serves 6 - 8

1 Tablespoon vegetable oil
1 shallot, minced
1 clove garlic, minced
2 Tablespoons tarragon or thyme, chopped
1 teaspoon salt
1 teaspoon freshly ground black pepper
1 cup mushrooms, chopped
2 Tablespoons sherry

1/2 pound chicken, diced
5 ounces chopped frozen spinach, thawed and drained
8 ounces spreadable cheese, garden vegetable variety
1/4 cup slivered almonds
1 sheet puff pastry, thawed
1 egg, lightly beaten
2 teaspoons lemon juice

Preheat oven to 400 degrees. In a large skillet, heat oil over medium-high heat. Add shallots and garlic, sauté until translucent. Add tarragon, pepper and salt. Stir until fragrant. Add mushrooms, sauté, 1 - 2 minutes. Add sherry, allow to boil off, about 1 minute. Add chicken and cook until no longer pink. Set aside.

In a large mixing bowl, combine spinach, cheese and almonds. Mix chicken mixture into cheese mixture. Defrost pastry according to package instructions. Put down large piece of parchment paper, flour it lightly, and roll puff pastry thin. In the middle third, spread filling evenly. On the diagonal and starting 1/2-inch from the filling, cut pastry into 1-inch strips. Braid the strips, overlapping in the middle, atop the filling. Mix egg and lemon juice together and brush the entire surface. Lift paper and gently place on baking sheet or jelly roll pan. Bake until browned about, 25 minutes. Allow to cool slightly and cut into 1-inch strips.

Crab, Shrimp and Asparagus Bake

Serves 8

4 eggs
1/2 cup evaporated milk
2 teaspoons Dijon mustard
1/2 teaspoon baking powder
1/2 teaspoon salt
1 Tablespoon sage, chopped

1 Tablespoon parsley, chopped
1/4 pound cooked shrimp, sliced
1/4 pound fresh crab, picked through
    and flaked
1 cup Swiss cheese, shredded
1/4 pound fresh asparagus tips, steamed

Preheat oven to 400 degrees. Grease a 9-inch pie plate. In a large bowl, whisk eggs, milk, mustard, baking powder, and seasonings. Stir in seafood and cheese. Pour mixture into the greased pie plate and arrange asparagus into mixture. Bake until set, about 20 minutes. Remove and let rest 5 minutes. Cut into wedges and serve.

Pepper Cheese Chicken Pinwheels

Serves 8

8 chicken breasts, pounded 1/4-inch thin
8 ounces spreadable cheese, garden
    vegetable variety
1 1/2 Tablespoons orange bell pepper,
    finely minced
1 1/2 Tablespoons yellow bell pepper,
    finely minced
1 Tablespoon flour

2 Tablespoons fresh chives, minced
1/4 cup sour cream
2 Tablespoons cornstarch
2 Tablespoons lemon juice
2 egg whites, lightly beaten
1 1/2 cups seasoned breadcrumbs
1/2 cup Parmesan cheese, grated
3 Tablespoons butter

Preheat oven to 375 degrees. Cut chicken breasts into 4x6-inch rectangles, set aside. In a medium bowl, mix cheese, peppers, flour, chives and sour cream. In a separate bowl, mix cornstarch, lemon juice and egg whites well, but not into a froth. Pour into a pie plate. In another pie plate, mix breadcrumbs and cheese. Spread about 2 Tablespoons cheese mixture evenly on each chicken breast. Roll tightly. Dip in egg wash, allowing excess to drip off. Roll in crumbs. Rest chicken on a wire rack to allow coating to set.

In a skillet, melt butter over medium heat. Sauté pinwheels, turning to brown all over for 2 minutes. Place in baking dish and cook, uncovered, for 25 minutes. Slice into 1/2 inch pinwheels pieces and arrange on a serving platter.

Any variety of spreadable cheese works well. Try cream cheese or goat cheese.

Brunch Baskets
Serves 20 - 30

WON TON CUPS
1 60-count package won ton wrappers
1 cup vegetable oil

HOT SAUSAGE FILLING
1 1/2 pounds bulk sausage (mild or hot)
1/2 cup roasted red peppers

1/3 cup black olives, chopped
2 cups shredded Monterey Jack/chedder cheese combo
1 (4 oz) can green chiles
up to 1 cup ranch dressing, homemade is preferred

To make sausage filling, preheat oven to 350 degrees. In a large skillet, fry sausage until cooked through, breaking meat constantly until it resembles coarse meal. Drain oil. In a large bowl, combine sausage, red pepper, olives, cheese, chiles and enough dressing to make a smooth, but not runny, consistency. Fill the won ton baskets with filling and bake until cheese has melted, 5-7 minutes. Serve while warm.

To make won ton cups preheat oven to 350 degrees. Separate won ton wrappers and lightly brush each side with vegetable oil. Press each wrapper inside each tin or mini muffin pan. Pierce each wrapper several times with a fork. Bake 5 minutes or until golden brown and crunchy.

Curried Chicken in Pastry Shells
Serves 12 - 18

2 to 3 packages puff pastry shells (12 shells) prepared as directed
1 1/2 teaspoons sweet curry powder
1 teaspoon ground coriander
1/2 teaspoon garam masala
1/2 teaspoon crushed red pepper flakes
1/2 teaspoon dry mustard
1 Tablespoon vegetable oil
2 1/2 cups onion, finely chopped
1/4 cup red pepper, finely chopped

1 Tablespoon ginger, peeled and grated
3 cloves garlic, minced
1 Tablespoon lime juice
3/4 cup chicken stock
1 Tablespoon sugar
1 teaspoon kosher salt
2 cups chicken, cooked and cubed
1 (4 oz) package cream cheese, softened
1/2 cup sour cream
1/2 cup slivered almonds, toasted

Prepare shells as directed, removing tops and pastry inside. Set aside. In a small pinch cup, combine curry, coriander, garam masala, red pepper flakes and mustard. In a skillet, heat oil over medium-high heat. Add onions, red pepper, ginger and garlic and sauté about 5 minutes, until lightly browned. Add spice mixture, cook until fragrant, stirring constantly, for about 1 minute. Add lime juice, stock, sugar, salt and chicken. Bring to a boil. Reduce heat, and simmer for 15 minutes. Uncover, cook 7 - 10 minutes more or until most of the liquid evaporates. Remove from heat. Cool 5 minutes. Stir in cheese, sour cream and almonds. To assemble, fill shells with chicken mixture. Replace tops. Bake at 375 degrees for 5 minutes.

For hotter palates, use hot curry and additional red pepper flakes.

GARAM MASALA

Garam Masala is a special spice blend used throughout Southern Asia. Generally, Garam Masala is added in a small quantity to add a subtle flavor to the dish.

Sweet and Spicy Bacon
Serves 6

1/4 cup brown sugar, packed
1/2 heaping teaspoon cayenne pepper
1/2 heaping teaspoon freshly ground
   black pepper
12 slices smokey bacon
3 Tablespoons pure maple syrup

Preheat oven to 375. In a small bowl, stir together sugar and peppers. Using a broiler pan or a jelly roll pan with a wire rack in it, arrange bacon in one layer. Brush top layer with maple syrup then sprinkle evenly with spiced sugar. Bake for 20 minutes. Turn slices over and sprinkle with spiced sugar (slices will be too hot to brush on syrup unless allowed to cool for a few minutes). Continue baking until bacon is crisp and brown, about 15 to 20 minutes. Transfer to paper towels to drain.

Apricot-Mustard Glazed Sausage Links
Serves 6

1/2 cup apricot preserves or orange
   marmalade
1/4 cup sweet-spicy mustard
1 Tablespoon rosemary, chopped
1 Tablespoon sage, chopped
1/4 teaspoon salt
1/2 teaspoon freshly ground black pepper
2 teaspoons vegetable oil
1 pound sausage links

In a saucepan over medium heat, whisk preserves until smooth and melted, about 1 minute. Add mustard and whisk another minute until mixture begins to simmer. Remove from heat and add herbs, salt and pepper. Stir completely. Set aside. In a large skillet, heat oil over medium heat. Add links and sauté until cooked through and browned, about 10 minutes. Drain. Transfer links to sauce pan with glaze. Stir over medium heat until links are coated and warm, about 1 minute. Transfer to a platter and serve hot.

An Original  *Ingredient*

FONTENELLE NATURE ASSOCIATION GUILD

In 1966, JLO members granted Fontenelle Forest $10,000 to secure employment of a full-time director and expand its educational programs. In 1969, the League pledged $40,000 for improvement at the Neale Woods Nature Center. By 1970, it was obvious the JLO had strong ties to this environmental treasure and, after "innumerable meetings," according to Sarah Ginn, President 1969-70, the JLO established the Fontenelle Forest Guild. The Fontenelle Nature Association Guild, as it is called today, continues to raise funds for educational programs at the Forest.

Chorizo Breakfast Burritos with Tomatillo Avocado Sauce
Serves 8

EGG FILLING
2 Tablespoons vegetable oil
1/2 cup roasted red peppers, chopped
2/3 cup bell peppers, chopped
1/2 cup red onion, chopped
1 1/2 teaspoons ground cumin
1 teaspoon salt
1 teaspoon freshly ground black pepper
1 clove garlic, minced and divided
1/2 pound ground chorizo, hot or sweet
1/2 teaspoon hot sauce
8 eggs
1/2 cup nonfat sour cream
1 cup Pepper Jack cheese, shredded

salt and freshly ground black pepper to taste
8 flour tortillas, 6-inch size

TOMATILLO-AVOCADO SAUCE
1 clove garlic, minced
5 tomatillos, roasted, husked and quartered
1 avocado, skinned
3 Tablespoons cilantro leaves, chopped
1 Tablespoon lime juice
1 teaspoon cumin
1/2 teaspoon salt
1/2 teaspoon freshly ground black pepper
cheese, diced tomatoes, hot sauce and chopped cilantro, for garnish

In a large skillet, heat oil over medium-high heat. Add peppers and onions and sauté until soft, about 3 minutes. Add cumin, salt, pepper and garlic. Sauté until fragrant, about 1 minute. Add chorizo and cook until no longer pink. Mix the vegetables completely into meat. Add hot sauce. In a medium bowl, combine eggs and sour cream. Add to meat mixture. Scramble, allowing eggs to settle a bit before stirring. Reduce heat to simmer, add cheese on top and mix completely until melted. Season to taste.

For sauce, place all ingredients in a food processor and blend to desired consistency. Spoon eggs into 6-inch tortillas, and top with sauce and wrap. Garnish with additional cheese, diced tomatoes, hot sauce and chopped cilantro, if desired.

The Owl and the Pussy Cat

In 1933 the Junior League took over the Children's Theater from the Omaha Community Playhouse and annually produced a play with League members in the cast. From left, children Courtney Campbell, Denman Kountze, Jr. and Sally Rullman admire Junior League members Kathryn Tukey as the cat and Josephine Coad as the owl in the April 1936 play "The Owl and the Pussy Cat" performed at the Omaha Community Playhouse. - *Reprinted with permission from the Omaha World-Herald*

English Muffin Breakfast Strata

Serves 10 - 12

1 pound ground mild sausage
olive oil
2 shallots, minced
2 cloves garlic, minced
1 (8 oz) package mushrooms, diced
1/2 cup bell pepper, chopped
1/4 cup fresh chives, minced
2 cups mild, nutty white cheese, shredded
2 cups tomatoes, diced
2 cups milk
10 eggs
1/2 teaspoon hot sauce
1 teaspoon salt
1/2 teaspoon freshly ground black pepper
1 Tablespoon mustard
4 English muffins, lightly toasted, buttered and cubed
1/2 cup basil, thinly sliced
1/2 cup Parmesan cheese, finely shredded

In skillet over medium-high heat, cook sausage until no longer pink. Remove sausage and set aside in large bowl. If needed, add olive oil to sausage rendering. Add shallots and cook about 2 minutes. Add garlic and cook another minute. Add mushrooms, bell peppers and chives and sauté for 4 - 5 minutes. Remove from heat. Mix cheese and tomatoes into the sausage. In another large bowl, whisk milk, eggs, hot sauce, salt, pepper and mustard. Spray a 9x13-inch baking dish with cooking spray. Spread muffin cubes evenly on the bottom. Top with sausage mixture and basil. Pour egg mixture evenly over the top. Cover and refrigerate 2 to 8 hours. Preheat oven to 325 degrees. Uncover strata, top evenly with parmesan cheese. Bake until set, about 60 - 70 minutes. Serve warm with a fruit salad.

Junior League Shop at Children's Hospital

Junior League members working in the Hospitality Shop at Children's Memorial Hospital. The League founded the shop in 1948, giving all proceeds to the hospital. In 1956, they turned the shop over to the Friends of Children's Hospital Guild. - *Reprinted with permission from the Omaha World-Herald*

Giant Jumble Project

From left Ann Wachter, Katie Best, Mary Pat Kleyla and Betty Coad were among the provisional Junior League members planning a "Giant Jumble" project in February 1955. Their hope was to procure more than $1,000 worth of new and used merchandise for the league's Jumble Shop. The Junior League assumed operation of the Jumble Shop from the Nebraska Society of the Colonial Dames in 1947 and continues to operate the shop today at 3038 North 90th Sreet. - *Reprinted with permission from the Omaha World-Herald*

American Girl

Since 1995 the Junior League of Omaha has hosted an American Girl Fashion Show to provide an entertaining and educational look at how generations of American girls have used clothing to express their own unique style and personality. Over 400 girls between the ages of 4 and 12 participate in the event by modeling traditional styles replicating the outfits of the popular American Girl dolls and showing the contemporary styles of the American Girl Today clothing. Year after year, the fashion show offers a unique, memorable experience for girls and their families and friends. From left are American Girl models Emily Swartzendruber, Megan Szwanek and Taylor Adams.

ENTREES

JOHNNY'S CAFE
4702 South 27th Street

Since opening in 1922, Johnny's Cafe has been one of Omaha's favorite steak houses. At the edge of the stockyards, it was once a place for cattlemen to celebrate a successful day of trading. Now families come from all around for the Nebraska-fed beef and seafood specialties guaranteed to accommodate nearly any appetite. - - *From the Bostwick-Frohardt Collection owned by KMTV and on permanent loan to the Durham Western Heritage Museum, Omaha, Nebraska*

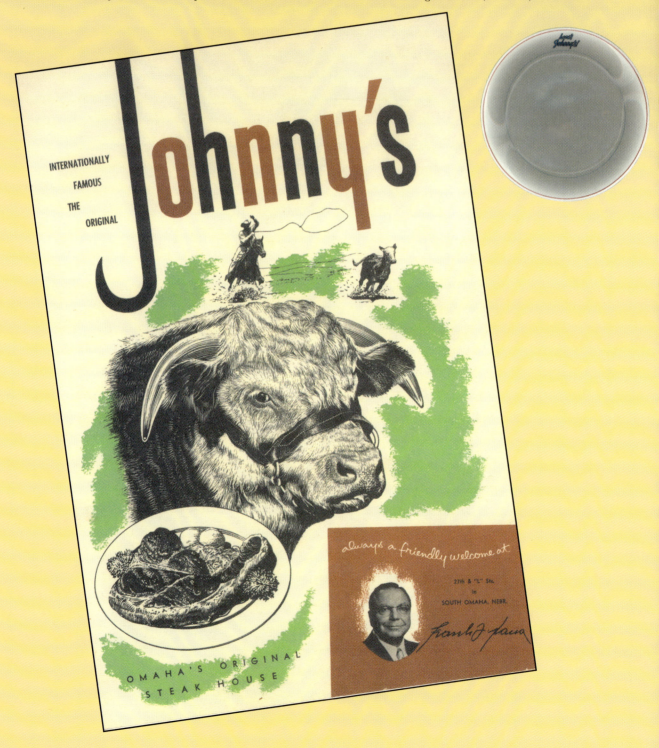

Johnny's Cafe Frisco Marinade

Makes 1 Quart

3 cups dry red wine
1 (9 oz) can frozen orange juice concentrate
1/4 cup dry crushed rosemary leaves (or 1 cup fresh)
1/4 cup garlic, minced
1 Tablespoon ground mustard
2 teaspoons freshly ground black pepper
2 teaspoons salt

Combine all ingredients and mix well. Refrigerate until ready to use. Marinate beef cut of choice overnight. Johnny's recommends flank, skirt, or sirloin steak. !O!

From Johnny's Cafe's Kawa family

Spicy Grilled Flank Steak

Serves 4 - 6

1/2 cup olive oil
1/4 cup white vinegar
1 1/2 teaspoons salt
1/4 teaspoon hot sauce

2 teaspoons oregano
2 teaspoons chili powder
1 teaspoon minced garlic
1 1/2 pounds flank steak

In a bowl, combine olive oil, vinegar, salt, hot sauce, oregano, chili powder and garlic. Mix well. Pierce the flank steak in several places with a fork. Place marinade and flank steak in a zippered plastic bag and marinate for 1 hour or overnight. Grill over medium-high heat for about 8 minutes each side, basting with the marinade. Slice and serve.

Grilled Skirt Steak with Watercress Sauce

Serves 4

2 pounds skirt steak, trimmed
5 cloves garlic, minced
2 teaspoons ginger, grated
1/3 cup soy sauce
1 Tablespoon yellow mustard seeds,
    toasted
2 Tablespoons mustard of choice
1 Tablespoon Dijon mustard
1/4 cup olive oil
1/3 cup balsamic vinegar
2 teaspoons freshly ground black pepper
1 teaspoon kosher salt

WATERCRESS SAUCE
1/4 cup mayonnaise
3/4 cup sour cream
1/4 cup buttermilk
1 shallot, chopped
1 teaspoon lemon pepper seasoning
2 cloves garlic, chopped
1 Tablespoon Dijon mustard
1 Tablespoon lemon juice
1 Tablespoon lime juice
1 pinch kosher salt
1 bunch watercress, leaves only

Cut the trimmed meat into four steaks. Place steaks in a glass dish. In a small bowl, combine garlic, ginger, soy sauce, mustard seeds, mustards, oil, vinegar, pepper and salt. Mix well. Pour over steaks, cover, refrigerate and marinate overnight. In a food processor, combine mayonnaise, sour cream, buttermilk, shallot, seasoning, garlic, mustard, lemon juice, lime juice, salt and watercress. Blend until green and pureed to desired consistency. Cover and refrigerate until ready to serve. Grill steaks over medium-high fire or grill pan for 3 - 5 minutes on each side. Transfer to dinner plates and serve with watercress sauce.

THE BLACKSTONE HOTEL

The Blackstone's Orleans Room in 1935 - *From the Bostwick-Frohardt Collection owned by KMTV and on permanent loan to the Durham Western Heritage Museum, Omaha, Nebraska*

The Blackstone Hotel was built in 1916 and was bought by Austrian immigrant Charles Schimmel in 1920. Schimmel and his four sons operated the hotel until 1968 when they sold it to Radisson Management Corporoation of Minneapolis. The Blackstone had a reputation for luxury. Their upscale Orleans Room was a favorite among the hotel guests and Omahans along with their more casual Cottonwood Room and the Plush Horse restaurants.

TUESDAY, AUGUST 21, 1934

Soups and Stews

Essence of Beef or Tomato in Gelee	.10
Consomme in Cup—Brunoise	.10
Fresh Vegetable Soup—Paysanne	.10

Cocktails, Relishes and Appetizers

Fresh Fruit	.25	Ind. Kraut Juice	.20
Fresh Shrimp	.30	Tomato Juice	.15
Crab Flakes	.30	Tomato Juice Cocktail	.20
Orange Juice	.15	Clam Juice Cocktail	.25
Pickled Herring	.45	Pineapple Juice	.20
Little Neck Clams	.45	Prune Juice	.20
Assorted Parisienne Canapes			.75

Delicacies From Lake and Ocean

Broiled Fresh Jumbo Whitefish, Mirabeau	.75
Fried Filet of Sole	.60
Chafing Dish of Fresh Jumbo Shrimps, Newburg	.75
Combination Seashore Dinner	.85
Broiled Fresh Lake Trout	.75
Fried Cisco Codfish Cakes, Tomato Sauce	.60
Boiled Salt Mackerel, New Parsley Potatoes	.55
Broiled Chicken Halibut Steak	.75
Smoked Whitefish—Cold Plate	.65

Chef's Special Dishes

Chicken Pot Pie	.50
Poached Eggs on Smithfield's Deviled Virginia Ham—"Richmond Inn"	.65
Ind. Boston Oven Baked Beans, Brown Bread	.35
Chicken Shortcake, Plantation Style	.75
Welsh Rarebit	.45
Combination English Grill	.90
Platter of Old Fashioned Fried Spring Chicken with Giblets and Liver	1.10
Chicken a la King	.45
Scrambled Egg and Salami	.60
Italian Spaghetti	.45

"Tasty-Pastry" Sandwiches
Toasted 5c Extra

Roast Pork	.20	Reuben Sandwich	.40
Swiss, Ham (Open)	.35	Chicken and Tomato	.45
American Cheese	.15	Chicken Salad	.25
Imported Swiss	.25	Tenderloin Steak	.55
Tunafish	.20	Sliced Chicken	.35
Salmon Salad	.20	Sliced Turkey	.35
Olive and Nut	.20	Baked Ham	.20
Bacon	.20	Smoked Tongue	.20
Hamburger on Bun	.20	Minced Ham	.15
Salami	.20	Fried Egg	.15
Liverwurst	.20	Hot Roast Beef	.45
Deviled Egg	.15	Denver	.25
Imported Sardines	.20	Corned Beef	.20
Chicken Shortcake on Smithfield's Deviled Ham			.60
Peanut Butter 15; with Jelly			.20
Open Toasted Cheese 25; with Bacon			.35
Cream Cheese on Nut Bread			.15
Lettuce, Tomato 15; with Bacon			.30
Sliced Egg 15; with Tomato and Green Pepper			.25
Blackstone Toasted Halves			.25
Ham or Bacon and Egg			.25

According to a 1976 World-Herald interview with Bernard Schimmel the Rueben sandwich was named for the late Reuben Kulakofsky one of the owners of the now-closed Central Market. In the 1920s, he and his poker group met in the Fern Room at the Blackstone Hotel. Among the group was the hotel's owner Charles Schimmel. Out of each pot, they'd save a nickel or dime and, later in the day they'd phone for a cold midnight lunch. They put the sandwiches together themselves and Reuben invented the corned beef and sauerkraut creation on dark rye. Reuben's became so popular that Charles said they must serve the sandwich at the Blackstone's Tasty-Pastry which later became the Golden Spur.

In 1956 Fern Snider, a former employee of the Blackstone, entered the sandwich in the National Sandwich Contest and won the top prize of $500 and a trip to New York City for the 1956 awards presentation.

The late Bernard Schimmel's secret for a perfect Reuben…use quality ingredients. For the dressing use homemade mayonnaise or buy Hellman's and add one fresh egg. Take out all the moisture you can from the sauerkraut so it is nice and crisp. Buy Kosher-style corned beef brisket. It has the right amount of fat to give the sandwich the flavor you want. It should be sliced thin and high. The thicker you slice this meat, the bulkier it gets and you lose the flavor. Use melted butter and put it on with a brush and use an electric sandwich grill to provide equal heat and pressure to both sides.

Bernard Schimmel

Reuben Sandwich

2 slices dark rye bread
2 thin slices Switzerland Ementhaler cheese
4 (or more) slices Kosher-style corned beef brisket
2 ounces sauerkraut, chilled and well-drained
1 ounce (or less) Thousand Island dressing (recipe follows)
Butter, softened

Mix Thousand Island dressing with sauerkraut that has been drained. Spread outside of each slice of dark rye bread with soft butter. Lay bread, unbuttered side up, side by side. Place Swiss cheese on each piece, corned beef on one piece, sauerkraut on corned beef and then put together for grilling on sandwich grill or skillet. Press together with spatula and cook until brown and hot through so cheese oozes. Eat immediately. !O!

Thousand Island Dressing

1/2 pint real mayonnaise
3 teaspoons chili sauce
1 teaspoon each of chopped pimentos and young onions
2 Tablespoons minced green pepper
1/2 cup sour cream
2 hard cooked eggs (optional)

Blend all ingredients except hard cooked eggs. Chop and fold the eggs into the dressing at time of service, if desired. Yields two-thirds pint.

Grilled Santa Maria Tri-Tips
Serves 8 - 10

6 cloves garlic, minced
1/2 cup orange juice
1/4 cup lime juice
2 Tablespoons tequila
2 Tablespoons chili powder
1 1/2 teaspoons celery seed
2 Tablespoons oregano, chopped
2 teaspoons kosher salt
1 Tablespoon freshly ground black pepper
2 Tablespoons chili seasoning blend
1/2 bunch cilantro leaves, chopped
2 pounds tri-tip beef steak

In a food processor, combine all ingredients, except the steak, and pulse briefly. Puncture steak with a fork, in several places. Place beef in a shallow glass dish. Pour the marinade over the steak. Cover and place in the refrigerator overnight or up to 72 hours. Turn meat occasionally. An hour before grilling, remove meat from the refrigerator. Using mesquite or hickory chips, if desired, grill over medium-high heat until internal temperature reaches 130 - 140 degrees or desired doneness. . Allow to rest until serving temperature reaches 145 - 155 degrees. Slice thinly against the grain. Serve with favorite red or green salsa, guacamole or Tex-Mex side.

Tri-tip leftovers are fabulous in sandwiches with crusty bread, in salads or reheated. Other names for it are triangle, culottes or bottom sirloin steak.

Kenny's Steak House at 72nd and Dodge Streets in the 1950s - *From the Catherine Lynn collection*

Beef Tenderloin Fillets with Stilton Portabello Sauce
Serves 6

6 (6 oz) beef tenderloin fillets
2 teaspoons tarragon, chopped
1/2 teaspoon freshly ground black pepper
5 Tablespoons butter, divided
8 ounces Portabello mushroom caps, sliced
1/2 cup shallots, diced
1/3 cup dry red wine
1/2 cup sour cream
3 ounces Stilton or blue cheese, crumbled and divided
fresh tarragon sprigs

Rub fillets with tarragon and pepper. In a large skillet, melt 2 Tablespoons of butter over medium-high heat. Cook fillets 4 - 5 minutes on each side or to desired degree of doneness. Remove fillets from skillet and keep warm. Melt remaining 3 Tablespoons of butter in skillet. Add mushrooms and shallot and sauté 3 - 4 minutes until tender. Add wine, and cook 1 - 2 minutes, stir in the sour cream. Sprinkle 1/4 cup cheese into sauce, stirring until melted. Arrange fillets on a serving platter and drizzle with sauce. Sprinkle with remaining cheese and garnish with fresh tarragon sprigs.

The Flat Iron Steak was the result of a Muscle Profiling Study done by the University if Nebraska and the University of Florida. Nobody knows steak better than Nebraskans! It does indeed have a Nebraska origin in part.

Blazin' Colorado Steaks

Serves 4

1/4 cup fresh lime juice	1/2 cup sour cream
3 chipotle peppers in adobo sauce	2 Tablespoons cilantro leaves, chopped
4 (8 oz) flat iron steaks (beef shoulder	tomatoes, diced
top blade)	cilantro or parsley, chopped
1 (4 oz) can green chiles, chopped	red onion, minced
1/2 cup whipping cream	

Place lime juice and chipotle peppers in a blender and puree until smooth. Place steaks and marinade in a zippered plastic bag. Turn steaks to coat. Seal bag and refrigerate overnight. Remove steaks from marinade. Discard the remaining marinade. Place steaks on a grill over medium heat. Grill steaks, covered, 10 - 14 minutes for medium-rare to medium doneness, turning once. Salt, if desired. Keep warm. Meanwhile, prepare sauce. Place chiles in a blender and puree until smooth. Pour pureed chiles into a small saucepan and add whipping cream. Cook until hot over medium heat for about 5 minutes, stirring frequently. Add sour cream and cilantro. Cook and stir 1 - 2 minutes until just heated through. Do not boil. Serve steak with sauce. Garnish with tomatoes, cilantro or parsley and red onion.

Cracked Pepper Crusted New York Strip with Whiskey Cream Sauce

Serves 4

1/3 cup whole black peppercorns	WHISKEY CREAM SAUCE
4 (6 oz) New York strip steaks	2 ounces whiskey
4 Tablespoons butter, melted	1 cup heavy whipping cream
	3 Tablespoons Worcestershire sauce
	salt to taste

In a food processor or blender, process peppercorns until finely crushed. Roll steaks in crushed peppercorns. In a large skillet, melt the butter. Over medium-high heat, sauté steaks 3 - 4 minutes each side, or until desired doneness is achieved. Remove from heat and keep warm. In a small saucepan, warm whiskey, cream, Worcestershire sauce and salt over low heat until heated through, do not boil. Serve steak over a pool of whiskey sauce.

Johnny's Cafe Cajun Blackened Strip Sirloin Steaks

Serves 6

1 1/2 Tablespoons salt
1 1/2 Tablespoons paprika
1 Tablespoon cayenne pepper
2 1/2 teaspoons dried onion, minced
2 1/2 teaspoons garlic powder
1 teaspoon thyme leaves

1 teaspoon marjoram leaves
1 teaspoon fennel seed
1/2 teaspoon cumin
6 (8 oz) boneless strip sirloin steaks
1/2 cup butter, melted

In an electric blender, blend salt, paprika, cayenne, onion, garlic powder, thyme, marjoram, fennel and cumin until mixed. Heat a cast iron skillet on the highest heat, until it is beyond the smoking stage and the bottom of the skillet turns white. Generously coat all sides of the steaks with the seasoning mix. Place steak in the skillet and top each with 1 Tablespoon melted butter, more or less to taste. Cook on each side for about 5 minutes, or until desired doneness. ¡O!

Grilled Espresso Steaks

Serves 4

2 Tablespoons espresso coffee beans, finely ground
1 Tablespoon garlic pepper
2 teaspoons salt

2 teaspoons brown sugar
1 teaspoon ancho chili powder
4 (6 oz) tri-tip beef steaks, cut 1-inch thick

Combine espresso, garlic pepper, salt, brown sugar and chili powder. Press mixture generously into beef steaks. Discard any remaining seasoning mixture. Place steaks in a glass dish. Cover and refrigerate 1 hour. Place steaks on grill over medium heat. Grill, uncovered, for 13 - 17 minutes for medium-rare to medium doneness, turning occasionally. Carve steaks into slices.

Columbo Lodge of the Sons of Italy
1238 South 10th Street

This recipe is used by the Columbo Lodge of the Sons of Italy, located on 10th Street in South Omaha. Homemade lunches are served at the hall on Thursdays from Labor Day to Memorial Day. Each week, 600 - 1,000 meals are served. Profits from the meals are channeled to a variety of charities and scholarships. The club has been serving these lunches since the early 1950s and the recipes have not changed. Some of the original members still work the meals in one capacity or another. For Thursday lunches, 3,000 meatballs are prepared each week.

Sons of Italy Meatballs
Serves 10 - 12, 2-inch meatballs

1 pound ground beef
1/2 pound ground veal
1/2 pound ground pork
2 eggs
2 Tablespoons butter
2/3 cup onions, finely chopped
3 Tablespoons parsley, chopped
1 teaspoon salt
1/4 teaspoon paprika
1 teaspoon lemon juice
1 Tablespoon garlic powder (or 1 fresh garlic clove, chopped)
4 Tablespoons Romano cheese, grated
1 teaspoon oregano or Italian seasoning
1/2 cup Italian breadcrumbs

Preheat oven to 400 degrees. Thoroughly mix meat and all other ingredients. When thoroughly mixed...mix some more. Roll mixture into 2 - 2 1/2 inch balls. An ice cream scoop makes the job faster and easier! Scoop the meat, round the top and pass to partner who finishes the process by rolling by hand. (Keeping the fingers wet keeps the meat from sticking to your hands.) Place meatballs in a casserole dish or baking pan. Cover meat with sauce of your choice. Bake covered for approximately 45 minutes. Check after 30 minutes. Serve with pasta, in sandwiches, or by themselves. Mangia and enjoy!

Tex-Mex Sloppy Joes
Serves 8

2 Tablespoons vegetable oil
1 onion, finely chopped
1 Tablespoon green chilies, diced
1/2 cup roasted or fresh red pepper, diced
4 cloves garlic, minced
1 Tablespoon steak seasoning
1 teaspoon dry mustard
2 pounds ground beef
2 Tablespoons brown sugar
2 Tablespoons cider vinegar
1 teaspoon hot sauce
2 Tablespoons Worcestershire sauce
1 (12 oz) jar chili sauce
1/2 cup tomato sauce
salt and freshly ground black pepper to taste
6 Kaiser rolls, sliced and toasted
grated cheese

In a skillet, heat oil. Add onion, chiles, pepper and garlic. Sauté until slightly browned. Add steak seasoning and dry mustard. Stir constantly until fragrant, less than 1 minute. Add meat, using spoon to break apart until it resembles coarse meal. Sauté until meat is no longer pink. Add sugar, vinegar, hot sauce and Worcestershire sauce. Mix thoroughly. Add chili sauce and tomato sauce. Simmer, uncovered, until thickened, about 10 minutes. Salt and pepper to taste. Serve on toasted Kaiser rolls with grated cheese on top of meat.

Ground turkey may be substituted for the ground beef.

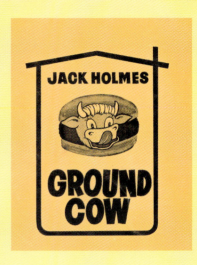

Jack Holmes Ground Cow restaurant was a family favorite at 7555 Pacific Street - *From the Joe Villella menu collection at the Douglas County Historical Society Archives*

Wedding Meatballs
Serves 8

2 pounds ground beef
1/2 cup ketchup
2 teaspoons onion, finely chopped
1 teaspoon Worcestershire sauce
2/3 cup saltines, crushed
2 large eggs
1 1/2 teaspoons salt
1/2 teaspoon freshly ground black pepper
1/2 teaspoon marjoram
1/2 teaspoon nutmeg
1 (8 oz) can cream of mushroom soup
1 cup milk
1 teaspoon sherry
2 Tablespoons butter
1/8 teaspoon garlic salt
1 cup mushrooms, sliced
1 Tablespoon pimentos, chopped

Preheat oven to 350 degrees. Combine beef, ketchup, onion, Worcestershire sauce, saltines, eggs, salt, pepper, marjoram and nutmeg. Mix well and shape into meatballs. Place in a deep dish. In a saucepan, place soup, milk, sherry, butter and garlic salt. Heat until butter is melted. Pour over meatballs. Cover and bake for 45 minutes. During the last 10 minutes, add mushrooms and pimentos.

Make the meatballs either into serving size 3-inch meatballs, or bite-size 1-inch meatballs. Both are great!

Hilltop House Hamburger Steak

Serves 8 - 10

5 pounds ground beef
1 pound ground pork
1 onion, diced
1 cup breadcrumbs
3 eggs

1 1/2 teaspoons salt
1/2 teaspoon freshly ground black pepper
1/2 teaspoon MSG (like Accent)
up to 3 cups chicken broth
Alamo or Lowry's seasoning salt

In a large bowl, combine meats, onion, breadcrumbs, eggs, salt, pepper and Accent. Add chicken broth, a little at a time, until mixture reaches a sticky, but workable consistency. Form into patties, about 5 ounces apiece. Season with seasoning salt. Grill or pan fry over medium-high heat until desired doneness is reached.

Hilltop House was famous for its hamburger steak. IO!

Wow Southwestern Tacos

Serves 10

MEAT FILLING
2 teaspoons vegetable oil
2 shallots, minced
3 cloves garlic, minced
2 Tablespoons chili powder
1 1/2 teaspoons ground cumin
1 1/2 teaspoons coriander
1 teaspoon dried oregano
1/2 teaspoon cayenne pepper
1 1/2 teaspoons fajita seasoning
1/2 teaspoon celery seed
1/2 teaspoon kosher salt
1 1/2 pounds ground beef

2 Tablespoons brown sugar
2 Tablespoons cider vinegar
1 (8 oz) can tomato sauce

SHELLS AND TOPPINGS
10 (6-inch) flour tortillas
vegetable oil, for frying
1/2 cup sour cream
2 tomatoes and avocados, chopped
2 cups iceberg lettuce, chopped
1 cup cheddar cheese, shredded
1 bunch green onions, sliced
1 cup Mexican-style corn

In a medium skillet, heat oil over medium-high heat. Sauté shallots and garlic until translucent, 3 minutes. In a pinch cup, combine chili powder, cumin, coriander, oregano, pepper, seasoning, celery seed and salt. Stir until mixed. Add spices to the onion mixture. Stir constantly and cook until fragrant, about 90 seconds. Add ground beef, cooking until it is no longer pink. Add brown sugar and vinegar. Cook until fragrant, about 1 minute. Add tomato sauce. Bring to a boil, then reduce to simmer until thickened, about 10 minutes.

In large skillet, add 1/2 inch of oil and heat. Using tongs, put one tortilla in oil (flat) for about 10 seconds, then turn it over. Bend tortilla in half, holding it with tongs in left hand and pressing frying side down with a spatula in right hand (reverse for left-handers). After 20 - 30 seconds, flip over using spatula, again holding fried side with tongs in left hand. Cook for another 30 seconds. Remove with spatula, holding shell up at the bend. Place bend-side up and drain on paper towels. Repeat process for each tortilla. Tortillas may be kept warm in a 200 degree oven.

Spoon meat mixture into taco shells. Top with sour cream, tomatoes, avocadoes, lettuce, cheese, onions and corn.

Wild West Beef and Smoked Gouda Grits

Serves 4

3 1/2 cups water
1 cup quick-cooking grits
1 cup smoked Gouda cheese, shredded
2 - 4 Tablespoons butter
1 Tablespoon olive oil
6 ounces Portabello mushrooms,
   coarsely chopped

1/2 cup red onion, chopped
1 (17 oz) package refrigerated fully-
   cooked beef tips with gravy
fresh parsley, chopped

In a medium saucepan, bring water to a boil. Slowly add grits, stirring constantly. Reduce heat to medium-low. Cover and cook 5 - 7 minutes or until thickened, stirring occasionally. Add cheese and butter; stir until completely melted. Remove from heat. Cover; set aside. In a large skillet, heat oil over medium-high heat. Add mushrooms and onion. Cook 4 - 5 minutes or until onion is tender, stirring occasionally. Stir in beef tips with gravy. Continue cooking until heated through, about 5 minutes, stirring occasionally. Divide grits evenly among four shallow bowls. Top with beef mixture. Garnish with parsley.

Johnny's Cafe Syrah Braised Short Ribs of Beef

Serves 7 - 8

5 pounds short ribs
short rib seasoning (see recipe)
4 ounces vegetable oil
1 pound bacon, chopped
1/2 cup onions, chopped
1/2 cup carrots, chopped

1/2 cup celery, chopped
1/2 gallon demi-glace
1 1/2 cups Syrah wine
salt and freshly ground black pepper to
   taste

Preheat oven to 350 degrees. Cut ribs between each bone. Season ribs with short rib seasoning. In a large skillet add oil, sear short ribs until golden brown on all sides. Remove ribs and reserve. To pan add bacon, onions, carrots and celery. Sauté for 10 minutes. Add demi-glace and wine to pan. In a large baking pan, add browned short ribs and pour sauce over the ribs. Cover and cook for 2 1/2 - 3 hours.

One of the great classic French sauces, demi-glace is a rich brown sauce which is itself a base for many other sauces. It is very time consuming to make but may be purchased. A product called Demi Glace Gold may be found at www.clubsauce.com.

SHORT RIB SEASONING

Use dried ingredients
5 Tablespoons salt
1 Tablespoon freshly ground black pepper
1 Tablespoon garlic powder
1 Tablespoon basil
1 Tablespoon rosemary
1 Tablespoon oregano

Mix all ingredients.

French Café Dijon Herb Encrusted Rack of Lamb Adorned with Sage Whipped Blue Potato

Serves 6 - 8

olive oil
salt and freshly ground black pepper
2 (8 - bone) racks of lamb
2 teaspoons Dijon mustard
1/2 ounce mint, chopped
1/2 ounce rosemary, chopped
1/2 ounce thyme, chopped
1/2 ounce chives, chopped
1/4 ounce parsley, chopped
5 Peruvian purple potatoes, boiled whole until soft
1/4 cup cream
1/4 cup butter
1 ounce sage, chopped

MACADAMIA-APPLE CRANBERRY CHUTNEY
olive oil
1 clove garlic, chopped
1 shallot, chopped
2 Granny Smith apples, chopped
1/4 cup dried cranberries
1/4 cup Macadamia nuts, chopped
2 Tablespoons honey
2 Tablespoons sugar
1 teaspoon apple cider vinegar
1 sprig rosemary
2 sprigs thyme

Preheat oven to 400 degrees. In a large skillet, heat several tablespoons of oil over medium-high heat. Season lamb with salt and pepper. Sear lamb until evenly browned on all sides. Place lamb in a large pan and place in oven for 6 - 8 minutes depending on desired doneness. Remove from oven and coat lamb with mustard, mint, rosemary, thyme, chives and parsley; cook for another minute. Let meat rest and cut into chops.

While lamb is cooking, place potatoes, cream, butter and sage in a food mill or mixer. Process until smooth. Season with salt and pepper to taste.

To make chutney, heat 2 Tablespoons oil in a skillet. Sauté garlic and shallot until soft. Add apples and sauté for another 4 - 5 minutes. Add cranberries, nuts, honey, sugar, cider vinegar, rosemary and thyme. Season with salt and pepper to taste. Serve with lamb and whipped potatoes. ¡O!

La Buvette Terrine of Frog Legs with Sturgeon Caviar and Oven Dried Tomato

Serves 4

2 shallots, minced
2 cloves garlic, minced
1 bay leaf
fresh thyme
grey salt
cayenne pepper
grape seed oil
5 pounds large frog legs, cleaned

dry white wine
chicken stock (unsalted)
4 roma tomatoes
grey salt
fresh thyme
1 clove garlic, minced
1/4 ounce good domestic caviar
   (Sevruga, Osetra or Beluga)

For the Terrine, in a sautoir sweat the minced shallot, garlic, bay leaf, thyme, salt and pepper in a few Tablespoons of grape seed oil over medium heat. Add the frog legs and sweat without adding color. Add the white wine and chicken stock (1:1) until the legs are just covered. Simmer the legs until cooked through and the meat falls off the bone. Strain the mixture discarding the sprigs of thyme and bay leaf. Return the liquid to high heat. Remove the meat from the bones, being careful of the feet. Put the meat, remaining shallots and garlic in a separate mixing bowl. Return the bones and feet to the liquid. Reduce the liquid and bones by 2/3. Taste the meat mixture and season if necessary. Re-wet with the reduced liquid. Line a sheet of aluminum foil with cling wrap. (This may take two sets of hands.) Heap the frog meat in a line along the short end of the foil, being careful to leave enough space on the sides, about 2 inches. Begin rolling the foil and plastic wrap, pinching in the ends to keep the mixture in a tight cylinder. When the log is rolled, twist the ends in opposite directions until the log feels firm. Refrigerate overnight.
For the tomatoes, preheat oven to 200 degrees. On a small baking sheet, coat tomatoes with grape seed oil and season with salt, thyme and crushed garlic. Bake in the oven overnight. The water will evaporate out of the tomato by midday. Put the dried tomato in a container and reserve the oil.
To assemble, carefully remove the log from the refrigerator and unwrap. The gelatin from the frog legs should hold everything tightly together. With a very sharp knife, slice the log into 1/2-inch medallions. To serve, place two medallions of the terrine on a plate. Place an oven dried tomato next to the slices then make a quenelle of the caviar and place that above the terrine.

Make sure the terrine is still visible, you'll want to show it off. Use some of the reserved tomato oil as a sauce and garnish with a sprig of thyme.

This moderately difficult preparation which will stun guests because of its elegance, flavor and uniqueness. |O!|

B & G Drive-In
85th and Dodge Streets

Not a hamburger, nor a Sloppy Joe, a loose-meat sandwich is crumbled beef with special seasonings served on hamburger buns with condiments mustard, ketchup and hamburger dill pickles. Maid-Rite restaurants and B & G Tasty Foods made this sandwich a popular item in the area. Pat Arndt shared this similar recipe with the Omaha World-Herald's Let's Swap Recipe Column. For an original, B & G's is still the place to go.

Loose-Meat Sandwiches

5 pounds finely ground beef
1/2 cup ketchup
3 heaping teaspoons creamy horseradish
3 teaspoons Worcestershire Sauce
5 heaping teaspoons salt
1 teaspoon monosodium glutamate
   (Accent is one brand name)
dash freshly ground black pepper
1 cup ground or chopped onion
1 cup water

Place meat in a large saucepan. Add ketchup, horseradish, Worcestershire sauce, salt, MSG, pepper, onion and water. Cook on low heat for 15 minutes, stirring constantly. Meat will be in very fine pieces. Let simmer about 1 1/2 hours. Add water if mixture becomes dry. Notes: Regular ground beef may be used.

Standing behind the B & G counter in the 1960s are (from left) Don Olson; Dale Munson, WOW radio; Gayle Gainsforth; Gary Marx, WOW Radio; and Ken Bliss. In the spring of 1953, Gainsforth and Bliss opened the B & G Drive at 85th and Dodge Streets and operated it until October 2000. The restaurant continues today at 7900 West Dodge Road. - *From Lori Ludwick, daughter of B & G's co-founder Gayle Gainsforth, and Tom and Michelle Foley, current B & G owners*

Hector's Enchiladas Guadalajara

Serves 4 - 6

2 cups poached or baked chicken,
  seasoned and shredded
6 - 8 (6-inch) flour tortillas
1 cup Chihuahua cheese, shredded (see
  notes)
1 cup Cotija cheese, shredded (see
  notes)

GREEN CHILE CREAM SAUCE
1 quart heavy whipping cream
1/2 (28-ounce) can Las Palmas green
  chile enchilada sauce

1/2 Tablespoon granulated garlic
1 teaspoon salt
1/2 cup Parmesan cheese, grated
cornstarch, dissolved in warm water

JALAPÉNO-CILANTRO SAUCE
2 fresh jalepenos, seeded
1/2 bunch fresh cilantro leaves, chopped
juice of 1 lime
1/2 (28-ounce) can Las Palmas green
  chile enchilada sauce
cornstarch, dissolved in warm water

Preheat oven to 350 degrees. Place chicken inside tortillas. Roll up and place in an oven safe baking dish. Green Chili Cream Sauce: In a large saucepan, combine cream, green chile sauce, garlic and salt. Bring to a simmer, watching closely to prevent the sauce from boiling over. Whisk in cheese, then cornstarch until a smooth. Set aside.

Jalapeño-Cilantro Sauce: In a blender or food processor, combine the jalapeños, cilantro, juice of 1 lime and green chile sauce. Blend until smooth. Pour contents into a medium saucepan and place over medium heat. Heat to a simmer, then add cornstarch until sauce becomes very thick, almost spreadable. Ladle the cream sauce over the enchiladas and sprinkle with Chihuahua cheese. Bake until warmed through and cheese is melted. Remove from oven and drizzle with Jalapeño-Cilantro Sauce and sprinkle Cotija cheese over the top. Let stand for 3 - 5 minutes then serve.

Chihuahua cheese and Cotija cheese are available at most Mexican grocery stores. |O!|

Red, White and Green Summer Sandwich

Serves 4

1 loaf French bread
4 Tablespoons sun-dried tomato spread
4 Tablespoons prepared basil pesto

8 ounces fresh Mozzerella cheese, sliced
3 ounces capicola, thinly sliced
4 leaves romaine lettuce

Cut the French loaf into four sections and slice each lengthwise for sandwiches. Spread the top slice with sun-dried tomato spread then spread the bottom slice with the pesto. Add a layer of cheese, capicola and lettuce.

This may be served as a party sandwich.

Zingy Chicken Enchiladas

Serves 6 - 8

ENCHILADA SAUCE
2 Tablespoons vegetable oil
1 Tablespoon garlic, minced
3/4 cup shallots or onion, minced
1 teaspoon ground cumin
2 Tablespoons chili powder
1/2 teaspoon paprika
1/2 teaspoon salt
1 teaspoon celery seed
1 teaspoon oregano
1 teaspoon fajita seasoning
3 dashes hot sauce
1/3 cup cider vinegar

1/4 cup brown sugar
1 1/2 cups beef broth
1 (16 oz) can tomato sauce
1 (6 oz) can tomato paste
salt and freshly ground black pepper to taste
1 (4 oz) can green or jalapeño chiles, diced
2 cups poached chicken breast meat, shredded
1 cup sour cream
6 - 8 flour tortillas, fajita-sized
2 cups colby-jack cheese, shredded

Preheat oven to 375 degrees. In a medium saucepan, sauté garlic and shallots in vegetable oil until translucent, over medium-high heat. In a pinch cup, mix together all spices; cumin, chili powder, paprika, salt, celery seed, oregano and fajita seasoning. Add to shallot mixture, stirring constantly, cook until fragrant, about 90 seconds. Add hot sauce, vinegar and brown sugar. Cook until sugar completely dissolves and some of the vinegar has evaporated. Add broth, sauce and paste. Bring to a simmer and cook, uncovered, for at least 10 minutes. Add 1 1/2 cups of the enchilada sauce and chilies to chicken, mix well. Spread 1/2 cup of the enchilada sauce in the bottom of a 9x11-inch dish. In a pie plate, swirl 1/2 cup of enchilada sauce. To assemble: spread sour cream on each tortilla. Spoon filling into tortilla, spread evenly, stopping short of the edge. Place plain side in sauce in pie plate. Push around the plate to coat lightly with sauce. Sprinkle with cheese. Roll tightly and place seam-side down in a baking dish. Repeat process until dish is full. Pour remaining sauce evenly over the top. Sprinkle with remaining cheese. Bake for about 35 minutes, uncovered, until bubbly. Let cool 5 - 10 minutes before serving. Top with additional sauce, cheese, or sour cream.

Prepare enchilada sauce ahead for easy preparation. It freezes well and has many uses.

Charlie's on the Lake Seafood Enchiladas

Serves 10

1 teaspoon butter
1 teaspoon red onion, chopped
1 teaspoon prepared salsa
1 teaspoon crushed red pepper flakes
1/2 teaspoon oregano
1 clove garlic, minced
1/4 cup green onions, chopped
5 ounces salad shrimp (about 70)
5 ounces bay scallops
2 Tablespoons flour

2 Tablespoons butter
2 Tablespoons sour cream
2 Tablespoons heavy cream
1 cup Monterey Jack cheese, shredded
1 cup prepared Alfredo sauce
1/2 cup Monterey Jack cheese, shredded
10 tortilla shells
1/2 cup sour cream
1/2 cup salsa
1 avocado, sliced

Preheat oven to 350 degrees. In a small saucepan, combine 1 teaspoon butter, red onion, salsa, red pepper, oregano, garlic and green onion. Sauté until onions are tender. Dust the seafood with flour. In a separate pan, sauté seafood in 2 tablespoons butter until 80% cooked. Add onion mixture to seafood and allow to cool. Add sour cream, heavy cream and 1 cup Monterey Jack cheese to seafood mixture. Chill in the refrigerator. To assemble the enchiladas, roll 2 ounces of the seafood mixture into each soft tortilla shell. Place in the baking dish, seam-side down. Repeat process for each enchilada. Cover with Alfredo sauce and additional cheese. Bake for 15 minutes. Serve with sour cream, salsa and avocado. !O!!

Eight Layer Casserole

Serves 9

1 pound wide egg noodles
2 pounds ground beef
1 (32 oz) can tomato sauce
2 teaspoons basil
2 teaspoons parsley
1/2 teaspoon onion flakes
1/2 teaspoon freshly ground black pepper
1 teaspoon garlic salt
1 teaspoon sugar

2 cups sour cream
1 (16 oz) package cream cheese, softened
1 cup milk
1 (20 oz) package frozen spinach, thawed and drained
1 cup colby-jack cheese, shredded
1 cup cheddar cheese, shredded

Preheat oven to 350 degrees. In a large stockpot, cook and drain noodles. In a large skillet, brown beef and drain. Add tomato sauce, basil, parsley, onion, pepper, garlic salt and sugar. Simmer 10 minutes. In a medium bowl, combine sour cream, cream cheese and milk. In a greased 9x13-inch pan, layer half of the cooked noodles, half of the meat mixture, all the cream cheese mixture and all of the spinach. Top with remaining meat and noodles. Sprinkle shredded cheeses over top. Bake 1 hour, until bubbly.

DUNDEE DELL MEATLOAF

5007 Underwood Avenue
Serves 8 - 10

1 onion
1/2 carrot
1/2 green bell pepper
1/2 cup mushrooms
3/4 cup barbecue sauce
3 eggs
2 1/2 pounds ground beef
1/4 cup garlic cloves, minced
1/2 teaspoon granulated garlic
1/2 teaspoon freshly ground black pepper
1/2 teaspoon thyme
1/2 teaspoon salt
1 cup breadcrumbs

Preheat oven to 350 degrees. In a food processor, make a mash out of the onion, carrot, green pepper and mushrooms. Then by hand, combine the vegetable mix, barbecue sauce and eggs with the ground beef. When everything is mixed completely add the cloves, garlic, pepper, thyme and salt. Add the breadcrumbs a little at a time until they are stiff but a workable consistency. Form a loaf on a sheet pan with parchment paper. Bake for 2 - 2 1/2 hours depending on the size and shape of your loaf. !O!!

The Canigia family from left Cirino, Ross, Eli, Yano, Al and Lou. - *Submitted by Chuck Caniglia*

CANIGLIA HISTORY

Caniglia's started with Giovanna Franco and Cirino Caniglia, childhood playmates in Carlentini Sicily. At the age of 17, Giovanna immigrated to join an older sister in Omaha. In Omaha she became reacquainted with Cirino and married the shy baker. They had five sons and one daughter while running a bakery where Cirino kneaded and baked his trademarked bread by hand from 10 p.m. to 3:00 a.m. He delivered it still warm to restaurant customers for their breakfast menus.

While in Baltimore awaiting military orders to go to England, Eli, the Caniglia's third oldest son, visited the Roma Café run by an Italian family a lot like the Caniglia's. They were making a dish they called "pizza" that was very much like cucurene, a double crusted meat and cheese pastry, Giovanna made at home. Eli wrote home to his father saying "we could make a fortune with something called pizza."

On August 3, 1946 the Caniglia's introduced pizza to Omaha. Their "pizzeria" a word the Caniglia's coined was located in a new addition to the bakery at Seventh and Pierce Streets. It was an immediate success although Omahans of non-Italian descent had to be taught how to eat this strange food.

As the restaurant took off so did the Caniglia restaurant dynasty.

Their daughter, Grace, married Tony Piccolo of Piccolo Pete's which opened in 1933. Piccolo Pete's is now run by their daughters, Donna Sheehan and Dee Graves, and grandson Scott Sheehan.

Their son, Ross, took over Caniglia's in the early 1970s. Before closing in 2005 the restaurant was run by sons Chuck, Ron and Bob Caniglia.

Lou opened Luigi's at 114th and Dodge Streets in 1979 and Luciano's in 1989. Both are now closed.

Son Eli opened the Venice Inn at 69th and Pacific Streets in 1956. His sons, Chuck and Jerry, still run the Italian Steakhouse which features a mix of Nebraska beef, Italian specialties, chicken and seafood.

Sebastiano "Yano" bought Marshall's Drive-Inn on North 30th Street in 1951 and renamed it the Royal Boy Drive-in. Each year's top carhop was richly rewarded with a brand new Studebaker. As drive-ins faded out, Yano turned the building into Mister C's in the early 1960s. Mister C's is still run by Yano and his wife Mary.

Al opened Al Caniglia's Drawing Room in Millard in 1971 and took over Top of the World restaurant in the Woodmen Tower. Both are now closed.

Lou, Al and Ross also opened a plush West Omaha restaurant known as the Palazzo 'Taliano at 84th and Center Streets. It is closed.

CANIGLIA'S

WELCOME YOU TO THE
PIZZARIA AND STEAK HOUSE

"Omaha's Original Pizza House"

1114 SOUTH 7TH STREET - OMAHA, NEBR.

Eli Caniglia

Tortellini Soup
Created by Randi Caniglia and submitted by Caniglia's Venice Inn

- 1 pound Italian sausage, casings removed
- 1 cup onion, coarsly chopped
- 2 cloves garlic
- 5 cups beef stock
- 1/2 cup water
- 2 cups tomatoes, chopped
- 1 cup carrots, chopped
- 1/2 teaspoon basil
- 1/2 teaspoon oregano
- 1 1/2 cups zucchini, sliced
- 3 Tablespoons parsley, chopped
- 1 green pepper, diced
- 8 ounces frozen cheese tortellini
- Romano cheese, grated
- Rotella rolls

In a skillet, brown sausage, drain, reserving 1 tablespoon of drippings. Fry onions and garlic in the drippings. Add stock, water, tomatoes, sausage, carrots, basil and oregano. Bring to a simmer and cook uncovered for 30 minutes. Skim fat. Add zucchini, parsley and peppers. Cover, simmer 30 minutes more. Add the tortellini and simmer a few more minutes. Sprinkle with Romano cheese. Serve with hot Rotella rolls. !O!

Explosive Pork Corkscrew Pasta with Habanero Pesto

Serves 10

1/4 cup garlic cloves, minced
1/2 cup onion, chopped
1 large bunch cilantro, leaves removed
   and divided
2 Tablespoons ginger, grated
1 teaspoon salt
1 teaspoon freshly ground black pepper
3 cups canned pineapple juice
1 cup soy sauce
2 pounds pork tenderloin, sliced into
   medallions
2 Tablespoons cooking oil

HABANERO PESTO

1 small habanero or serrano pepper,
   chopped
1/2 cup green onions, sliced
1/2 cup olive oil
1/4 cup grated Parmesan cheese, grated
1/2 teaspoon salt
1/2 teaspoon freshly ground black pepper
1 teaspoon cornstarch, mixed in 1
   teaspoon water
1 (16 oz) bag corkscrew pasta
1/4 cup sour cream

In a food processor, puree garlic, onion, half of the cilantro leaves, ginger, salt and pepper. In a large saucepan add puree, pineapple juice and soy sauce. Mix well. Pour the marinade into a shallow dish and add medallions. Marinate in the refrigerator for 24 hours.

Separate the medallions and the marinade, reserving marinade. In a skillet, heat oil on medium-high heat. Sear medallions for about 30 seconds per side, until lightly browned. Pour the reserved marinade over medallions. Cover and stew on low heat for 2 hours. To make the pesto, puree chopped pepper, onions and remaining cilantro in a food processor. Add olive oil, cheese, salt and pepper. Pulse and set aside. After the medallions have stewed, strain and reserve marinade. Return marinade to the skillet. Shred all the pork and set aside. Let the marinade settle until cool in order to remove any fat which may form on top. Simmer the marinade and reduce for 15 - 20 minutes. Add cornstarch and water to thicken, if necessary. As the marinade reduces, cook, drain and set aside pasta. Add pork back into the marinade and. To assemble, layer in this order: pasta, medallion reduction sauce, 1 Tablespoon sour cream per person and 2 teaspoons of pesto. Toss and enjoy!

Be careful when cutting the pepper; use dishwashing gloves. Wash your hands well after cutting. Substitute other mild pepper, if desired, or add another habanero pepper for extra heat.

Pesto Bow Tie Pasta with Pepper

Serves 4 - 6

2 large bunches fresh basil leaves
4 cloves garlic, minced
1/2 cup Parmesan cheese
1/2 cup pine nuts, toasted
juice of 1 lemon
1/2 cup olive oil
salt and freshly ground black pepper to
   taste

1 (10 oz) package bow tie pasta
1 red pepper, sliced
1 green pepper, sliced
2 bunches green onion, sliced
2 medium tomatoes, cut into wedges

In a food processor, combine basil, garlic, cheese, nuts, juice, and oil; blend. Season with salt and pepper. Cook pasta according to package directions. To cooked pasta, add peppers, onions and tomatoes. Add pesto and toss.

Jam's Red Chili Macaroni and Cheese

Serves 8

1 medium onion, minced
4 cloves garlic, minced
1 Tablespoon olive oil
1 Tablespoon chili powder
1 teaspoon ground cumin
2 cups dry sherry
2 cups chicken stock
2 cups heavy cream
1/2 cup roux (see note)

1/2 cup blue cheese, crumbled
1/2 cup Monterey Jack cheese, shredded
1/2 cup cheddar cheese, shredded
1 teaspoon salt
1 teaspoon freshly ground black pepper
1 bag elbow macaroni
1 cup breadcrumbs
2 Tablespoons butter, melted

Preheat oven to 350 degrees. In a medium pan, add the onion and garlic. Sauté in olive oil over medium heat until soft and starting to caramelize. Add chili powder and cumin, then heat until fragrant, 30 seconds or so. Deglaze with dry sherry and then simmer for 15 minutes. Add chicken stock and cream. Bring to a high simmer, then reduce heat and simmer on low for 25 minutes. Thicken by whisking in the roux. Continue to simmer for 5 more minutes. Whisk in cheeses. Season with salt and pepper. Boil macaroni according to package directions. Drain, then mix with the sauce. Place macaroni and sauce in an oven safe baking dish. Mix breadcrumbs and melted butter; sprinkle over macaroni mixture. Bake for 20 minutes, then broil until browned. Add bacon, chopped tomato, or vegetables to the macaroni and cheese before baking, if desired

To make roux, melt butter and add enough flour to make a mixture resembling wet sand. |O!|

Penne Alfio

Serves 4

1 Tablespoon olive oil
4 boneless, skinless chicken breasts, diced
2 cloves garlic, minced
1/2 teaspoon salt
1/2 teaspoon crushed red pepper flakes
1 teaspoon oregano
1 teaspoon thyme

1 teaspoon basil
2 ounces sun dried tomatoes in olive oil, chopped
1 (14 oz) can artichoke hearts packed in water, chopped into bite-size pieces
1 (14 oz) can chicken broth
1 (12 oz) box penne pasta
1/4 cup Parmesan cheese, grated

In a large skillet heat oil and add chicken and garlic. Brown chicken, then add salt, red pepper, oregano, thyme and basil. Stir until fragrant, for about 1 minute. Add tomatoes, artichokes and broth. Simmer on medium heat for 30 minutes. Cook pasta according to package directions. Spoon sauce over pasta and sprinkle with cheese.

All-Star Spaghetti with Meat Sauce
Serves 6 - 8

2 Tablespoons olive oil
1 cup onion, chopped
1/2 cup green pepper, chopped
4 cloves garlic, minced
1 large carrot, peeled and chopped
1 1/2 cups mushrooms, chopped
1 Tablespoon dried Italian seasoning blend
2 teaspoons pizza seasoning (see note)
1 1/2 pounds ground beef
2 Tablespoons brown sugar
2 Tablespoons balsamic vinegar
2 Tablespoons red wine
1 (32 oz) can diced tomatoes, undrained
1 (6 oz) can tomato paste
4 bay leaves
1 pound spaghetti, cooked and drained
salt and freshly ground black pepper to taste
1 cup Parmesan cheese, finely grated
1/8 teaspoon crushed red pepper flakes
Parmesan cheese, finely grated
1/4 cup fresh parsley, chopped

In a large skillet, heat oil over medium-high heat. Add onions, pepper, garlic and carrots. Sauté until lightly browned. Add mushrooms and sauté for 1 minute. Add seasonings and stir until fragrant, about 1 minute. Add meat and brown. Add sugar, vinegar and wine. Stir one minute. Add tomatoes and paste; stir. Bring to a high simmer, then reduce heat and add the bay leaves. Cover and simmer for 30 minutes. Cook spaghetti according to package directions. Discard bay leaves from the sauce. Season to taste with salt and pepper. Add cheese and red pepper, stir until melted. Divide pasta, ladle with sauce. Sprinkle with parsley and additional parmesan.

A pizza seasoning blend should include ground fennel, fennel seeds, red pepper and cayenne.

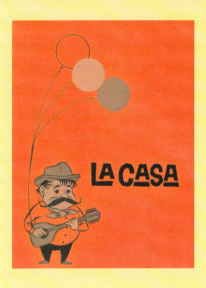

For authentic Italian cuisine, check out La Casa Pizzeria, home of Omaha's original Neapolitan pizza. The original location is at 4432 Leavenworth Street or try their West Omaha location at 8216 Grover Street. - *From the Joe Villella menu collection at the Douglas County Historical Society*

Fettuccini Carbonara
Serves 6

1 teaspoon salt
1/4 cup olive oil
1/2 pound bacon, diced
1/4 cup capers
1/2 cup dry white wine
3 eggs, beaten
3/4 cup Parmesan cheese, finely grated
1/4 cup Romano cheese, finely grated
1/2 teaspoon crushed red pepper flakes
3 cloves garlic, minced or pressed
1 pound fettuccini
Kosher salt and freshly ground black pepper to taste
1/4 cup parsley, chopped

Place heatproof pasta bowl in oven and heat oven to 200 degrees. In a large stockpot, bring water to boil and add salt. In a skillet, heat oil over medium-high heat. Add bacon and stir until lightly browned and crisp, 6 - 7 minutes. Add capers and cook for 1 minute. Add wine and simmer until slightly reduced, another 6-8 minutes. Remove from heat and cover. In a small bowl, beat eggs, cheeses, pepper and garlic and set aside. Cook pasta according to package directions. Drain pasta, reserve 1/3 cup of pasta water. Transfer drained pasta to the warmed serving bowl, adding water if necessary. Immediately pour egg mixture over hot pasta, sprinkle with Kosher salt and toss well. Pour bacon and caper mixture over pasta, season generously with pepper. Toss well. Garnish with parsley. Serve immediately.

Warming the bowl makes all the difference and is important to fully cook the eggs.

Gorgonzola and Fresh Thyme Pasta

Serves 2

1 1/2 cups heavy cream
6 ounces Gorgonzola cheese, crumbled
1 teaspoon fresh thyme
1/8 teaspoon ground nutmeg

salt and white pepper, to taste
1 (10 oz) package pasta
1 - 2 apples, sliced and peeled
1/2 cup walnuts, toasted

In a small pot, combine cream, cheese, thyme and nutmeg. Cook gently until sauce reduces by one quarter. Add salt and pepper to taste. Cook pasta according to package directions. Toss sauce with pasta, apples and walnuts.

Pasta with Lemon-Parmesan Cream Sauce

Serves 4

6 Tablespoons butter
6 Tablespoons fresh lemon juice
1 Tablespoon lemon zest
1 cup whipping cream
3/4 cup Parmesan cheese, grated

3/4 pound thin pasta or linguine
1/2 cup parsley, finely chopped
salt and freshly ground black pepper to
taste

Melt butter in a pan over medium-low heat. Add lemon juice and zest. Simmer for 5 minutes, stirring occasionally. Whisk in whipping cream and cheese. Bring to simmer and remove from heat. Sauce may be prepared 1 hour ahead. Let stand uncovered at room temperature. Cook pasta until tender but still firm to bite. Drain well. Add pasta and parsley to sauce. Toss over medium heat until sauce coats pasta. Season with salt and pepper.

Tomato Prosciutto Pasta

Serves 6

1 Tablespoon olive oil
3 cloves garlic, minced
4 ounces prosciutto, diced
1 (56 oz) can whole tomatoes, drained
   and liquid reserved

1 (14 oz) box bucatini rigati pasta
1 cup basil, sliced into thin strips
3 ounces Parmesan cheese, grated

In a Dutch oven, heat olive oil over medium heat. Add garlic and prosciutto and sauté until golden. Add tomatoes, breaking them up with a spoon. Cover, leaving room for steam to escape so sauce will thicken. Simmer for 20 minutes, covered, and 20 minutes, uncovered. Add reserved tomato liquid, as needed, to thin. Cook pasta according to package directions. Pour sauce over hot pasta. Toss with basil and cheese.

Tortellini Primavera

Serves 4

1 cup mushrooms, sliced
1/2 cup onion, chopped
1 clove garlic, minced
2 Tablespoons butter
1 (10 oz) package chopped spinach,
   thawed and well drained
1 (8 oz) package cream cheese, softened
1 tomato, diced

1/4 cup milk or cream
1/4 cup Parmesan cheese, grated
1 teaspoon Italian seasoning
1/4 teaspoon salt
1/4 teaspoon freshly ground black pepper
8 ounces cheese-filled tortellini, cooked
   and drained

In a large skillet, melt butter. Sauté mushrooms, onion and garlic, stirring occasionally. Add spinach, cream cheese, tomato, milk, cheese, seasoning, salt and pepper. Mix well and cook until mixture just begins to boil. Stir in tortellini and cook until thoroughly heated.

Chicken Mushroom Lasagna

Serves 8 - 10

8 lasagna noodles, cooked
1/4 cup butter
1 pound fresh mushrooms, sliced
1/2 teaspoon salt
1/4 teaspoon white pepper
1/4 cup flour
3 cups milk

2 chicken breast halves, skinned, boned,
    cooked and chopped
15 ounces ricotta cheese
12 ounces mozzarella cheese, shredded
1/2 cup Parmesan cheese, grated
1/2 cup fresh parsley, chopped

Preheat oven to 325 degrees. Cook, drain and rinse noodles. Spread out noodles on waxed paper to cool. In a large saucepan, melt butter. Add mushrooms, salt and pepper. Sauté until tender, about 5 minutes. Stir in flour; then slowly add milk while stirring. Cook over medium-high heat until sauce thickens, stirring constantly. Stir in half of the parsley. Spread 1/3 cup of the sauce in the bottom of a 9x13-inch baking dish. Layer one-third each: noodles, chicken, ricotta, mozzarella and Parmesan. Repeat layers two more times, ending with Parmesan cheese on top. Sprinkle top with remaining parsley. Bake 45 minutes or until bubbly. Let stand for 10 minutes to set before serving. Freezes well.

Brandied Cranberries

Serves 8 - 10

4 cups fresh cranberries
2 cups sugar

1/2 cup apricot brandy
zest of 1/2 orange

Preheat oven to 275 degrees. Mix all ingredients together and place in a 9x13-inch baking pan. Cover tightly with foil. Bake for 4 - 5 hours. Leave covered and allow to cool. Place in a serving bowl after cooling and refrigerate.

This fantastic holiday recipe may be made one day ahead.

Onion Jam
Makes 2 cups

2 Tablespoons olive oil
4 cups onions, chopped
1 1/2 Tablespoons thyme, chopped
1/2 teaspoon granulated garlic
1/2 teaspoon kosher salt
freshly ground black pepper, to taste
1/4 cup brown sugar

1 teaspoon soy sauce
1/4 cup balsamic vinegar
1/4 cup red wine or cooking sherry
1/4 cup beef stock
salt and freshly ground black pepper to
    taste

In a skillet, heat oil over medium heat. Add onions; cook for 6 - 9 minutes, until translucent. Add thyme, garlic, salt and pepper. Cook and stir constantly until fragrant, about 1 minute. Add sugar. Cook until golden brown, 10 - 15 minutes, stirring occasionally. Add soy sauce, vinegar, wine and beef stock. Cook for another 10 minutes until thickened, stirring often. Season to taste. Refrigerate and serve chilled.

Great in mashed potatoes, as a sandwich spread, or as steak sauce. Process, if desired, for smoother consistency. This compliments the Grilled Skirt Steak with Watercress Sauce on page 118.

Taste Pesto
Serves 6

12 fresh basil leaves, washed, dried, and
    coarsely chopped
3 garlic cloves, coarsely chopped

2 Tablespoons pine nuts, lightly toasted
1/8 teaspoon kosher salt
3 Tablespoons olive oil

In a food processor, blend the basil, garlic, nuts and salt until thoroughly mashed. Add the oil, a few drops at a time, until you have a smooth paste. Pesto may also be made in a blender. Pour in the oil first, then the garlic, nuts and finally the basil leaves. Blend on low to a smooth paste. Season with kosher salt. Pesto may be prepared and refrigerated or frozen. Bring to room temperature before using. This recipe is doubled very easily.

"If you own a mortar and pestle, use it to make this pesto. You will definitely notice the difference in flavor when the fresh herbs are stone-ground!" - Don Poty, Owner Taste ¡O!¡

Shrimp Pasta

Serves 4

1 pound raw shrimp, shelled with tails
    left on
1/2 cup Riesling or other favorite white
    wine
1/2 cup lemon juice
3 Tablespoons olive oil
1 cup spinach, chopped

1 cup tomatoes, chopped
1 clove garlic, minced
1 (10 oz) package pasta
1/2 cup feta, crumbled or Parmesan
    cheese, grated
salt and freshly ground black pepper to
    taste

In a large pot, combine shrimp, Riesling, lemon juice, oil, spinach, tomatoes and garlic. Simmer for 12 minutes. Cook pasta according to the package directions. Toss sauce with cooked pasta. Sprinkle with feta or Parmesan cheese. Serve hot or cold.

This is great when created the day before a brunch or dinner, allowing the flavors to really blend.

Omaha Country Club
Baked Tomatoes and Rigatoni with Garlic

Serves 4

4 Tablespoons olive oil, divided
8 garlic cloves, peeled and sliced
1 sprig of rosemary, chopped
4 large beefsteak tomatoes, split in half
    and seeded
salt and freshly ground black pepper

8 ounces rigatoni
2 Tablespoons butter

Preheat the oven to 300 degrees. Brush a 12x12-inch baking sheet with 1 Tablespoon olive oil. Place 8 piles of garlic slices on the sheet, 3 inches apart, with a pinch of rosemary on top. Season each tomato half with salt and pepper and place over the garlic, skin-side up. Brush the tomatoes with oil. Bake them in the oven for 40 - 60 minutes, or until very soft. Remove the skin from the tomatoes and set aside. Cook the rigatoni in boiling, salted water with 1 Tablespoon of oil until done, 7 - 10 minutes. Drain and toss with butter, and season to taste.

Place the pasta in a buttered rectangular baking dish and cover with the baked tomatoes and garlic. Press the tomatoes down to even out the pasta. |O|

THE BOHEMIAN CAFE
1406 South 13th Street

The Bohemian Cafe has been a local favorite in Omaha since opening in 1924. The restaurant, at 1406 South 13th Street, offers traditional international cuisine specializing in Czech and Eastern European fare. Dumplings and kraut, roast duck, wiener schnitzel, hasenpfeffer and soups fill the dinner menu along with homemade apple strudel and kolaches for dessert. The exterior boasts an opulent display of tile work and Czech detailing, while the interior is simple and inviting. Ann and Josef Libor bought the Bohemian Cafe in 1947 and now fourth-generation family members work at the restaurant. - *From the Joe Villella menu collection at the Douglas County Historical Society*

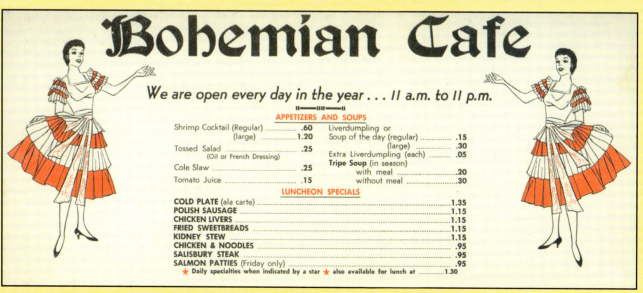

Sam Nisi's Spare Time Cafe

1211 South Fifth Street

Mr. and Mrs. Sam Nisi in the Spare Time cooler with their son, Ross. Spare Time at 1211 South Fifth Street was known from coast to coast as the place to go for a good Nebraska steak. *- From the William Wentworth collection at the Douglas County Historical Society collections*

"I remember the great big cooler when you entered Spare Time where you could pick your own steak."

- From the Burnice Fiedler collection

Herb-Crusted Pork Tenderloin

Serves 4 - 6

1 (2 lb) package pork tenderloin
kosher salt and freshly ground black
   pepper
1 bunch sage, finely chopped
2 Tablespoons garlic, minced

1 cup Dijon mustard
1/2 cup breadcrumbs or panko flakes
   (Japanese breadcrumbs)
1/4 cup olive oil

Preheat oven to 350 degrees. Season pork with salt and pepper. Sear or grill pork until lightly browned on all sides. Combine the sage, garlic, mustard, breadcrumbs and olive oil. Roll the seared pork in the mixture. Bake for 15 - 20 minutes until meat reaches 140-145 degrees internal temperature. Pork may also be grilled, wrapped in foil. Slice thin and serve with rice, couscous or polenta.

Dill, thyme or rosemary also work well in this recipe.

Pork Chops with
Parmesan Sage Cornbread Crust

Serves 6

1 large corn muffin, processed into fine
   crumbs
1 cup Parmesan cheese, grated
1/4 cup sage, chopped
2 teaspoons lemon pepper seasoning
1 teaspoon lemon zest
1 teaspoon kosher salt
2 egg whites, lightly beaten

2 Tablespoons cornstarch
2 Tablespoons lemon juice
1/2 teaspoon salt
2 Tablespoons butter
2 Tablespoons olive oil
6 bone-in center pork loin chops
lemon or orange wedges, for garnish

In a pie plate or cake pan, combine cornbread crumbs, Parmesan cheese, sage, lemon pepper, lemon zest and salt. In a separate bowl, whisk together egg whites, cornstarch, lemon juice and salt. Pour into another pie plate. Dredge each chop in egg mixture, turn to coat. Press chop into crumb mixture, turning to coat completely. Let rest on a wire rack for 20 - 30 minutes to allow coating to set.

In a large skillet, melt butter with oil over medium-high heat. Add chops and cook until golden brown on both sides, about 3 - 4 minutes per side. Cook, turning often, until internal temperature reads 140 - 145 degrees, about 20 minutes. Baste chops with pan juices, while cooking. Transfer to serving platter and let rest, lightly tented with foil, until internal temperature reads 150 - 155 degrees. Transfer to plates, and garnish with lemon or orange wedges.

The pork may be browned for 3 - 4 minutes a side and baked in a 425 degree oven until done. This recipe also works well with boneless chops and bone-in chicken. Wheatfield's Ron's Cornbread (page 182) works well for the breadcrumbs.

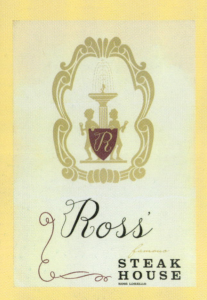

Ross' Steakhouse, 909 South 72nd Street, shortly before it closed November 2, 1996.
- Photographed by Bill Kratville

The story goes that when Ross Lorello and his wife Josephine started Ross' Steak House, 72nd Street was a dirt road. The first night Ross' was open 14 cars went by. Traffic soon picked up and Ross' grew to one of Omaha's most popular steak houses. Ross' Lyonnaise potatoes were always a favorite.

Seared Pork Tenderloin with Gorgonzola Sauce

Serves 4

1 1/2 pounds pork tenderloin
1 Tablespoon freshly ground black pepper
1 Tablespoon fennel seed, crushed
1/2 teaspoon kosher salt
1 teaspoon ground paprika
1 teaspoon ground cumin
2 Tablespoons olive oil

GORGONZOLA SAUCE
2 Tablespoons olive oil, divided
1 Tablespoon butter
12 ounces cremini mushrooms, sliced
2 Tablespoons shallots, minced
2 Tablespoons garlic, minced
1/2 cup white wine
1 cup whipping cream
4 green onions, sliced
6 ounces Gorgonzola cheese, crumbled

Cut pork into eight 1-inch medallions; flatten slightly with the heel of your hand. In a small bowl, combine pepper, fennel seed, salt, paprika and cumin. Rub spice mixture onto both sides of the medallions; set aside. In a large skillet, heat olive oil over medium-high heat. Add pork and cook about 4 minutes per side.

In a large pot, heat 1 Tablespoon olive oil and butter over medium-high heat. Add mushrooms; cook until mushrooms are caramelized, about 6 minutes. Add remaining olive oil, shallots and garlic. Cook 3 minutes. Add the white wine, and stir. Cook until wine almost evaporates, about 2 minutes. Add the cream. Cook until reduced and slightly thickened, about 2 minutes. Add the onions and cheese. Stir until the cheese melts. Serve over medallions.

Bangkok Pork with Peanut Sauce

Serves 6

3 cloves garlic, minced
1 shallot, minced
3 Tablespoons cilantro leaves, chopped
2 Tablespoons oyster sauce
2 Tablespoons soy sauce
2 Tablespoons brandy or apple cider vinegar
2 teaspoons Saté seasoning (see note)
6 (6 oz) center loin boneless pork chops
bean sprouts and cilantro, for garnish

PEANUT SAUCE
1/2 cup coconut milk
1 teaspoon red curry paste
2 Tablespoons crunchy peanut butter
1 Tablespoon water
3 Tablespoons dry roasted peanuts, chopped
2 teaspoons sugar
2 teaspoons fish sauce
2 teaspoons lime juice

In a bowl, whisk together garlic, shallots, cilantro, oyster sauce, soy sauce, brandy and Saté seasoning. Cut chops in half and place in a shallow dish. Pour marinade over pork. Cover and refrigerator overnight.

In a small saucepan, heat coconut milk over medium heat. Stir until bubbly, 30 - 60 seconds. Add curry paste, stirring constantly until broken down and bubbly. Add peanut butter, water, peanuts, sugar, fish sauce and lime juice. Prepare grill or grill pan. Grill pork about 3 to 4 minutes per side, until just pink inside (145 degrees). Tent lightly with foil until temperature reaches 150 - 155 degrees. Brush peanut sauce generously on pork halves and serve more on the side. Garnish with bean sprouts and cilantro. Serve with rice.

If unavailable use 1/4 teaspoon each of as many of the aforementioned as available. Saté is an eastern Indian Spice blend and is available as a blend from many spice companies.

Slow Roasted Pork Roast with Hoisin

Serves 6

1 Tablespoon olive oil
1 (5 - 6 lb) boneless pork shoulder
1 1/2 cups hoisin sauce
3 bunches green onions, sliced on the
    diagonal

1/2 cup scotch whiskey
3/4 cup water

Preheat oven to 300 degrees. In a Dutch oven, heat oil over high heat. Add pork shoulder, fat-side down. Brown on all sides, about 12 minutes. Remove pot from heat. Add hoisin sauce and onions to pork. Cover and bake until the pork is very tender, about 2 3/4 hours. If mixture is dry, add 1/4 cup water to the Dutch oven. Transfer pork to a cutting board and tent with foil. Spoon off excess fat from pan juices. Stir whiskey and 3/4 cup water into juices. Boil 2 minutes. Add more water if sauce is too thick or boil to reduce if too thin. Cut pork crosswise and pour pan sauce over to serve. Garnish with green onions.

Bourbon-Glazed Grilled Pork Chops

Serves 6

6 (6 oz) center loin boneless pork chops
1/4 cup hoisin sauce
2 Tablespoons rice wine vinegar
2 Tablespoons bourbon
2 Tablespoons pure maple syrup or
    honey

1 Tablespoon lime juice
1/2 teaspoon ground ginger
1 1/2 teaspoons chili garlic sauce or 1/3
    cup ketchup-style chili sauce
1/2 teaspoon salt
1/2 teaspoon freshly ground black pepper

Trim pork chops and place in a shallow dish. In a small bowl, combine hoisin sauce, rice vinegar, bourbon, maple syrup, lime juice, ginger, chili garlic sauce, salt and pepper. Cover, place in the refrigerator and marinate overnight. Heat a grill pan over medium-high heat. Grill pork, 3 - 4 minutes each side collecting excess marinade. Internal temperature should reach 145 degrees. Tent lightly with foil or cover pan for 5 minutes. Serve over rice. Spoon sauce over chops.

The Fountain Room in Kiewit Plaza, 36th and Farnam Streets, 1960. - From the Burnice Fiedler collection

Curried Pork Chops

Serves 6

6 (6 oz) pork chops, boneless loin chops
2 Tablespoons unsalted butter
1 Tablespoon olive oil
1/4 cup dry white wine
1 cup heavy whipping cream
1 beef bouillon cube
1 1/2 Tablespoons curry powder
1 apple, cored and chopped

Season pork chops with salt and pepper. In a large skillet, melt butter and olive oil. Cook pork chops until browned on both sides. Remove pork chops. Add white wine, cream, bouillon, curry and apple. Add back the pork chops. Cook on medium heat until sauce is bubbly and pork chops are cooked through. Serve chops with sauce.

For a lighter alternative, substitute whole milk or light cream and two teaspoons of flour for the heavy cream.

Grilled Honey Mustard Maple Pork Chops

Serves 6

2 Tablespoons brown sugar
1 Tablespoon butter, melted
1 Tablespoon olive oil
2 Tablespoons honey
1 Tablespoon soy sauce
1 1/2 Tablespoons mustard
2 Tablespoons pure maple syrup
1 teaspoon garlic powder
2 Tablespoons balsamic vinegar
2 Tablespoons rosemary, chopped
6 (6 oz) center loin boneless pork chops
Salt and freshly ground black pepper to taste

In a small bowl, whisk together brown sugar, butter, olive oil, honey, soy sauce, mustard, syrup, garlic powder, vinegar and rosemary. Cut pork chops in half and place in a glass baking dish. Pour marinade ingredients over pork chops and cover. Refrigerate overnight. Heat grill pan. Grill chops approximately 3 - 4 minutes per side. Internal temperature needs to reach 140 - 145 degrees. Remove from heat and cover. Allow to rest for 8 - 10 minutes. The internal temperature should go no higher than 150 - 155 degrees. Salt and pepper to taste. Transfer to platter, scooping up glaze. The grill pan allows the marinade to caramelize and get nice and sticky.

Prosciutto Pork Tenderloin Medallions

Serves 6

1 1/2 pounds pork tenderloin
2 Tablespoons olive oil
1/4 cup prosciutto, chopped
2 Tablespoons sage leaves, chopped
2 Tablespoons parsley, chopped
2 Tablespoons sun-dried tomatoes in oil,
   drained and chopped

1/4 cup onion, chopped
1/2 cup dry white wine or chicken broth
1/2 cup heavy whipping cream or half
   and half
1/4 teaspoon salt
1/2 teaspoon freshly ground black pepper

Cut pork diagonally across grain into 1/2-inch slices. In a 12-inch skillet, heat oil over medium-high heat. Cook prosciutto, sage, parsley, tomatoes and onion about 5 minutes, stirring frequently, until onion is tender. Add pork. Cook 10 minutes, turning pork occasionally, until pork is light brown. Stir in wine, cream, salt and pepper. Heat to high simmer; then reduce heat. Simmer uncovered about 20 minutes, stirring occasionally, until pork is no longer pink in center and sauce is thickened.

Roasted Pork Tenderloin

Serves 2 - 4

2 sweet onions, sliced
2 Tablespoons brown sugar
2 Tablespoons balsamic vinegar
1/2 teaspoon salt

1/2 teaspoon freshly ground black pepper
1/2 cup golden raisins
1 pound pork tenderloin

Preheat oven to 375 degrees. In a skillet, sauté onions until soft. Add brown sugar, vinegar, salt, pepper and raisins until glazed. Sear pork tenderloin in the skillet. Place pork tenderloin in a baking dish and top with the sautéed onion mix. Bake for 45 minutes.

Hiro Don Katsu (Pork Filet)

Serves 4 - 6

1 1/2 pounds pork tenderloin, cut into 1/2-inch slices
salt and freshly ground black pepper to taste
2 cups flour
2 eggs, beaten
2 cups panko flakes (Japanese breadcrumbs)
6 cabbage leaves
3 radishes
1/2 cup Worcestershire sauce
2 Tablespoons shoyu or soy sauce
2 Tablespoons ketchup
vegetable oil, for deep frying
4 lemon slices
mustard, to taste

Season the tenderloin with salt and pepper. Dredge the slices in flour and shake off the excess. Dip in the egg, then the breadcrumbs. Place on a wire rack and refrigerate for 30 minutes. Cut out the hard stalk of the cabbage leaves and slice each leaf, lengthwise, in half. Layer three pieces together, roll up tightly and slice into fine threads. Soak the cabbage threads in cold water. Cut the radish into thin slices, then into fine strips. Add to the cabbage threads. Once crisp, drain.

In a small bowl, combine the Worcestershire sauce, soy sauce and ketchup. Set aside. In a deep skillet, heat 2 inches of vegetable oil to 350 degrees. Add the pork, turning once when it becomes golden and crispy. Continue to cook for 5 - 6 minutes until golden brown. Drain well on paper towels. Heap generous servings of the cabbage and radish onto plates. Arrange the pork in front and garnish with lemon and mustard. Serve the sauce on the side. !O!

Volunteer Bureau

A map of the city pinpoints some 60 welfare agencies serviced by the Volunteer Bureau, which was co-sponsored by the United Community Services and the Junior League of Omaha from 1955 until 1960. Pictured (left to right) are Mrs. William Otis, Mrs. Fred Golan and Mrs. Lloyd Peterson. - *Reprinted with permission from the Omaha World-Herald*

Pork Piccata
Serves 6 - 8

1 1/2 pounds pork tenderloin,
  cut into 6 - 8 cutlets
1/2 cup flour
1 teaspoon freshly ground black pepper
1 teaspoon lemon zest
3 Tablespoons butter
1/2 cup lemon juice
3/4 cup dry vermouth or dry white wine
lemon slices
1/2 cup capers

Pound cutlets thin (about 1/8-inch). In a small dish, combine flour, pepper and lemon zest. Dredge cutlets in flour mixture. In a large skillet, melt butter over medium-high heat. Sauté cutlets, turning once, until golden brown, about 5 - 6 minutes. Remove pork chops from pan. Add lemon juice and vermouth to skillet. Stir constantly for 3 minutes, until sauce is slightly thickened. Place pork chops back in the pan to warm. To serve, place pork chops on a platter. Top with sauce. Garnish with lemon slices and capers.

Brine for Meat
Serves 10

1/2 cup kosher salt
7 cups hot water
2 cups cider vinegar, apple cider or hard
  cider
1/2 cup brown sugar
1 Tablespoon peppercorns
16 dried juniper berries
1 Tablespoon allspice
1 Tablespoon crushed red pepper flakes
4 bay leaves
2 celery ribs, chopped
1 carrot, sliced
8 cloves garlic, minced
1 onion, sliced

In an 8 quart stockpot, dissolve salt in water. Add cider, sugar, peppercorns, juniper berries, allspice, pepper flakes, bay leaves, celery, carrot, garlic and onion. Bring to a boil over high heat. Remove and cool. Add meat and refrigerate for recommended time:

Boneless pork or venison: 4 hours
Tenderloin: 8 hours
Roast: 48 hours
5-7 pound roaster chicken: 48 hours
10 pound turkey: 48-72 hours

Bake or grill as desired.

An Original **JLO** *Ingredient*

RACE FOR THE CURE

For many years, women's health care issues were taboo. However, the JLO broke the silence by bringing the Susan G. Komen Breast Cancer "Race for the Cure" to Omaha in October of 1994. League members planned everything from the race route to registration forms, securing finish line equipment and established the JLO Mammography Fund. For over eight years the JLO was active in establishing this outreach project. Proceeds from the race were directed towards breast cancer research, education and screening for area women through the Nebraska Department of Health's "Every Women Matters" program. Chair Kate Sommer revealed in a 1994 JLO This Month article that, "Our money isn't going towards mammography but to the next step along the road to diagnosis." Today, the Omaha Race for the Cure attracts thousands of runners and continues to celebrate a survivor's victory, courage and determination.

Baked Heartland Apple Pork Chops

Serves 4

1 pound Granny Smith apples, peeled,
   cored and sliced
2 Tablespoons olive oil
4 (6 oz) bone-in pork chops

1/4 cup white wine
1 cup whipped cream
1/3 cup Dijon mustard

Preheat oven to 400 degrees. Place apples in a greased 9x13-inch dish. Bake 15 minutes. Meanwhile, in a skillet, brown pork chops in olive oil for 6 - 7 minutes on each side over medium heat. Place browned pork chops on top of baked apples. Pour wine over pork chops and apples. Mix whipped cream and mustard, pour over apples, pork chops and wine. Bake 15 minutes uncovered.

Sweet and Savory Pork

Serves 4

1 pound lean pork, cubed
1 Tablespoon soy sauce
1 egg, lightly beaten
1/2 cup flour
1/2 teaspoon salt
1/4 cup water
2 Tablespoons oil

1 (16 oz) can pineapple cubes plus juice
1 green pepper, cut into 1-inch strips
1/4 cup vinegar
1/4 cup brown sugar
1/2 cup grape tomatoes
2 Tablespoons cornstarch

Place pork in a zippered bag with soy sauce. Let stand for 20 minutes. In a bowl, mix egg, flour, salt and water until smooth. Add pork, turn to coat each cube in batter. In a skillet, fry pork in hot oil until brown. In a microwaveable bowl with a lid, combine pineapple, green pepper, vinegar, brown sugar and tomato. Microwave and boil for 2 minutes. Mix cornstarch with enough water to make a thin mixture. Add to the boiling sauce, stirring, and cook until thickened. Toss with pork and serve at once with rice.

Slow Cooked Tangy Pork Chops

Serves 4

5 (6 oz) boneless pork chops
1/2 teaspoon salt
1/8 teaspoon freshly ground black pepper
2 medium onions, chopped
2 celery ribs, sliced
1 green pepper, sliced
1 (14 1/2 oz) can petite-diced tomatoes
1/2 cup ketchup

2 Tablespoons cider vinegar
2 Tablespoons brown sugar
3 Tablespoons Worcestershire sauce
1 Tablespoon lemon juice
1 beef bouillon cube or 1 teaspoon beef base
2 Tablespoons cornstarch
2 Tablespoons water

Season pork chops with salt and pepper. Place pork chops in a slow cooker. Add onions, celery, green pepper and tomatoes. In a small bowl, whisk ketchup, vinegar, brown sugar, Worcestershire sauce, lemon juice and bouillon cube. Pour over meat and vegetables. Cover and cook on low for 5 1/2 - 6 hours. Mix cornstarch and water until smooth. Stir into liquid in the slow cooker. Cover, cook on high for 30 minutes until sauce thickens. Serve over noodles or rice.

Asian Marinade for Pork Tenderloin

Serves 4 - 6

1/2 cup soy sauce
1/2 cup water
2 Tablespoons fresh lemon juice
1 Tablespoon brown sugar
1 Tablespoon olive oil

1 clove garlic, minced
1/4 teaspoon hot pepper sauce
1/2 teaspoon freshly ground black pepper
1 1/2 pounds pork tenderloin

In a small bowl, mix soy sauce, water, lemon juice, brown sugar, olive oil, garlic, hot pepper sauce and pepper. Place pork tenderloin in a shallow dish. Pour marinade over pork. Cover and place in the refrigerator for 3 hours. Preheat grill and place pork tenderloin on sizzling grill. Cook for 15 - 20 minutes, or until inner temperature reaches 140 degrees, turning once. Remove from grill. Tent and allow to rest until temperature reaches 155 degrees.

This marinade works well with other meats.

Grilled Ham Steaks
Serves 6 - 8

2 pounds fully-cooked ham steaks,
  1/2 - 1 inch thick
1/2 cup ginger ale
1/2 cup orange juice

1/4 cup brown sugar, packed
1 1/2 teaspoons dry mustard
1/2 teaspoon ground ginger
1/4 teaspoon ground cloves

Place ham slices in a heavy-duty zippered plastic bag or shallow dish. In a bowl, combine ginger ale, orange juice, brown sugar, mustard, ginger and cloves. Stir until sugar dissolves. Pour mixture over ham slices and marinate in the refrigerator 8 hours. Turn ham occasionally. Drain ham and reserve marinade. Grill ham over medium heat 6 minutes on each side. Baste once with reserved marinade.

This dish may be made ahead of time. Freeze the ham slices and the marinade together in a heavy-duty zippered freezer bag. Thaw and grill.

Sam Comento's Steak House located on the 900 block of Seventh Street was Omaha's first real Italian restaurant. Pictured is the staff in 1942. - *From William Wentworth collection at the Douglas County Historical archives*

156

Cascio's Steak House
10th and Hickory Streets.

Cascio's Steak House was started by Al Cascio and continues serving great food today under the management of Al's nephew Larry Cascio. The chicken fried steak is a local favorite. - *From Lou Marcuzzo*

Tandoori-Spiced Grilled Chicken
with Mint-Cucumber Yogurt Sauce
Serves 6 - 10

1/4 cup malt vinegar
2 Tablespoons lemon juice
1 teaspoon turmeric
1 teaspoon kosher salt
1 Tablespoon garam masala
1 Tablespoon garlic powder
1 1/2 Tablespoons ginger, grated
1 1/2 Tablespoons ground cumin
2 Tablespoons paprika
2 Tablespoons ground coriander
2 teaspoons sugar
3 cups plain yogurt
15 skinless chicken thighs

MINT SAUCE
1/2 cup plain yogurt
1/2 cup cucumber, seeded and diced
1/2 cup tomatoes, diced
2 teaspoons shallots, minced
2 teaspoons fresh mint, chopped
1/2 teaspoon ground cumin
1/2 teaspoon kosher salt
lemon or lime wedges, for garnish
mint leaves, for garnish

In a bowl, whisk together vinegar, juice, turmeric, salt, garam, masala, garlic, ginger, cumin, paprika, coriander, sugar and yogurt. Pour mixture into a shallow dish. Add chicken, turn to coat and marinate, covered, overnight. Prepare grill. Using tongs, allow excess marinade to drip off before putting on the grill. On a broil pan or wire rack, placed in a jelly roll pan, grill chicken for 25 - 30 minutes, until juices run clear. Turn occasionally.

For sauce, in a bowl, whisk together yogurt, cucumber, tomatoes, shallots, mint, cumin and salt. Refrigerate for at least 1 hour. Serve mint sauce over chicken. Garnish with lemon or lime wedges and additional mint leaves.

Teriyaki Beer Grilled Chicken
Serves 10

2/3 cup soy sauce
1/4 cup mirin (Asian rice wine) or sweet sherry
1/4 cup cider vinegar
1/4 cup sugar
1 (12 oz) bottle beer (not dark)

2 tablespoons ginger, grated
1 teaspoon garlic-chili sauce (see note)
2 teaspoons cornstarch
2 teaspoons water
2 pounds bone-in chicken, skinned and trimmed

In a saucepan, combine soy sauce, mirin, vinegar, sugar, beer, ginger and garlic-chili sauce. Simmer the mixture for 20 - 25 minutes. Mix cornstarch and water. Add to saucepan. Cook until sauce reduces and thickens. Allow to cool completely. Place chicken in a shallow dish. Pour cooled sauce over the chicken. Cover chicken and marinate in the refrigerator overnight. Prepare grill, broiler or grill pan. Discard marinade. Grill chicken, turning occasionally, until juices run clear, about 25 minutes.

Garlic-chili sauce is a common ingredient in Asian cooking. Regular supermarkets display it in ethnic food sections.

Grilled Savory Barbecued Chicken

Serves 6 - 8

1/3 cup vegetable oil
2 cups onion, chopped
5 cloves garlic, minced
2 shallots, minced
1 1/2 Tablespoons ancho chili powder
1 Tablespoon chipotle chili powder
1 Tablespoon ground cumin
1 teaspoon crushed red pepper flakes
2 teaspoons chili seasoning blend
2 (6 oz) cans tomato paste
1 1/4 cups ketchup

1/2 cup Dijon mustard
1/2 cup spicy mustard
1 cup honey
1 cup cider vinegar
2/3 cup soy sauce
1/2 cup Sioux Z Wow marinade (see
    resource guide)
1/2 cup hoisin sauce
freshly ground black pepper to taste
8 assorted chicken pieces, skinned

In a medium pan, heat oil over medium heat. Sauté onions, garlic and shallots for 10 - 12 minutes. Add chili powders, cumin, red pepper and chili seasoning. Mix well, cooking until fragrant. Add tomato paste, ketchup, mustards, honey, vinegar, soy sauce, Sioux Z Wow marinade, hoisin sauce and pepper. Lower the temperature and simmer uncovered for 45 minutes. Remove from heat and cool. Place chicken in a shallow glass dish and pour cooled marinade over chicken. Cover, refrigerate and marinate chicken for 3 hours. Grill until juices run clear, turning often.

Chipotle Honey Lime Grilled Chicken

Serves 4

2 chipotle chiles in adobo sauce
2 teaspoons olive oil
2 cloves garlic, minced
1 shallot, sliced
3 tablespoons lime juice
2 Tablespoons honey

2 Tablespoons fresh oregano
1 Tablespoon red wine vinegar
1 teaspoon ground cumin
2 teaspoons salt
1 teaspoon freshly ground black pepper
8 chicken thighs, skinned and trimmed

Mix all ingredients, except the chicken, in food processor. Puree until finely chopped and thoroughly blended. In a shallow dish, place chicken. Pour puree over chicken, coat completely, cover and chill overnight. Prepare grill or grill pan. Remove excess marinade from chicken. Grill chicken, bone-side down, first. Grill until juices run clear, turning occasionally, about 30 minutes. Transfer to platter and serve.

SHALLOT PEPPER BLEND

1 teaspoon kosher salt
1 teaspoon freshly ground black pepper
2 teaspoons dried tarragon
2 teaspoon shallots or chives
a pinch of ground bay leaf.

Makes 2 Tablespoons. Also available online at www.Penzys.com.

Champagne Mustard Chicken
Serves 4

8 chicken thighs, skin and fat removed
2 Tablespoons shallot pepper blend
2 Tablespoons olive oil
2 shallots, minced
2 cloves garlic, minced
8 ounces mushrooms, sliced
1 cup champagne

2 cups plain yogurt
1/2 cup Dijon mustard
1/4 cup fresh chives, chopped
salt and freshly ground black pepper to taste

Season chicken generously with shallot pepper blend. In a skillet, heat oil over medium-high heat. Add chicken and brown well on both sides, about 10 - 15 minutes. Remove chicken, set aside, and cover with foil. Add shallots and garlic to the skillet. Sauté until lightly browned. Add mushrooms and cook for another 2 minutes. Add champagne, yogurt and mustard. Reduce heat and simmer until sauce starts to thicken, 20 minutes. Add chives. Return chicken to sauce. Turn to coat. Simmer until cooked through. Season to taste

Orange Mushroom Peppered Chicken
Serves 4

1 Tablespoon lemon pepper
2 teaspoons orange zest
1 teaspoon salt
8 boneless, skinless chicken thighs
1 Tablespoon olive oil
3 cloves garlic, minced
1 cup mushrooms, chopped

2 shallots, minced
3/4 cup orange juice
3/4 cup chicken stock
1/2 cup spicy mustard
3 Tablespoons honey
1 teaspoon hot sauce

In a small cup, mix lemon pepper, zest and salt. Sprinkle liberally on chicken and press into chicken, if necessary. Cover and refrigerate for 3 hours. In a skillet, heat oil over medium-high heat. Sauté chicken until brown, about 3 minutes per side. Transfer to a platter and set aside. Add to the skillet, garlic, mushrooms and shallots. Sauté until translucent, 3 minutes. In a medium bowl, combine juice, stock, mustard, honey and hot sauce. Add ingredients to skillet. Simmer until sauce thickens, 3 minutes. Return chicken to the skillet, heat through, until juices run clear, 10 minutes. Serve chicken over white rice or egg noodles. Drizzle with sauce.

Snappy Coconut-Crusted Chicken with Zowee Mustard Sauce

Serves 4

8 ounces panko flakes (Japanese breadcrumbs)
4 ounces coconut flakes, toasted
1/4 cup sesame seeds, toasted
1 (1 lb) box ginger snaps, finely crushed
2 Tablespoons cornstarch
2 Tablespoons lemon juice
2 egg whites
1/2 teaspoon salt
2 teaspoons lemon pepper seasoning

1 pound boneless, skinless chicken breast
3 Tablespoons butter

ZOWEE MUSTARD SAUCE
1/2 cup sour cream
2 Tablespoons grainy mustard
2 Tablespoons Sioux Z Wow Marinade (see notes)

In a large zippered bag, combine panko, coconut, sesame seeds and ginger snaps. Shake to combine ingredients evenly. Place coconut mixture in a pie plate. In a small bowl, combine cornstarch, juice, egg whites, salt and lemon pepper. Mix well, but not into a froth. Pour mixture into another pie plate. Cut chicken breasts into four cutlets and pound thin. Dredge each cutlet in egg mixture. Press into the coconut mixture turning to coat completely. Place cutlets on a wire rack to rest for 30 minutes. In a large skillet, melt butter over medium-high heat. Sauté chicken cutlets until both sides are golden brown. Add butter, as needed for the dipping sauce, mix the sour cream, mustard and marinade.

Sioux Z Wow marinade may be purchased locally at PHG. See resource guide. Garlic-chili or cocktail chili sauce and a splash of oyster sauce or rice vinegar may be substituted.

Spicy Asian Grilled Chicken

Serves 4

1 1/2 cups chili sauce
3/4 cup red wine vinegar
1 1/2 Tablespoons prepared horseradish
3 cloves garlic, minced

1 teaspoon kosher salt
1 teaspoon freshly ground black pepper
4 bone-in, skinless chicken breasts or 8 chicken thighs, skinned and trimmed

In a shallow dish, mix all the ingredients except chicken. Reserve 1 cup of the marinade; refrigerate separately. Add chicken to the remaining marinade, cover and refrigerate overnight. Prepare grill or grill pan. Remove chicken and discard marinade. Grill, basting with reserved marinade, until juices run clear (15 minutes for breast and 30 minutes for thighs). Thoroughly heat reserved marinade, and serve with chicken.

Caribbean Jerk Chicken

Serves 6 - 8

1 package Italian salad dressing mix
2 Tablespoons brown sugar
2 Tablespoons oil
2 Tablespoons soy sauce

1 teaspoon cinnamon
1 teaspoon thyme
1/2 teaspoon cayenne
2 1/2 pounds chicken pieces, skinned

In a small bowl, mix dressing mix, brown sugar, oil, soy sauce, cinnamon, thyme and cayenne until well blended. Pour dressing over chicken; cover and refrigerate overnight to marinate. Drain chicken and discard marinade. Place on a greased grill over hot coals, 5 - 7 inches from heat. Grill or broil 40 - 45 minutes or until cooked through, turning frequently.

Garlic and Honey Glazed Chicken Pizza

Serves 8

1/4 cup sesame seeds, toasted
2 cloves garlic, minced
1 teaspoon dried red pepper flakes
1/2 cup soy sauce
5 Tablespoons honey
3 Tablespoons sugar
1 1/2 cups red wine vinegar

1 cup olive oil, divided
5 chicken breasts, cut into small pieces
1 pizza crust, unbaked
2 cups Gruyere cheese, grated
1 red onion, thinly sliced
4 green onions, diced

Preheat oven to 425 degrees. In a small skillet, toast sesame seeds over medium heat. Shake skillet until seeds are golden, about 4 minutes. Empty onto a plate to cool. In a small bowl, combine garlic, pepper, soy sauce, honey, sugar and vinegar. Set aside. In a large skillet, heat 1/2 cup olive oil. Sauté chicken in oil until opaque. Remove chicken and drain on a paper towel. Pour garlic mixture into the skillet. Cook over medium-high heat, stirring occasionally, until sauce is reduced to a syrup, about 30 minutes. Return chicken to skillet and cook, stirring constantly, until pieces are lightly glazed. Remove from heat and set aside. Brush pizza crust lightly with oil. Top with cheese, glazed chicken and onions. Drizzle remaining oil evenly over the top. Sprinkle with sesame seeds. Bake 10 - 12 minutes.

Slice the pizza in to small wedges or strips and serve as an appetizer.

Balsamic Maple Chicken
Serves 4

8 chicken thighs, skin and fat removed
1/4 cup olive oil
1/4 cup pure maple syrup
1/4 cup balsamic vinegar
2 Tablespoons Dijon mustard

2 Tablespoons rosemary, chopped
1 Tablespoon sage, chopped
1 teaspoon freshly ground black pepper
3/4 teaspoon kosher salt
rosemary sprigs

Generously season chicken with salt and pepper and place in a shallow dish. In a small bowl, mix oil, syrup, vinegar, mustard, rosemary, sage, pepper and salt. Pour over chicken cover, marinate and refrigerate at least 4 hours or overnight. Preheat oven to 350 degrees. Spoon chicken and marinade into a 9x11-inch baking dish. Bake for 50 - 60 minutes. Remove chicken from the oven and place on a platter and lightly tent with foil. Pour juices into a saucepan. Over medium heat, cook until reduced to a thick syrup, about 5 minutes. Pour syrup over chicken. Garnish with rosemary sprigs. Season to taste.

Also works with boneless chicken. Reduce baking time to 25 - 30 minutes.

Italian Artichoke Tomato Chicken
Serves 4

8 chicken thighs, skinned and trimmed
2 teaspoons salt
1 Tablespoon freshly ground black pepper
1 teaspoon dried tarragon
2 Tablespoons olive oil
2 shallots, minced
2 cloves garlic, minced
2 Tablespoons oregano
2 Tablespoons basil
1 cup mushrooms, sliced

2 cups asparagus
1 (14 1/2 oz) can diced Italian-style tomatoes
1 (6 oz) jar marinated artichoke hearts, drained and rinsed
1/2 cup sherry
1 Tablespoon cornstarch
2 Tablespoons water
1/4 cup Parmesan or romano cheese, finely grated

Preheat oven to 375 degrees. Season chicken with salt, pepper and tarragon. In a skillet, heat oil over medium-high heat. Sauté chicken until browned, about 3 minutes per side. Place in an 8x11-inch baking dish and set aside. Sauté shallots until translucent, 3 minutes. In a small bowl, mix garlic, oregano and basil. Add to the shallots and mix until fragrant, about 1 minute. Add mushrooms, asparagus, tomatoes and artichoke hearts. Cook until asparagus is softened, about 5 minutes, stirring occasionally. Add sherry, bring to a simmer and cook uncovered for 10 minutes. Mix cornstarch in cold water. Add to mixture, stir until thickened, about 1 minute. Pour pan of vegetables over chicken. Sprinkle cheese over the top and bake until bubbly, about 1 hour. Garnish with chopped parsley and additional cheese.

An Original Ingredient

WELLSPRING

Beginning in 1990, the JLO made a commitment to women trapped in the world of prostitution. Nearly $15,000 was given to develop and facilitate a project to help women who were incarcerated; review rehabilitation options and provide career opportunities. League members interacted with the women in all phases: providing childcare needs, counseling on healthy relationships and planning special activities for participants; such as fieldtrips, craft days and a special Mother's Day celebration. In 1992, the Junior League of Omaha received the BMW Corporation Community Impact National Merit Award for the Wellspring program.

Juiciest Ever Roasted Chicken with Crispy Vegetables
Serves 4 - 6

1 teaspoon kosher salt	2 lemons, quartered
2 teaspoons freshly ground black pepper	extra sprigs of herbs
2 Tablespoons chives, finely chopped	3 potatoes, cut into 1-inch wedges
2 Tablespoons rosemary, finely chopped	2 onions, quartered
2 Tablespoons thyme, finely chopped	1 cup baby carrots
2 Tablespoons Parmesan cheese, finely grated	2 cloves garlic, minced
5 - 6 pounds roasting chicken, washed, dried and giblets removed	salt and freshly ground black pepper

Preheat oven to 500 degrees (yes, 500 degrees). In a small bowl, mix salt, pepper, chives, rosemary, thyme and cheese. Rub entire chicken above and under the skin with herb and cheese mixture. Put lemon quarters inside of the chicken, and additional herb sprigs, if desired. On the bottom of a large roasting pan, place potatoes, onions and carrots in a single layer. Sprinkle with garlic and with remaining herb and cheese mixture. Place roasting rack atop the vegetables. Place chicken, breast-side down, legs toward the back of oven on the lower rack. Bake for 1 hour, turning breast-side up, once, about halfway through. Every 20 minutes, lift one or both sides of the roasting rack. Stir the vegetables underneath to prevent sticking. After 1 hour, remove the chicken and allow to rest on a board for 15 minutes before carving. Transfer vegetables to a serving bowl. Remove lemons and additional herb sprigs. Season to taste.

When the herbs begin to singe, tent the entire bird lightly with foil. Increase baking time if chicken is over 6 pounds.

Experiment with fresh or dried seasonings of choice and with different potatoes and root vegetables.

Greek Chicken with Capers, Raisins and Feta
Serves 4

4 (4 oz) boneless, skinless chicken breast halves	2 cloves garlic, minced
2 Tablespoons flour	1 1/2 cups chicken stock
1 teaspoon oregano	1/3 cup golden raisins
1 teaspoon mint	2 Tablespoons lemon juice
1 Tablespoon olive oil	2 Tablespoons capers
1 cup onion, sliced	1/4 cup feta cheese, crumbled
	4 lemon slices, for garnish

Place each chicken breast half between 2 sheets of plastic wrap. Flatten to 1/4-inch thickness using a meat mallet or rolling pin. In a shallow dish, combine flour, oregano and mint. Dredge chicken in flour mixture. In a large skillet, heat oil over medium-high heat. Add chicken and cook 4 minutes on each side. Remove chicken from pan; keep warm. Add onion and garlic to pan; sauté 1 - 2 minutes. Stir in stock, raisins and lemon juice. Cook 3 minutes. Return chicken to pan. Cover, reduce heat, and simmer for 5 - 8 minutes or until chicken is done. To serve, divide the chicken among 4 plates. Add capers to sauce in pan. Spoon 1/3 cup sauce over each serving and top with 1 Tablespoon cheese. Garnish with lemon slices.

Bruschetta Chicken
Created by Randi Caniglia and submitted by Caniglia's Venice Inn

Serves 4

1/2 cup flour
2 eggs, slightly beaten
4 boneless, skinless chicken breasts
1/4 cup Romano cheese, grated
1/4 cup breadcrumbs
1 Tablespoon butter, melted

2 tomatoes, seeded and chopped
3 Tablespoons basil, chopped
2 cloves garlic, minced
1 Tablespoon olive oil
1/2 teaspoon salt
1/4 teaspoon freshly ground black pepper

Preheat oven to 375 degrees. In shallow separate bowls, place flour and eggs. Dip chicken in the flour, then in the egg. Place chicken in a greased 9x13-inch baking dish. In a small bowl, combine cheese, breadcrumbs and butter. Sprinkle over chicken. Loosely cover dish with aluminum foil. Bake 20 minutes. Uncover, and bake for 10 minutes more, until the top is browned. In a bowl, combine tomatoes, basil, garlic, olive oil, salt and pepper. Spoon over baked chicken. Return to oven for 5 minutes until heated through. ¡O!¡

Apricot Roasted Chicken

Serves 4

6 ounces apricot preserves
1/4 cup olive oil
1 Tablespoon white wine vinegar
1/4 teaspoon sea salt
1/2 teaspoon freshly ground black pepper

1 teaspoon garlic powder
1 teaspoon ground sage
16 prunes, pitted
4 skinless chicken breast halves

Preheat oven to 425 degrees. In a large bowl, mix preserves, olive oil, vinegar, salt, pepper, garlic, sage and prunes. Add chicken and toss all of the ingredients until the chicken is evenly coated with the sauce. Arrange the chicken pieces in a pan. Roast until the chicken is thoroughly cooked and the juices run clear, about 30 to 40 minutes.

For a buffet, substitute chicken thighs. They will stay moist longer. Boneless thighs may also be used.

Chicken on the Ritz
Serves 6

2 cups Ritz crackers, crumbled
3/4 cup Parmesan cheese, grated
2 Tablespoons dried parsley
1 Tablespoon garlic powder

2 teaspoons salt
1/8 teaspoon freshly ground black pepper
1 cup butter
6 boneless, skinless chicken breasts

Preheat oven to 350 degrees. In a zippered bag, place crackers and crumble with hands or a rolling pin. Add cheese, parsley, garlic powder, salt and pepper. Cover a 9x13-inch pan with foil. Spray with nonstick cooking spray. In a small pan, melt butter. Dip 1 chicken breast in melted butter then add to the zippered bag to coat with cracker mixture. Place on pan. Repeat with other breasts. Sprinkle any remaining crumbs on chicken breasts in pan. Drizzle remaining butter on top. Bake for 45 minutes. May be assembled several hours before baking and stored in the refrigerator.

A family favorite, especially for the children

Apple and Brie Chicken with Cider Sauce
Serves 4

4 Tablespoons butter, divided
1 small apple, cored and sliced
4 slices brie cheese
4 (5 oz) skinless, boneless chicken
  breasts, halves pounded
1/2 teaspoon salt
1/2 teaspoon freshly ground black pepper
1 Tablespoon flour

CIDER SAUCE
1 1/2 cups apple cider
1 cup white wine
1 1/2 cups chicken stock
2 Tablespoons grainy mustard
1 Tablespoon pure maple syrup

Preheat oven to 450 degrees. In a large sauté pan, warm 1 Tablespoon of butter over medium-high heat. Add the apples and sauté until softened. Remove the pan from the heat and set aside. Place 1 slice of brie and a few of the apple slices in the center of each chicken breast. Fold chicken over like a taco. Secure the breast with 1 or 2 toothpicks. Season the outside of the chicken with salt and pepper, and pat with a little flour. In the sauce pan, warm 1 Tablespoon of butter over high heat. When the butter foams, add the chicken breasts and brown them on both sides. Reserve pan drippings. Transfer the chicken to a sheet pan and bake in the oven for 12 to 14 minutes. While the chicken is baking, make the sauce.

For the Cider Sauce, pour the cider, wine, stock, mustard and syrup into the sauce pan with the drippings. Simmer the sauce over high heat until reduced to about 1 1/2 cups. Swirl in the remaining 2 Tablespoons of butter. Season to taste with salt and pepper. To serve, divide the chicken among 4 plates. Remove the toothpicks and pour a little sauce over each serving.

The wine may be omitted if more stock and cider are used. Adding 1/4 cup heavy cream makes a thick, rich sauce. Do not slice the apples too thin or they will be mushy.

Picnic Parmesan Crusted Chicken Breasts

Serves 4

3 eggs, beaten
3 Tablespoons Dijon mustard
1 1/2 cups breadcrumbs
1/2 cups Parmesan cheese, grated

1 teaspoon salt
1 teaspoon freshly ground black pepper
1 Tablespoon oregano, chopped
4 chicken breasts

Preheat oven to 400 degrees. In a small bowl, whisk eggs and mustard. In a separate bowl, blend breadcrumbs, cheese, salt, pepper and oregano. Grease a 9x12-inch glass baking dish. Dip chicken in egg mixture, then coat liberally in crumbs. Place coated chicken in the baking dish. Bake for 20 - 30 minutes until golden brown and juices are clear.

Great served cold or at room temperature. Pack it in a picnic basket for an outdoor concert, like Jazz on the Green or Shakespeare on the Green. Pair with White Sangria on page 44

Smokey Barbecued Turkey Burgers

Serves 6

1 1/2 pounds ground turkey
1 egg, beaten
1/3 cup oatmeal
1 shallot, diced
1/2 teaspoon granulated garlic
1/2 teaspoon freshly ground black pepper
1/4 teaspoon kosher salt

2 teaspoons liquid smoke
2 Tablespoons chiles, diced
1/3 cup prepared barbecue sauce
6 hamburger buns, split and buttered
6 slices smoked Gouda cheese
1 avocado, sliced

In a medium bowl, mix together turkey, egg, oatmeal, shallot, garlic, pepper, salt, liquid smoke and chiles. Shape into 6 patties. Brush barbecue sauce on one side of the turkey burger. Lay basted side down on the heat. Grill, covered, for 5 - 7 minutes. Flip, baste other side with barbeque sauce and continue grilling for another 5 - 7 minutes. Top each burger with 1 cheese slice. Grill until cheese melts. Meanwhile, place buns on the grill to brown. Top buns with avocado slices. Serve on grilled buns with condiments of choice.

Gorat's Steak House
4217 Center Street

In October 1944, Sicilian immigrants Louis and Nettie Gorat opened Gorat's Steak House. It started as a one-room restaurant. The steakhouse has been through several expansions, however it remains at the same location today. The menu expanded to include seafood and chicken. Their son Pal was 15 when his parents opened the restaurant and he immediately went to work. Sixty-two years later he is still a fixture at Gorat's. His wife Shirley also worked at the restaurant for close to 30 years before retiring several years ago.

Gorat's has always had something other Omaha steak houses don't. They have Warren Buffet. Pal's connection with Buffet began at Rose Hill Elementary school where they were classmates. They've continued their friendship over the years. Buffet is a frequent visitor at Gorat's, ordering his customary T-bone steak, rare, and a double order of hash browns. For over a decade the restaurant has earned a national reputation for hosting the annual Berkshire Hathaway dinners. The restaurant begins taking reservations from Berkshire shareholders on April 1 and at 4:00 a.m. the phones start ringing. With three people answering the phones, Gorat's is booked for the weekend by 2:30 p.m.

Pal and Shirley's children are now involved in Gorat's with son Mark serving as general manager, daughter Deb Branecki helping with the bookkeeping and daughter Pam Kenney assisting with the computers.

According to Deb, in the last five years Gorat's has seen couples who had their wedding reception at the restaurant now celebrating their 50th anniversary. Children and grandchildren of Gorat's original customers now come in with stories of how they remember the place as a child. Customers who have left Omaha come in saying there are three things they have to do when back in Omaha, get a Runza, have a Goodrich malt and eat a steak at Gorat's.

Sensational Stuffed Red Snapper

Serves 2

2 - 3 Tablespoons clarified butter
salt and freshly ground black pepper to
   taste
2 (6 oz) red snapper fillets
1/3 cup flour
1/2 cup lump crab meat, picked through
   and flaked

2 teaspoons sliced almonds, toasted
1 Tablespoon parsley, finely chopped
1 cup dry white wine
1 bunch spinach, washed and stems
   removed
1 orange, thinly sliced

Preheat oven to 400 degrees. In a medium ovenproof skillet, heat the butter over medium heat. Liberally salt and pepper the fish, then lightly dredge in flour, shaking off the excess. Place the fish skin-side up in the pan and sear fillets to brown about 30 seconds. Turn fish over to skin-side down. Evenly spread the crab, almonds and parsley over the fillets. Cook 2 minutes and then deglaze the pan with the wine. Bake for 4 - 5 minutes, until the fish flakes easily with a fork. Remove fish from oven. Serve on a bed of spinach leaves garnished with orange slices.

Moroccan Style Red Snapper

Serves 4

1 1/2 lemons, divided
1/3 cup garlic, minced
1/2 cup sharmoulla (Moroccan spice
   found at specialty food stores)
2 potatoes, peeled and quartered
2 carrots, peeled and sliced
1 green pepper, cut into strips
1 red pepper, cut into strips

2 tomatoes, cut into wedges
salt and freshly ground black pepper to
   taste
1 1/2 pounds dense fish (bluefish,
   halibut, snapper or salmon)
1/4 cup water
1/2 cup olive oil
1/2 cup kalamata or alfonson olives

Add the juice of 1 lemon and garlic to sharmoulla and blend well. Toss 1/4 cup of the sharmoulla mixture with potatoes, carrots, peppers, tomatoes, salt and pepper. Spread the remaining sharmoulla over fish. In a stock pot, layer half the vegetables, fish, then the rest of the vegetables. Add 1/4 cup of water, cover and simmer over low heat for 30 minutes. To serve, plate the vegetables and fish on a large serving platter, drizzle with olive oil and garnish with olives.

Recipe may also be made in a casserole dish and baked in a 375 degree oven for 30 - 40 minutes. Check potatoes for doneness. When tender, add olives and juice and rind of 1/2 lemon. Cook for an additional 5 minutes.

CLARIFIED BUTTER

Clarified butter is unsalted butter which has been slowly melted, evaporating most of the water and leaving the milk solids from the golden liquid on the surface. After skimming the foam off the top, the clear (clarified) portion is poured off and used in the recipe.

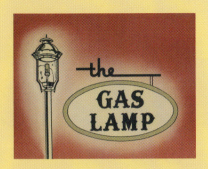

The Gas Lamp was a well-loved restaurant at 30th and Leavenworth Streets. - *From the Joe Villella menu collection at the Douglas County Historical Society*

Hawaiian Macadamia Sole
Serves 4 - 6

1 1/2 pounds sole fillets, skinned
2 teaspoons lemon pepper
1/2 cup coconut flakes, toasted
1/2 cup panko flakes (Japanese breadcrumbs)
1/2 cup Macadamia nuts, finely crushed
1/4 cup sesame seeds, toasted
3 Tablespoons lemon juice
3 Tablespoons cornstarch
3 egg whites, lightly beaten
1 teaspoon salt
2 Tablespoons vegetable oil
salt and freshly ground black pepper

Generously season both sides of fillets with lemon pepper. In a pie plate, mix together coconut, panko, nuts and sesame seeds. In a small bowl, mix lemon juice, cornstarch, egg whites and salt. Pour mixture into another pie plate. Dip each fillet into egg mixture, allowing excess to drip off. Place in crumb mixture, press, turn to coat completely. Rest fillets on a wire rack for 30 minutes, allowing coating to set. In a large pan, heat oil over medium-high heat. Sauté fillets, turning once, 2 minutes per side. Salt and pepper to taste.

This recipe may be used for any mild, white fish, or pork or chicken cutlets. Nice with a tropical salsa or a light, slightly sweet, mustard sauce.

Pecan Crusted Tilapia
Serves 4

4 tilapia fillets
1/4 cup flour
4 Tablespoons milk
1 egg, lightly beaten
1 cup pecans, finely crushed
4 Tablespoons butter
4 lemon slices
4 sprigs of fresh parsley

Preheat oven to 350 degrees. On a small plate, roll each tilapia fillet in the flour until coated. In another bowl, mix the milk and egg. Increase the amount of milk and egg if larger fillets are used. Place crushed pecans in a separate bowl. Spray a baking sheet with cooking spray. Dip each floured fillet in the egg mixture, then into the crushed pecans, pressing them into the fish. Place the fillets on the baking sheet. Top each fillet with 1 Tablespoon of butter. Bake for 30 minutes or until fish flakes. Garnish each fillet with a slice of lemon and a sprig of fresh parsley.

Easy, tastes delicious and looks beautiful!

Crab Stuffed Flounder Rolls

Serves 4

1/2 pound fresh lump crabmeat, picked
   through and flaked
1/4 cup pecans, chopped
1/4 cup green onions, sliced
1 Tablespoon red bell pepper, minced
1 Tablespoon fresh lemon juice
1/4 teaspoon salt
1/8 teaspoon freshly ground black pepper
3 Tablespoons plus 2 teaspoons Creole
   seasoning, divided

4 (4 oz) flounder fillets
1/2 cup flour, divided
1 egg, lightly beaten
1/4 cup milk
3 Tablespoons pecans, finely ground
1 Tablespoon olive oil
8 lemon wedges

In a bowl, combine the crabmeat, pecans, onions, red pepper, juice, salt, pepper and 1 Tablespoon of seasoning. Set aside. Rub 2 teaspoons of Creole seasoning over the fillets. In a shallow dish, combine 1/4 cup flour and 1 Tablespoon seasoning. Set aside. In a second shallow dish, combine egg and milk. Set dish next to the seasoned flour. In a third shallow dish, combine 1/4 cup flour, 1 Tablespoon seasoning and ground pecans. Place this dish next to egg mixture. Lay fillets flat and spread about 1/4 cup crab mixture on top of each fillet. Gently roll, jellyroll style, and secure with 1 or 2 toothpicks. Dredge each stuffed fillet first in the flour mixture, second in the egg mixture and third in the pecan mixture. Allow to rest for 20 minutes on a wire rack. In a large skillet, heat oil over medium-high heat. When hot, add the fish. Cook each fillet 2 minutes on each side until done. Garnish with lemon wedges.

Halibut may be substituted for the flounder.

Pan Sautéed Asian Cod

Serves 4

2 pounds cod, thawed, rinsed and dried
1 clove garlic, minced
1 shallot, minced
2 Tablespoons soy sauce
2 Tablespoons sesame oil
1 teaspoon sugar
1 teaspoon ground ginger

1/2 teaspoon freshly ground black pepper
2 Tablespoons lime juice
1 teaspoon fish sauce
1 teaspoon rice vinegar
2 teaspoons Asian chili garlic sauce
1 Tablespoon cilantro leaves, chopped
5 Tablespoons orange juice

In a bowl, mix all the ingredients, except the cod, thoroughly. Pour into a zippered bag or shallow marinating dish. Add the cod and coat entirely. Cover and refrigerate marinate for at least 90 minutes, but no more than 4 hours, turning occasionally. Heat grill pan over medium-high heat. Add fish, do not shake off excess marinade. Grill until cooked through, about 4 - 5 minutes. Turn occasionally to caramelize sauce.

Island Fish Bake

Serves 6

3 pounds island fish, such as snapper or
   tilapia, rinsed and dried
2 Tablespoons olive oil
2 Tablespoons ginger, minced
2 Tablespoons garlic, minced

1 bunch cilantro, cleaned, stems
   removed and chopped
2 Tablespoons soy sauce
1 can coconut milk
juice and zest of 1 lime

Preheat oven to 350 degrees. Place fish in a greased, 9x13-inch glass baking dish. Brush each fillet with olive oil. Sprinkle ginger, garlic and cilantro on top of fillets. In a small bowl, mix the soy sauce, milk, juice and zest together. Gently pour over fillets without disturbing aromatics. Bake for 15 - 30 minutes, depending on fish thickness, until fish flakes with a fork.

Easy summer outdoor party dish. Serve with a Mango Splash, page 43

Caribbean Halibut with Vegetables

Serves 4

2 pounds halibut steaks
salt and freshly ground black pepper
3 tomatoes, peeled, seeded and chopped
1/2 cup green pepper, minced
1/4 cup yellow pepper, minced

1/2 cup onion, minced
6 Tablespoons butter
3 Tablespoons lemon juice
1/2 teaspoon hot sauce

Preheat oven to 400 degrees. Grease a shallow baking dish and arrange the fish. The dish should be large enough to hold all the fish in 1 layer. Season with salt and pepper. Spread the tomatoes, peppers and onion over the fish. In a small pan, melt the butter with the lemon juice and hot sauce. Drizzle the butter mixture over the fish and vegetables. Bake for 25 minutes. Baste with pan juices every 10 minutes.

A colorful dish!

Barbecued Salmon
Serves 8

1 cup brown sugar, packed
1/2 cup honey
1 Tablespoon liquid smoke
1/2 cup apple cider vinegar

1/4 teaspoon chipotle powder
salt and freshly ground black pepper
4 pounds whole salmon fillet

Preheat grill to high heat. In a small bowl, mix together brown sugar, honey, liquid smoke, vinegar and chipotle powder. Season sauce to taste. Brush 1 side of the salmon with the basting sauce. Place the salmon on the grill, basted side down. After 7 minutes, generously baste the top, and turn over. Cook for 8 more minutes, then brush on more basting sauce. Turn salmon and cook for 2 more minutes. Garnish with chipotle powder.

Miso Glazed Salmon
Serves 4

1/4 cup brown sugar, packed
2 Tablespoons soy sauce
2 Tablespoons miso

2 Tablespoons hot water
4 (6 oz) salmon fillets
chives, chopped

In a small bowl, whisk brown sugar, soy sauce, miso and hot water. On a broiler pan, arrange salmon. Spoon glaze over the fish. Broil 10 minutes, basting twice with the glaze. Sprinkle with fresh chives. Salmon may also be grilled.

Salmon with Strawberry Mango Salsa

Serves 2

SALSA
1 cup strawberries, stemmed and quartered
1/2 cup mango, diced
1/4 cup red bell pepper, diced
2 Tablespoons red onion, diced
1 1/2 Tablespoons rice wine vinegar or lime juice
2 teaspoons mint, chopped
1 1/2 teaspoons brown sugar
1 - 2 canned chipotle chiles in adobo sauce, rinsed, seeded and finely minced
salt

SALMON
2 (6 oz) skinless salmon fillets
1 Tablespoon olive oil
salt and freshly ground black pepper

In a bowl, combine strawberries, mango, red pepper, onion, vinegar, mint, sugar and chiles. Stir together with a rubber spatula or wooden spoon. Season with salt, cover and refrigerate for at least 1 hour or up to 8 hours. Preheat broiler. Brush salmon on both sides with oil and season with salt and pepper. Place on a baking sheet. Broil 4 inches from element for 4 - 6 minutes or until done. Transfer to plates and spoon salsa over salmon.

Market Days

In April 1993, the Junior League kicked off their first Market Days event at the Peony Park Ballroom. Under the leadership of honorary chairman Jeanne Skutt and co-chairs Melanie Wright and Lissa Sutton (pictured above) the event raised $40,000 with nearly 2,000 people attending. Over the next 10 years the event continued to grow with vendors from across the Midwest selling fresh food, flowers, gourmet gadgets, unique gifts, art and planting tools. Attendees also were treated to cooking and gardening demonstrations from some of the metro area's experts. - *Reprinted with permission from the Omaha World-Herald*

RoJA Shrimp Alambres with Jicama Mandarin Slaw and Ancho Chili Tartar Sauce

Serves 2

8 jumbo shrimp, peeled and deveined,
  tail on
2 jalapeños, seeded and cut into quarters
  lengthwise
8 slivers of Monterey Jack cheese, cut
  the same size as the jalapeños
8 thin slices of bacon
4 10-inch skewers, soaked in water for
  30 minutes

JICAMA MANDARIN SLAW
4 cups green cabbage, thinly sliced
1 cup jicama, peeled and julienned
1/2 pablano pepper, julienned
1/2 red pepper, julienned

1/2 cup mandarin oranges in syrup
1/2 bunch cilantro leaves, chopped
juice of one lime

ANCHO CHILE TARTAR SAUCE
2 Tablespoons ancho chile paste
juice of one lime
1/4 cup yellow onion, chopped
1/4 cup celery, chopped
2 cups mayonnaise
1 jalapeño, seeded and chopped
1 Tablespoon Cajun seasoning
1/2 bunch parsley, chopped
1 lemon for garnish

Assemble the Alambres by stacking the shrimp, jalapeños and cheese next to each other. Wrap them with bacon from the top to the bottom until none of the ingredients are exposed. At this point place the Alambre on the skewer. One on each end. Repeat this until there are 4 Alambres on 2 skewers. Place the Alambres in the refrigerator and preheat the grill

For the slaw, toss the cabbage, jicama, pablano pepper, red pepper, mandarin oranges, cilantro and the juice of 1 lime in a bowl. Refrigerate.

For the sauce, place the ancho chili paste, juice of 1 lime, yellow onion, celery, mayonnaise, jalapeño, seasoning and parsley in a food processor. Process until smooth. Toss some of the tartar sauce with the slaw and reserve the rest for the shrimp. Refrigerate both the slaw and the sauce.

Place the Alambres on the grill, season to taste. Grill until both sides are crispy and the bacon and shrimp are cooked through. To serve, place a little slaw on a plate with the Alambres removed from the skewers. Serve with sauce and lemon for garnish. ¡O!

Dijon Fish Fillets
Serves 4 - 6

1 1/2 pounds fish fillet, like Walleye,
  Flounder or Cod
salt and freshly ground black pepper
5 Tablespoons butter, melted
1 Tablespoon grainy Dijon mustard

1 1/2 teaspoons lemon juice
1 teaspoon Worcestershire sauce
panko flakes (Japanese breadcrumbs)
fresh parsley, chopped
lemon wedges

Preheat oven to 450 degrees. Butter a 9x13-inch glass baking dish. Arrange fish fillets in prepared dish. Season with salt and pepper. In a small bowl, combine butter, mustard, lemon juice and Worcestershire sauce. Spread mixture over each fillet covering completely. Sprinkle breadcrumbs over each fillet. Bake fish until just cooked through, about 10 minutes. Garnish with parsley and lemon wedges.

Crab Cakes with Avocado Tartar Sauce
Serves 8 - 12

4 eggs, divided
1 cup green onion, sliced
1 cup red pepper, chopped
2 Tablespoons mayonnaise
3/4 teaspoon orange zest, grated
salt and freshly ground black pepper
1 pound lump crab meat, picked through
  and flaked

3 cups breadcrumbs, divided
3/4 cup flour

AVOCADO TARTAR SAUCE
2 ripe Haas avocados, peeled and pitted
1/4 cup prepared tartar sauce
1 Tablespoon lime juice
1 cup peanut oil, for frying

In a bowl, mix 1 egg, onion, red pepper, mayonnaise and orange zest. Salt and pepper to taste. Add the crab and 1 cup of the breadcrumbs and mix. Shape 1/4 cupfuls into 24 2-inch round cakes, making each cake 1-inch thick. Place flour, seasoned with salt and pepper, on waxed paper. In a small bowl, beat remaining eggs. Place remaining crumbs in a pie plate. Coat cakes: first in the flour mixture, then in the eggs, then in the breadcrumbs. Place cakes on a baking sheet. Chill 30 minutes.

In a food processor, puree 1 1/2 of the avocados and tartar sauce. Pour the puree into a small bowl. Dice the remaining avocado half. Stir into the tartar sauce mixture. Add the lime juice. Cover and chill.

In a large skillet, heat the peanut oil over medium-high heat. In three batches, fry cakes 3 minutes per side, until golden and crispy. Drain on paper towels. Serve with the avocado tartar sauce for dipping.

BREADS and ROLLS

Sweet Magnolia Banana Chocolate Chip Espresso Muffins

Makes 16 muffins

4 teaspoons espresso powder
1/2 cup milk
6 bananas
1 cup sugar
1/2 cup brown sugar, packed
1 cup butter, melted
2 eggs

3 cups flour
3 teaspoons baking soda
1/2 teaspoon salt
1/4 teaspoon nutmeg
1/4 cup cocoa
1/2 cup chocolate chips

Preheat oven to 350 degrees. In a small bowl, combine espresso powder and milk. In a large mixing bowl, combine bananas, sugars, espresso mixture, butter and eggs. Mix until well combined. Into a large bowl, sift the dry ingredients. Add the wet mixture to the dry ingredients and stir well. Fold in chocolate chips. Scoop the batter into muffin tins and bake for 30 minutes or until a tester comes out clean. ¡O!

Gingerbread Muffins with Lemon Curd

Makes 12 muffins

LEMON CURD
2/3 cup white sugar
3/4 teaspoon cornstarch
1/3 cup lemon juice
5 egg yolks, lightly beaten
1/4 cup butter, cubed
2 teaspoons lemon peel, grated

GINGERBREAD MUFFINS
2 cups flour

1/4 cup white sugar
2 1/2 teaspoons baking powder
2 teaspoons ground ginger
1 teaspoon cinnamon
1/4 teaspoon salt
1/4 teaspoon ground cloves
1 egg
3/4 cup milk
1/4 cup vegetable oil
1/4 cup molasses

In a heavy saucepan, whisk the sugar, cornstarch and lemon juice until smooth. Heat to a simmer, cook and stir for 2 minutes or until slightly thickened. Stir in a small amount of the lemon mixture into the egg yolks to temper. Add the egg yolks to the pan. Heat to a simmer, stirring constantly. Cook and stir 1 - 2 minutes longer or until mixture reaches 160 degrees and coats the back of a metal spoon. Remove from heat, gently stir in butter and lemon peel until blended. Pour into a bowl and cover with plastic wrap. Refrigerate until serving.

Preheat oven to 375 degrees. In a bowl, combine the flour, sugar, baking powder, ginger, cinnamon, salt and cloves. In another bowl, whisk the egg, milk, oil and molasses until smooth. Stir wet ingredients into dry ingredients, just until moistened. Fill paper-lined muffin cups half full. Bake for 15 - 20 minutes or until a tester comes out clean. Cool for 5 minutes before removing from pan to a wire rack. Serve warm with lemon curd.

Branana Muffins

Makes 12 muffins

1 cup flour
1 Tablespoon baking powder
1/4 cup sugar
1/2 teaspoon salt
1/4 teaspoon cinnamon
1/4 teaspoon nutmeg
2 cups bran flakes

2/3 cup skim milk
2/3 cup banana, mashed
2 egg whites
1/4 cup butter, melted
1/3 cup applesauce
1/2 cup raisins

Preheat oven to 400 degrees. Stir together flour, baking powder, sugar, salt and spices. In a separate bowl, mix cereal, milk and bananas. Let stand 2 minutes. In a small bowl, beat egg whites until foamy and add to the cereal mixture. Add butter and applesauce and beat. Stir the flour mixture and raisins into the wet ingredients. Spray a muffin tin lightly with cooking spray and fill the cups half full. Bake for 25 minutes or until golden brown.

Low cholesterol, big taste!

Pumpkin Loaves with Caramel Glaze

Makes 2 loaves

3 1/3 cups flour
3 1/4 cups sugar, divided
2 teaspoons baking soda
1 1/2 teaspoons salt
1 teaspoon ground cinnamon
1 teaspoon ground nutmeg
1 (15 oz) can solid-pack pumpkin
1 cup vegetable oil
4 eggs, lightly beaten

2/3 cup water
1/2 cup pecans, chopped

CARAMEL GLAZE
1/4 cup butter
1/4 cup brown sugar, packed
1/4 cup heavy whipping cream
2/3 cup powdered sugar
1 teaspoon vanilla

Preheat oven to 350 degrees. In a large bowl, combine the flour, 3 cups sugar, baking soda, salt, cinnamon and nutmeg. In a separate bowl, combine the pumpkin, oil, eggs and water. Mix well. Stir the wet ingredients into the dry ingredients and mix until just combined. Fold in the pecans. Pour into 2 greased 9x5-inch loaf pans. Bake for 50 to 60 minutes or until a tester comes out clean. Cool for 10 minutes before removing from pans to wire racks.

For the glaze, in a saucepan, combine the butter, remaining 1/4 cup sugar, brown sugar and cream. Cook over low heat until sugar is dissolved. Cool for 20 minutes. Stir in the powdered sugar and vanilla until smooth. Drizzle over cooled loaves.

An Original  *Ingredient*

OPERATION ROLE MODEL

In 1984, Father Jim Scholz established the Employability Program at Sacred Heart School. Junior League members interfaced with Sacred Heart School to enhance this program by developing Operation Role Model in 1990. The members of the JLO produced videotapes of minority role models for use in the Employability classroom and provided much needed audio/visual equipment. The videos represented a variety of job opportunities to over 150 students, and exposed the students to lessons of motivation, leadership and other life skills. Nominated by the Junior League, Sacred Heart and the Employability Program received President George Bush's Point of Light Award.

Coconut Bread
Makes 3 small loaves

5 eggs
1 1/2 cups vegetable oil
2 cups sugar
2 cups bananas, mashed
1 teaspoon salt
1 teaspoon vanilla

1 heaping teaspoon baking soda
1 heaping teaspoon cinnamon
2 cups flour
2 packages instant coconut pudding mix
1/2 cup walnuts

Preheat oven to 350 degrees. In a large mixing bowl, beat eggs, then add oil and sugar. Mix in bananas, salt and vanilla. In a separate bowl, sift together the soda, cinnamon and flour. Add dry ingredients into the wet along with the pudding mix. Fold in the walnuts. Bake in loaf pans for 45 minutes to 1 hour or until a tester comes out clean.

Triple Berry Bread
Makes 1 loaf or 12 muffins

1 1/2 cups flour
1/2 teaspoon baking soda
1/2 teaspoon salt
1 1/2 teaspoons cinnamon
1 cup sugar

2 eggs, well beaten
2/3 cup vegetable oil
1/2 cup chopped pecans
2 cups frozen berry mixture, blueberries, raspberries and blackberries, thawed

Preheat oven to 350 degrees. In a medium bowl, mix flour, soda, salt, cinnamon and sugar. Thoroughly mix in eggs and oil. Gently fold in pecans, then berries. Grease and flour a 9x5-inch loaf pan. Gently pour batter into pan. Bake for 1 hour or until a tester comes out clean.

To make muffins, spoon batter into a lightly greased muffin tin. Bake 15 - 20 minutes in a 400 degree oven. Cool 5 minutes before removing from pan.

Pepper Herb Cheese Bread

Makes 1 loaf

3 eggs
1 cup plain yogurt
3/4 cup vegetable oil
1/2 cup buttermilk
1 Tablespoon mustard
1 1/2 cups colby jack cheese, grated
1/2 cup green onion, sliced
1 Tablespoon rosemary, chopped

2 Tablespoons chives, chopped
2 cups flour
1 Tablespoon sugar
1 teaspoon baking powder
1/2 teaspoon baking soda
1 1/2 teaspoons salt
2 teaspoons freshly ground black pepper

Preheat oven to 350 degrees. Lightly spray loaf pan with cooking spray. In a medium bowl, whisk eggs, yogurt, oil, buttermilk, mustard, cheese, onion, rosemary and chives. In a large bowl, sift all remaining ingredients together. Make a well in the center. Add wet ingredients to dry and mix until just moistened. Pour batter into loaf pan, and spread evenly. Bake for 50 - 60 minutes or until a tester comes out clean. Cool on wire rack for 10 minutes. Remove from loaf pan and cool for 1 hour.

May also be made into 24 mini muffins. Great compliment to Ham and Cheese Chowder, page 56.

French Bread With Garlic Aioli

Serves 8

1 egg
1 Tablespoon garlic, crushed
1 Tablespoon Dijon mustard
juice of 1 lemon
salt and white pepper

1 cup canola oil
1/4 cup pickled jalapeños, sliced
1 cup artichoke hearts, thinly sliced
5 ounces Parmesan cheese, shredded
1 loaf French bread, sliced open-faced

Mix the egg, garlic, mustard and lemon juice in a blender. Season with salt and pepper. Slowly add the canola oil to the mixture in a thin stream. Blend until the mixture thickens. Refrigerate for 1 hour. Once the mixture has been chilled, add the jalapeño, artichoke hearts and cheese. Preheat oven to 400 degrees. Spread garlic mixture onto French bread and bake until golden and bubbly.

Gruyére Bread Ring

Serves 6

1 cup milk
1/2 cup butter
1 cup flour

4 eggs, slightly beaten
1 cup Gruyére cheese, shredded

Preheat oven to 400 degrees. Grease a cookie sheet and set aside. In a saucepan, heat milk and butter to a high simmer. Mix in flour. Stir vigorously over low heat, about 1 minute or until mixture forms a ball. Remove from heat. Beat in eggs all at once, continuing until smooth. Fold in 2/3 cup cheese. Divide dough in half. Drop dough by tablespoonfuls onto cookie sheet to form two 4-inch rings, smooth with a spatula. Sprinkle with remaining cheese. Bake 40 - 50 minutes or until puffed and golden.

Ron's Wheatfield Cornbread

Serves 12 - 16

3 cups flour
2 cups cornmeal
1/2 cup sugar
1/4 cup baking powder

1 teaspoon salt
2/3 cup butter, melted
2 1/2 cups milk
3 eggs, well beaten

Preheat oven to 350 degrees. In a large bowl, mix flour, cornmeal, sugar, baking powder and salt. Add butter and milk and stir until combined. Fold beaten eggs into the mix until just incorporated. Bake in a 9x13-inch pan for 35 - 45 minutes or until center springs to the touch. Serve with maple butter or honey butter. |O!

Use extra cornbread to make Pork Chops with Parmesan Sage Cornbread Crust, page 143.

Paris Puffins

Makes 12 muffins

1/3 cup shortening
1/2 cup sugar
1 egg
1 1/2 cups flour
1 1/2 teaspoons baking powder
1/2 teaspoon salt

1/4 teaspoon nutmeg
1/2 cup milk
1/2 cup butter, melted
1/2 cup sugar
1 teaspoon cinnamon

Preheat oven to 350 degrees. In a large mixing bowl, combine shortening, sugar and egg. In a smaller bowl sift together the flour, baking powder, salt and nutmeg. Add the dry ingredients alternately with milk to the shortening mixture. Fill greased muffin tins 2/3 full. Bake 20 - 25 minutes. Cool slightly. Dip muffin tops in melted butter, then roll in a mixture of sugar and cinnamon.

Cheddar Bread

Serves 6 - 8

1 package active dry yeast
1 teaspoon sugar
1 1/4 cup warm water, 110-115 degrees
2 Tablespoons butter
2 Tablespoons sugar

1 teaspoon salt
1 1/4 cups sharp cheddar cheese, grated
3 cups flour, divided
1/2 cup chopped pecans
2 Tablespoons butter, melted

In a small bowl, dissolve yeast and 1 teaspoon sugar in water and whisk to blend. Set aside. In a large bowl, combine butter, 2 Tablespoons sugar, salt, cheese and 1 1/2 cups flour. Mix with a mixer or by hand. Stir in yeast mixture and add remaining 1 1/2 cups flour. Fold in pecans. Stir until smooth, then cover and let rise until double, about 30 minutes. Knead by hand for 1 minute. Place in a greased loaf pan. Cover and allow to rise again for 45 minutes. Bake at 375 degrees for 45 - 55 minutes. Cool on a wire rack and brush with melted butter. When slightly cooled, remove from pan.

Black Bread
Makes 2 loaves or 3 rounds

2 cups rye flour
1 cup unprocessed bran flour
1/2 cup wheat germ flour
3 cups whole wheat flour
2 Tablespoons active dry yeast
2 Tablespoons sugar
1 1/2 teaspoons salt

3/4 cup milk
1 cup water
1/2 cup butter
1/3 cup dark molasses
3 eggs, divided
3/4 cup white flour
1/4 cup corn meal

In a large bowl, mix rye flour, bran flour, wheat germ flour, and whole wheat flour. In a mixing bowl, combine yeast, sugar and salt. Add 3 cups of the flour mixture to the yeast mixture. In a saucepan, heat the milk, water, butter and molasses to 110 - 120 degrees and add to the flour and yeast mixture. With an electric mixer, mix on low for 2 minutes with a regular mixing paddle. Add 1 egg, 1 egg white and 2 cups of the flour only mixture. Switch to a dough hook and add the remaining flour only mixture and up to 3/4 cup white flour. Mix with a dough hook for 3 minutes. It will be sticky. Divide the dough into 2 halves, for loaf pans, or 3 sections for rounds.

For the loaves: grease the pans and shape into each. For the rounds: sprinkle cornmeal on a cookie sheet and shape dough into rounds. Let the dough rise for 1 hour or until double in size. Punch down and allow to rise 1 more hour. Mix the white of the remaining egg with a couple of teaspoons of water and brush the tops of the loaves. Cut 3 slashes across the top of each and bake in a preheated oven at 350 degrees for 1 hour.

This incredible rich, black bread goes great with Herb Bean Soup, page 58.

Baguette Bread
Makes 2 loaves

1 package dry yeast
1 Tablespoon sugar
1 Tablespoon salt

5 cups flour
2 Tablespoons cornmeal

In a large bowl, pour 2 cups warm water (110 degrees). Sprinkle yeast, sugar and salt over water. Whisk to combine. Stir in flour, adding gradually. Cover dough with a damp towel, let rise in a warm place to double, about 1 hour. Grease a baking sheet or French bread pan. Sprinkle with corn meal. Divide dough into 2 halves and form into loaves, and place in pan. Cover with a damp towel, rise for another hour to double. Preheat the oven to 425 degrees. Bake for 10 minutes to brown and continue baking at 375 degrees for 20 minutes. Pat loaves for a hollow sound before removing from oven. Remove from pan and cool on wire racks.

DESSERTS

Hilltop House Restaurant
49th and Dodge Streets

In January 1941, Raymond Matson left the insurance industry and with his wife, Mildred, opened the Hilltop House restaurant. They were manager and hostess for 39 years. Hilltop House gained national attention for serving home-cooked food in a relaxing atmosphere. The original 70-seat suburban restaurant was built on land owned by Mildred's parents, Alfred and Mabel Hansen, who also owned the nearby Mildred, Ellwood and Ambassador apartment buildings. Over the years, the Matson's added the Cape Cod Room, Danish Room, Duck Room, Garden Room and the Red Rooster Bar and Lounge to become a 450-seat operation. Specialties included their hamburger steak, creamed chicken over tea biscuits, chicken salad and cinnamon rolls. In 1979, the Matsons retired and sold the restaurant to a group of investors. Today, the building is used for offices and retail stores. *- Submitted by Linda Matson Andersen, Ray and Mildred's daughter*

-Harbor Room

Memories...

The Matson's bar, the Red Rooster, was in the southeast section of the restaurant. It was the bar of choice in town with Gold Cadillacs a favorite drink.

Bavarian Mint Dessert

1/2 pound butter
2 cups powdered sugar
6 eggs, separate yolks and
  stiffly beat whites
5 squares semi-sweet chocolate, melted
2 1/2 teaspoons peppermint extract
vanilla wafer crumbs

In a mixer, cream together butter and powdered sugar. To mixture add egg yolks, chocolate and peppermint extract. Fold in stiffly beaten egg whites. Cover bottom of a 9x9-inch pan with vanilla wafer crumbs. Pour mixture over crumbs, then sprinkle additional vanilla crumbs on top. Place in refrigerator and chill until firm (1 - 3 hours). **¡O!**

-Hilltop House's main entrance as seen through The Cape Cod Room

Simple Single Pie Crust

Makes 1 (9-inch) pie shell

1 3/4 cups flour
1 teaspoon sugar
1/2 teaspoon salt

1/2 cup vegetable oil
1/2 Tablespoon cold milk

In a medium-sized bowl, sift flour, sugar and salt. Make a well in the flour mixture. In a measuring cup, whisk together oil and milk. Pour the liquid mixture into the well made in the flour mixture. Mix with a fork or hands. Press the dough onto the sides and bottom of a 9-inch pie plate to form a pie crust. Put the plate in the freezer for 5 - 10 minutes to set. Use in place of any unbaked pie crust.

To make a crust for a savory pie, add 2 teaspoons of seasoning blend of choice or dry herbs.

Thai Pepper Fresh Mango Pie

Serves 8

CRUST
2 cups flour
1 1/4 teaspoons salt
3 Tablespoons sugar
3/4 cup vegetable oil
3 Tablespoons milk

FILLING
4 ounces cream cheese, softened
1/2 cup powdered sugar
1/2 cup ripe mangoes, peeled and
  mashed
2 Tablespoons lemon juice
2 Tablespoons cornstarch
1/2 cup sugar
2 additional ripe mangoes, peeled and
  sliced

Preheat oven to 425 degrees. To make the crust in a mixing bowl, sift the flour and salt. Stir in the sugar. Add the oil and milk. Stir with a fork until the flour is moistened. Form the pastry into a ball. Press into the bottom and sides of a 9-inch pie pan. Form a fluted edge by pinching the rim with your fingers. Bake the crust for 12 - 15 minutes. Cool completely.

In a mixing bowl, combine the cream cheese and powdered sugar. Mix well. Spread the mixture evenly on the bottom of the cooled pie crust. In a small saucepan, combine the mangoes, lemon juice, cornstarch and sugar. Cook over medium heat until thick, about 5 minutes. Fold the mango slices into the cooked mixture. Arrange the mango mixture in the pie crust on top of the cream cheese filling. Chill the pie in the refrigerator for at least 2 hours before cutting. If desired, top slices with whipped cream before serving. ¡O!

Apple-Rhubarb Crisp

Serves 4 - 6

3 cups Granny Smith apples, peeled, cored and thinly sliced
1/2 cup sugar
1/2 pound rhubarb, sliced into 1/2-inch pieces
2 teaspoons cornstarch
1 pinch salt
2 Tablespoons lemon juice
2 teaspoons pumpkin pie seasoning

TOPPING
1/4 cup flour
1/4 cup sugar
3/4 cup brown sugar, packed
1 pinch salt
2 teaspoons vanilla
1/2 cup oatmeal
1/2 cup coconut flakes
6 Tablespoons butter, softened and sliced into 6 pieces
1/2 cup sliced almonds
1 Tablespoon sugar

Preheat oven to 375 degrees. In a medium bowl, gently toss fruit and sugar. Blend cornstarch and salt, and pour on to fruit, stirring to coat. Toss with lemon juice and pumpkin pie seasoning. Transfer to a 9x11-inch baking dish. For the topping, combine flour, sugars and salt in a food processor. Drizzle vanilla on top and pulse to combine. Add oatmeal, coconut, butter and nuts. Pulse until incorporated. Spread topping evenly over fruit and sprinkle 1 Tablespoon of sugar on top. Bake until well-browned and fruit is bubbling around the edges, 30 - 40 minutes. Cool on a wire rack for 15 minutes. Serve with vanilla ice cream.

Recipe suitable for berries and stone fruits, as well. Walnuts and pistachios work great.

Rhubarb Pudding

Serves 6

2 cups sugar, divided
1 egg, beaten
3 Tablespoons butter, melted and divided
1/2 cup milk
2 teaspoons baking powder

1 cup flour
1 teaspoon vanilla
1/8 teaspoon salt
2 cups rhubarb, diced
1 1/2 cups boiling water

Preheat oven to 350 degrees. In a large bowl, combine 1 cup sugar, egg, 2 Tablespoons butter, milk, baking powder, flour, vanilla and salt. Pour into a greased 8x8-inch baking dish. Arrange rhubarb over batter. Sprinkle 1 cup sugar and 1 Tablespoon butter on top of the rhubarb. Cover with boiling water. Bake until brown and bubbly, 40 minutes.

Recipe may be doubled and baked in a 9x13-inch pan. Classic summer dessert.

Sumptuous Strawberry Rhubarb Pie

Serves 8

3/4 cup sugar
3 Tablespoons flour
1 egg, beaten
1/2 teaspoon vanilla
2 cups rhubarb, finely sliced
1 cup strawberries, finely sliced
1 unbaked (9-inch) pie crust

TOPPING
1/3 cup butter
1/2 cup brown sugar, packed
3/4 cup flour

Preheat oven to 400 degrees. In a bowl, beat sugar, flour, egg and vanilla. Fold in rhubarb and strawberries. Pour into the pie crust.

For the topping, blend butter, brown sugar and flour to make a crumbly topping. Sprinkle topping evenly over filling. Bake for 35 - 40 minutes or until topping is brown and filling starts to bubble.

Open-Face Peach Pie

Serves 8

2 Tablespoons flour
3/4 cup sugar
1/4 teaspoon nutmeg
dash of salt

1 unbaked (9-inch) pie crust
3 large peaches, peeled and sliced
1/2 teaspoon vanilla
1 cup heavy cream

Preheat oven to 450 degrees. Mix flour, sugar, nutmeg and salt. Pour half of this mixture into the bottom of the pie shell. Cover the bottom of the pie shell with peaches. Sprinkle remaining flour mixture over peaches. In a bowl, combine vanilla and cream and mix well. Pour cream mixture over peaches and flour mixture. Bake for 15 minutes. Lower the oven temperature to 350 degrees and continue baking for 45 minutes.

Nantucket Cranberry Pie

Serves 8

2 cups fresh cranberries
1/2 cup chopped walnuts
1/2 cup sugar
3/4 cup butter, melted

1 cup sugar
1 cup flour
1 teaspoon almond extract
2 eggs, beaten

Preheat oven to 325 degrees. Grease a 10-inch pie pan. Arrange cranberries on the bottom of the pan and sprinkle with nuts and 1/2 cup sugar. In a bowl, combine butter, 1 cup sugar, flour, almond extract and eggs. Pour over top of cranberries. Bake for 50 - 60 minutes until edges are brown and center is lightly colored. Serve with whipped cream or ice cream.

Fresh cranberries are difficult to find year round and are usually a seasonal or holiday item. Stock up at Thanksgiving and stick several bags in your freezer.

Bourbon Chocolate Pecan Pie

Serves 8

1 cup sugar
4 Tablespoons cornstarch
2 eggs, beaten
1/2 cup butter, melted and cooled
3 Tablespoons bourbon

1 cup semi-sweet chocolate chips
1 cup chopped pecans
1 unbaked (9-inch) pie shell
whipped cream

Preheat oven to 350 degrees. In a bowl, combine sugar and cornstarch. Beat in eggs, butter, bourbon, chocolate chips and pecans. Pour into the pie shell and bake for 40 minutes. Cool and cut into 8 pieces. Top with whipped cream.

This dessert is very rich but the slices do not serve well if cut smaller than 8.

Krunchy Kahlua Pecan Pie

Serves 6

PIE
2 Tablespoons butter
1/3 cup sugar
3 eggs
1/4 teaspoon salt
3/4 cup dark corn syrup
1/4 cup Kahlua
3/4 cup pecan halves
1 unbaked (9-inch) pie shell

TOPPING
1/2 cup heavy cream
2 Tablespoons Kahlua
12 pecan halves, toasted
1/4 cup chocolate, shaved

Preheat oven to 350 degrees. In a bowl, cream together butter and sugar. Beat in eggs 1 at a time. Stir in salt, corn syrup and Kahlua. Arrange pecans on the bottom of the pie shell and pour pie mixture over pecans. Bake for 40 minutes. Cool thoroughly.

For the topping, whip cold cream with Kahlua until soft peaks form. To serve, dollop whipped cream on pie slices and garnish with pecans and chocolate shavings.

Chocolate Pistachio Phyllo Rolls

Serves 24

1/3 cup heavy cream
1/4 teaspoon cinnamon
6 ounces semi-sweet chocolate, coarsely
    ground
1 cup pistachio nuts, shelled and coarsely
    ground, reserve 2 Tablespoons

6 sheets phyllo dough, thawed
3/4 cup unsalted butter, melted
1 Tablespoon powdered sugar

Preheat oven to 350 degrees. In a small saucepan, heat cream and cinnamon over medium heat until it begins to simmer. Add chocolate, stirring to melt. Set aside 2 Tablespoons of the nuts. Stir the remaining nuts into the chocolate mixture. Spoon chocolate into a zippered plastic bag and cut 1 inch off 1 corner. Lay 1 sheet of phyllo dough on a work surface and cover remaining sheets with a damp kitchen towel. Lightly brush phyllo dough surface with melted butter. Lay another sheet of phyllo dough on top, brushing with more melted butter. Immediately pipe chocolate along the short side of the dough, 1 1/2 inches from the edge. Tightly roll into a log, lightly brushing with butter at each turn and tucking in the ends. Brush log with butter and cover with a damp kitchen towel. Repeat process to make 2 more logs. Transfer to a parchment-lined baking sheet. Bake 15 minutes. Rotate baking sheet and brush logs again with butter. Sprinkle with reserved nuts. Continue baking until golden, about 15 minutes. Cool completely and then dust with powdered sugar. With a very sharp knife, cut each log into 8 pieces.

White Chocolate Bread Pudding

Serves 6

3 cups dense bread cubes, French or Italian
3 Tablespoons butter, melted
2 cups heavy cream
1/2 cup whole milk
1/4 cup sugar
5 ounces white chocolate, finely chopped
1 egg
4 egg yolks
1/8 teaspoon nutmeg
1/8 teaspoon cinnamon

Preheat oven to 350 degrees. On a baking sheet, lightly toast bread cubes in the oven. Remove from oven and allow to cool. Drizzle toasted bread cubes with the melted butter and set aside. In a saucepan, heat cream, milk and sugar over medium heat, stirring constantly, until sugar is dissolved. Add white chocolate. Remove from heat and stir until the chocolate is melted. In another bowl, whisk the whole egg and egg yolks together. Temper the egg mixture by adding a small amount of the hot cream mixture to the egg yolks while stirring. This step is very important in order to bring the temperature of the egg yolks up without making scrambled eggs! Add tempered egg yolks to the cream mixture while stirring. Add the nutmeg and cinnamon. Butter and sugar a 9x9-inch glass baking dish. Arrange bread and pour custard mixture over the bread. Allow to soak for 30 minutes. Make sure all the bread is submerged. Place the glass baking dish in a 9x13-inch metal pan. Place in the preheated oven, then fill metal pan with hot water so half of the glass dish is in a hot water bath. Bake for 45 minutes or until golden brown. Let stand for 30 minutes and enjoy warm or cold.

Great with any type of berry sauce poured on top.

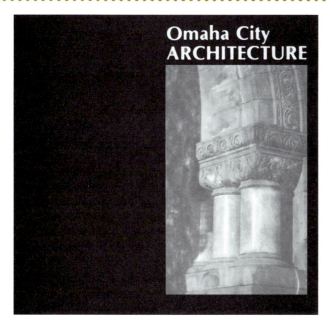

Omaha Architecture Book

In 1977, the Junior League published *Omaha City Architecture* with Landmarks, Inc.

Bishop's Buffet
102nd and West Dodge Road

Bishop's Buffet at the Westroads Shopping Center in 1968 - *From the Burnice Fiedler collection*

Chocolate Pie

1 (3 oz) package instant French vanilla pudding mix
1 (3 oz) package instant chocolate fudge pudding mix
2 cups milk
2 cups vanilla ice cream
9-inch graham cracker crust
1 (8 oz) carton frozen non-dairy whipped topping, thawed
Chocolate curls shaved from a 2-pound milk chocolate bar, for garnish

With an electric mixer, combine pudding mixes and milk. Add ice cream and beat until just thickened. Pour into the graham cracker crust. Top with whipped topping. With a potato peeler, shave part of the chocolate bar onto top of pie. Chill before serving.

Chocolate Citrus Zucchini Cake

Serves 10 - 12

1/2 cup butter, softened
1/2 cup vegetable oil
2 cups sugar
2 eggs
1/2 cup buttermilk
1 teaspoon vanilla
1/4 cup cocoa
1/2 teaspoon baking powder
1 teaspoon baking soda
2 1/2 cups flour
1/2 teaspoon salt
2 cups zucchini, grated and wrung dry

1 cup chocolate chips
zest of 1/2 lemon
zest and juice of 1/2 orange
2/3 cup chopped pecans, toasted

ICING
1 (8 oz) package cream cheese, softened
3 Tablespoons butter, softened
2/3 cup powdered sugar
3 Tablespoons cream

Preheat oven to 350 degrees. In a large bowl, cream butter, oil and sugar. Add eggs, buttermilk and vanilla, beat well. In a separate bowl, sift cocoa, baking powder, soda, flour and salt. Stir into the egg mixture. Fold in the zucchini, 1/2 of the chips, 1/2 of the lemon and orange zest and 1/2 of the orange juice. Reserve the remainder of the zest and juice for the icing. Pour the batter into a greased and sugared 9x13-inch baking dish or fluted tube pan. Sprinkle remaining chips on the top. Bake for 40 - 45 minutes. Cool completely.

For the icing, blend the cream cheese and butter until smooth. Add powdered sugar, remaining citrus zest and juice. Mix well and add the cream slowly, 1 Tablespoon at a time, until the icing is thin enough to pour. Drizzle glaze over cooled cake.

Black Russian Cake

Serves 10 - 12

1 box yellow cake mix
1 (5 oz) box chocolate pudding mix, not
    instant
1/2 cup sugar
1 cup vegetable oil

3/4 cup water
1/4 cup vodka
1/2 cup Kaluha, divided
4 eggs
1/2 cup powdered sugar

Preheat oven to 350 degrees. In a large bowl, combine all ingredients, except the 1/4 cup Kaluha and powdered sugar. Pour batter into a well-greased fluted tube pan and bake for 45 minutes. Allow cake to cool for 5 minutes, then remove from pan. Poke holes in the top of the cake with the tines of a fork. Whisk together the remaining 1/4 cup of Kaluha and powdered sugar. Drizzle the glaze over the top of the cake.

Coconut Cake with Caramel-Rum Sauce

Serves 10 - 12

1 cup sugar
1/2 cup unsalted butter, softened
1 Tablespoon vanilla
1/2 teaspoon almond extract
2 eggs
1 cup flour
1 teaspoon baking soda
3/4 cup sour cream
3/4 cup plus 2 Tablespoons sweetened,
  shredded coconut

1/2 cup cream of coconut

SAUCE
1/2 cup sugar
2 Tablespoons water
1 Tablespoon dark rum
2 Tablespoons unsalted butter
1/2 cup heavy cream

Preheat oven to 350 degrees. Spray a 9-inch springform pan with cooking spray. In a large mixer, cream sugar, butter, vanilla and almond extract until fluffy. Beat in eggs, 1 at a time. In a separate bowl, sift flour and baking soda, then add to the butter mixture. Mix until just combined. Stir in sour cream, 3/4 cup coconut and cream of coconut. Pour the cake batter into the pan. Sprinkle with remaining 2 Tablespoons of coconut. Bake until cake is golden brown, about 55 minutes, and tester comes out clean. Cool pan completely on a rack. Using a small knife, cut around the sides of the pan. Release pan sides.

For the sauce, in a heavy saucepan, combine sugar and water. Stir over low heat until sugar dissolves. Increase heat to high and boil without stirring until syrup turns a deep amber color. Brush down sides of the pan with a wet pastry brush and swirl it occasionally. Remove pan from heat and carefully add rum, mixture will bubble vigorously. Return pan to heat and bring to a boil. Whisk in 2 Tablespoons butter, stirring to melt. Add cream and simmer until sauce is reduced to 3/4 cup, about 3 minutes. Remove pan from heat. Cut cake into slices and serve with hot caramel-rum sauce.

Cake and sauce may be prepared 1 day ahead. Wrap cake tightly and store at room temperature. Refrigerate sauce and reheat over low heat, stirring frequently, before serving.

Nebraska's Fresh Crop Apple Cake

Serves 10 - 12

4 cups apples, peeled, cored and coarsely
  chopped
1 3/4 cups sugar
1/2 cup oil
2 teaspoons vanilla
1 cup chopped walnuts
2 eggs, beaten
2 cups flour

2 teaspoons cinnamon
1 1/2 teaspoons baking soda
1 teaspoon salt

ICING
1 1/2 cups powdered sugar
2 Tablespoons brewed coffee
2 Tablespoons butter, melted

Preheat oven to 350 degrees. In a large mixing bowl, toss the apples and sugar. To this mixture add, by hand, the oil, vanilla, nuts and eggs. In a separate bowl, blend the flour, cinnamon, baking soda and salt. Add the dry ingredients to the apple mixture and blend well, by hand. Pour batter into a greased 9x13-inch pan. Bake for 45 - 60 minutes.

For the icing, in a small bowl, beat the powdered sugar with the coffee and butter. Add more coffee and/or butter, if needed, to make the icing thin enough to pour. Drizzle the icing over the warm cake.

On autumn afternoons, many Omahans take a drive to Nebraska City. They enjoy the scenic fall foliage and a trip to the city's well-known apple orchards.

Sugar Plum Cake

Serves 10 - 12

3 eggs
2 cups sugar
1 cup vegetable oil
1 small jar baby food, plums or prunes
1 small jar baby food, apricots or
   peaches

2 cups flour
1 teaspoon baking soda
1/2 teaspoon salt
1 teaspoon ground cloves
1 teaspoon cinnamon
1/2 cup chopped pecans

Preheat oven to 325 degrees. In a large mixing bowl, combine eggs, sugar, oil and both jars of baby food. Mix with an electric mixer or whisk, until mixture is well-blended. In a separate bowl, combine the flour, baking soda, salt, cloves and cinnamon. Add the flour mixture to the egg mixture and mix well. Stir in pecans. Spray a fluted tube pan with cooking spray and sprinkle with sugar. Pour batter into the pan. Bake for 55 - 60 minutes, or until tester comes out clean.

A wonderful treat after a trip to the Orpheum to see The Nutcracker.

Extraordinary Oatmeal Cake

Serves 15

1 cup quick oatmeal
1/2 cup butter
1 1/4 cups boiling water
1 cup sugar
1 cup brown sugar, packed
2 eggs
1 1/3 cups flour
1 teaspoon baking soda
1/2 teaspoon salt
1 teaspoon cinnamon

1/2 teaspoon nutmeg

FROSTING
3/4 cup sugar
1/4 cup milk
6 Tablespoons butter
1/2 cup sweetened, shredded coconut
1 cup chopped walnuts
1 cup powdered sugar
1 teaspoon vanilla

Preheat oven to 350 degrees. In a large bowl, place oatmeal and butter. Pour boiling water over the ingredients and stir to blend. Let mixture stand for 20 minutes. Add sugars and eggs, mixing well to combine. In another bowl, mix flour, soda, salt, cinnamon and nutmeg. Add the dry mixture to the wet mixture and mix well. Pour batter into a greased and floured 9x13-inch pan. Bake for 45 minutes. Cool the cake before frosting.

For the frosting, in a small saucepan, combine sugar, milk, butter, coconut and walnuts. Stir and simmer for 3 minutes. Cool frosting slightly. Mix in the powdered sugar and vanilla. To achieve the desired spreading consistency, add more powdered sugar and/or milk. Frost cake and serve.

This cake is a family favorite. It also may be made into cupcakes and freezes well.

The Best Ever Coconut Pound Cake

Serves 12 - 16

6 eggs, separated
1 cup shortening
1/2 cup butter
3 cups sugar
1/2 teaspoon almond extract

1 teaspoon coconut extract
1 cup milk
3 cups cake flour, sifted
2 cups sweetened, shredded coconut

Preheat oven to 300 degrees. Separate eggs, placing whites in a large bowl, and yolks in another. Beat whites into stiff peaks and set aside. Beat egg yolks with shortening and butter until well-blended. Gradually add sugar, beating until light and fluffy. Add extracts and milk. On low speed, beat in flour alternating with milk, beginning and ending with the flour. Add the shredded coconut and beat until well-blended. Gently fold the egg whites into batter. Pour into a greased 10-inch tube pan. Bake for 2 hours or until tester comes out clean. Cool in pan on wire rack for 15 minutes. Remove from pan and cool completely.

Chocolate Oatmeal Cake

Serves 18

1 1/2 cups boiling water
1 cup old fashioned oatmeal
1 cup butter, softened
2 cups sugar
2 eggs

1 Tablespoon vanilla
1 cup flour
1/2 teaspoon salt
1 teaspoon baking soda
1/2 cup cocoa

Preheat oven to 350 degrees. In a large bowl, combine oatmeal and water. Stir and let stand 8 - 9 minutes. Add butter to the oatmeal mixture and let stand until melted. Add sugar and mix. Beat eggs, then and to the mixture. Add vanilla. In a bowl, sift flour, salt, soda and cocoa. Combine wet ingredients with dry ingredients. Mix well. Pour into an ungreased 9x13-inch pan. Bake 30 to 35 minutes. Cool and frost.

If desired, frost with a cream cheese or sour cream frosting.

Mint Chocolate Candy Cake

Serves 12

CAKE
1/2 cup butter, softened
1 cup sugar
4 eggs, beaten
1 (16 oz) can chocolate syrup
1 teaspoon vanilla
1 cup flour

MINT TOPPING
1/2 cup butter
2 cups powdered sugar
2 Tablespoons milk
1 teaspoon peppermint extract
3 drops green food coloring

CHOCOLATE TOPPING
6 Tablespoons butter
1 cup mint chocolate chips

Preheat oven to 350 degrees. In a bowl, cream together butter and sugar. Blend in eggs, syrup, vanilla and flour. Pour batter into an ungreased 9x13-inch pan. Bake for 30 minutes. Set aside and cool completely.

For the mint topping, beat butter, powdered sugar and milk. Blend in peppermint and food coloring. Spread mixture over the cooled cake and refrigerate.

For the chocolate topping, melt butter with chocolate chips in a saucepan. Spread over the mint topping and refrigerate. Serve cold.

This cake is best made a day before serving.

Wine Cake

Serves 10 - 12

1 package yellow or chocolate cake mix
1 package instant vanilla pudding
2/3 cup vegetable oil

2/3 cup white wine or cream sherry
4 eggs
1 teaspoon nutmeg

Preheat oven to 350 degrees. Grease and flour a fluted tube pan. In a bowl, mix all ingredients with a hand mixer. Bake for 45 - 50 minutes. Cool in pan, then sprinkle with powdered sugar.

This is an easy cake to make in a pinch and it freezes well. It may also be made with an orange cake mix.

Carrot Cake
Serves 10 - 12

2 cups flour
1 teaspoon baking soda
2 teaspoons cinnamon
1 teaspoon salt
2 cups sugar
1 1/2 cups oil or unsweetened
   applesauce
3 eggs

2 cups carrots, finely grated
1 cup crushed pineapple, drained
1 cup sweetened, shredded coconut
1 cup chopped walnuts
1 cup raisins
1 teaspoon vanilla
cream cheese frosting or powdered sugar

Preheat oven to 350 degrees. Grease and flour a 9x13-inch baking pan. In a bowl, sift together flour, soda, cinnamon and salt. Set aside. In a large mixing bowl, beat sugar, oil and eggs with an electric mixer until well mixed. Gradually add flour mixture. Fold in carrots, pineapple, coconut, walnuts, raisins and vanilla. Pour batter into pan and bake for 1 hour. Frost with cream cheese frosting or dust with powdered sugar.

Cinnamon Cake
Serves 12

4 eggs, beaten
1 cup sugar
1 cup brown sugar, packed
2 teaspoons vanilla
2 cups flour
2 Tablespoons cinnamon
1 teaspoon nutmeg
2 teaspoons baking powder

pinch of salt
1 cup milk
4 Tablespoons butter

TOPPING
1/2 cup sugar
1 Tablespoon cinnamon
1/4 cup butter, melted

Preheat oven to 350 degrees. Lightly grease and flour a 9x13-inch baking pan. In a bowl, beat the eggs and add in sugars and blend. Add vanilla. In another bowl, mix dry ingredients and add to wet mixture. Scald milk and butter. To scald, in a glass measuring cup, cut up butter into pieces and combine with milk. Microwave for about 1 minute, heating to just below boiling, Quickly add the milk mixture to other ingredients and gently blend. Pour into the pan. Bake for 40 - 45 minutes until tester comes out clean.

For the topping, combine sugar and cinnamon and sprinkle over hot cake. Drizzle melted butter over the top. Serve warm.

Great on a crisp fall night or serve as a coffee cake.

Golden Toque

Brought to America in 1961 by French chef Pierre Berard, the Honorable Order of the Golden Toque is the highest acclaimed recognition a chef may receive in America. To qualify, chefs must have 20 years experience, achieved high professional standing and devotion and distinguished service in the culinary profession and arts. Chefs must be nominated by at least two members in good standing. It takes an average of three years to get though the qualification process. Membership is restricted to only 100 lifetime members.

At one time Omaha had five Golden Toque members, the only city with more than two members. Chefs included:
Al Buda - Blackstone Hotel
Richard Bolamperti - Louie Cantoni's Restaurant
Joe Incontro - Chieftan Hotel and the Indian Hills Restaurant
Lou Turco - The Townhouse
Paul Goebel - Holiday Inn, and later, The New Tower Inn

Joe Villella, from the Rome Hotel, was also inducted as an Honorary Member. Goebel, who just celebrated 50 years in the restaurant business, is the only living member. He continues to hold the title as the youngest member ever inducted.

Omaha's five Golden Toque chefs in 1979. From left: Richard Bolamperti, Lou Turco, Al Buda, Joe Incontro and Paul Goebel.

Savory Grilled Fruit Sundaes
Serves 4

8 cups nectarines, peaches, pineapple or apricots, pitted and halved

1/2 cup sugar
1/2 gallon vanilla ice cream

Use any combination of fruits. Sprinkle fruit flesh with sugar. Allow the fruit to sit for 1 - 2 minutes, allowing the sugar to absorb. Spray a large piece of aluminum foil with cooking spray. Place the fruit, sugar side down on the aluminum foil. Grill on medium-low heat until fruit is soft to the touch. Place ice cream scoops into 4 bowls. Top with fruit.

Simply Elegant Sundaes
Serves 4

1/2 gallon ice cream, any flavor
1/2 cup chocolate sprinkles or pecans, toasted and finely chopped

1/2 cup Chambord or cassis liqueur
fresh raspberries and mint leaves, for garnish

Shape ice cream into 3-inches balls with a scoop. Roll in chocolate sprinkles or pecans. Place ice cream balls on a cookie sheet and place in the freezer. To serve, pour a shallow layer of the liqueur on each dessert plate. Place an ice cream ball in the center. Garnish with fresh raspberries and a mint leaf.

Apple Brickle Dip
Serves 10 - 12

8 ounces cream cheese, softened
1/2 cup brown sugar, packed
1/4 cup sugar

1 teaspoon vanilla
1 (7 oz) package toffee bits
6 apples, cored and sliced

In a large bowl, combine cream cheese, sugars, and vanilla. Mix well. Stir in toffee bits. Chill and serve with apple slices.

Pumpkin Dip

Serves 10 - 12

8 ounces cream cheese, softened
2 cups powdered sugar
1 (15 oz) can solid pack pumpkin

1/2 teaspoon ground ginger
1 teaspoon cinnamon
1/4 teaspoon ground cloves

In a large bowl, blend all ingredients until smooth. Chill at least 30 minutes. Serve with gingersnaps.

Mocha Ice Cream Cake

Serves 10 - 12

2 cups 60% cocoa baking chips (like Ghirardelli), divided
3/4 cup butter
2 Tablespoons boiling water
2 Tablespoons instant espresso powder
1 1/2 cups sugar
2 teaspoons vanilla
1/2 teaspoon salt

4 eggs
1 cup flour
2 pints coffee or vanilla ice cream, softened
1/2 cup heavy cream
2 Tablespoons butter
chocolate covered coffee beans, for garnish

Preheat oven to 350 degrees. Grease a 10-inch springform pan or square baking pan and set aside. In a small saucepan, melt 1 cup cocoa chips and butter. Remove from heat and allow to cool 15 minutes. In a small mixing bowl, combine boiling water and espresso powder. Add half of the espresso mixture to the chocolate mixture and blend. Save the rest of the espresso for the glaze. Mix in sugar, vanilla and salt. Stir until combined. Add eggs, beating well. Gently stir in the flour until just mixed through. Pour into the pan and bake for 30 minutes or until tester comes out clean. Cool completely. Spread softened ice cream evenly over brownie to create a smooth surface. Place in the freezer to harden.

For the glaze, in a small saucepan, stir cream with 2 Tablespoons butter and reserved espresso mixture. Add 1 cup cocoa chips to the saucepan, stirring over low heat. When mixture is smooth, set aside to cool. Spread over the set ice cream and return to the freezer for another 2 hours. Allow to sit at room temperature for 10 minutes before serving. Garnish with 2 - 3 chocolate covered coffee beans, if desired.

The inside of the Peony Park ballroom, 78th and Cass Streets, in 1970. Joe Malec opened Peony Park in 1917. The ballroom was built six years later. It seated 1,600 people and served more than 100,000 meals in a year. Peony Park was demolished in 1996. - *From Louie Marcuzzo*

Extravagant Espresso Cream
Serves 2

1/2 cup whole milk
1 1/2 teaspoons unflavored powdered gelatin
3 teaspoons instant espresso powder
1/4 cup sugar

1 1/2 cups heavy cream
pinch of salt
1 package ladyfingers or shortcake shells
fresh mint, for garnish
berries, for garnish

In a saucepan, pour milk and sprinkle the gelatin on top. Let stand for 5 minutes. Over medium-low heat, stir until gelatin is dissolved. Do not let the milk boil. Add the espresso powder, sugar, cream and salt. Stir over low heat until the sugar dissolves. Remove from the heat and let cool slightly. Pour into a bowl, cover and refrigerate. Keep refrigerated, stirring every 20 minutes during the first hour. Chill at least 6 hours or until set. Serve with ladyfingers or in shortcake shells garnished with fresh mint and berries.

Swedish Cream
Serves 10 - 12

2 1/3 cups heavy cream
1 1/4 cups sugar
1 envelope unflavored gelatin

2 cups sour cream
2 teaspoons vanilla
1 teaspoon almond extract

In a saucepan, combine the cream, sugar and gelatin. Cook over low heat, stirring constantly, until mixture just comes to a boil, about 10 minutes. Cool mixture to lukewarm. Whisk in sour cream, vanilla and almond. Lightly prepare a mold with cooking spray. Pour mixture into the mold and chill. Make at least 1 day ahead. Keeps up to 1 week covered and chilled in the refrigerator.

To serve, remove from mold onto a serving platter. Garnish with fresh fruit. Three kinds of berries, green grapes and quartered kiwi are pretty together surrounding the white, creamy mixture.

Chocolate Chip Cheesecake

Serves 12 - 16

1 cup chocolate cookie crumbs
2 Tablespoons butter, softened
2 pounds cream cheese, softened
1 cup sugar
2 cups sour cream

3 eggs
1 Tablespoon vanilla
1 1/2 cups semi-sweet chocolate chips,
    divided

Preheat oven to 350 degrees. In a bowl, combine the cookie crumbs and butter. Blend until smooth. Press the cookie crust into the bottom of a 9-inch springform pan. Refrigerate while preparing the filling.

To prepare the filling, in a large bowl, beat the cream cheese until smooth. Blend in sugar and sour cream. Add the eggs and vanilla, mix until smooth. Fold in 1 cup of the chocolate chips. Pour filling into the prepared crust and smooth the top with a spatula. Sprinkle the remaining 1/2 cup chocolate chips evenly over the top. Bake for 30 - 40 minutes. Turn oven off and leave cheesecake in oven for 1 hour to set. Remove from oven and chill until firm, 3 - 4 hours.

Blackstone Hotel
Original Schimmel Cheesecake

Serves 9

2 cups graham cracker crumbs
1/2 cup sugar
1/2 cup butter
3 eggs
12 ounces cream cheese, softened
1/2 teaspoon vanilla

pinch of salt
1/2 cup sugar
1 1/2 cups sour cream
2 Tablespoons sugar
1 teaspoon vanilla

Preheat oven to 375 degrees. In a bowl, combine the graham cracker crumbs, sugar and butter. Press the mixture into the bottom and sides of a 9-inch springform pan. Reserve extra crumbs for topping. Refrigerate the crust.

In a bowl, combine the eggs, cream cheese, vanilla, salt and sugar. Mix well. Pour the filling into the crust and bake for 20 minutes. Remove and allow to rest for 15 minutes. Increase oven heat to 475 degrees. In a bowl, combine sour cream, sugar and vanilla and mix well. Carefully spread on top of the cheesecake and return to the oven for 10 minutes. When the cake has cooled, sprinkle remaining cracker crumbs on top and refrigerate until ready to serve.

iOi

REED'S ICE CREAM COMPANY

Partners Charles Reed and C.F. Becker opened Reed's Ice Cream Company's Omaha plant in 1929, located at 3106 North 24th Street. Reed's created 63 neighborhood bungalows and drive-in ice cream shops throughout the area like the one pictured here in 1936 at 4967 Dodge Street, Reed's served over 20,000 people daily during peak season. - - *From the Bostwick-Frohardt Collection owned by KMTV and on permanent loan to the Durham Western Heritage Museum, Omaha, Nebraska*

COOKIES and CANDY

THE FONTENELLE HOTEL
1806 Douglas Street

A Hotel Greeters Banquet at the Fontenelle Hotel, June 17, 1937. - *From the Bostwick-Frohardt Collection owned by KMTV and on permanent loan to the Durham Western Heritage Museum*

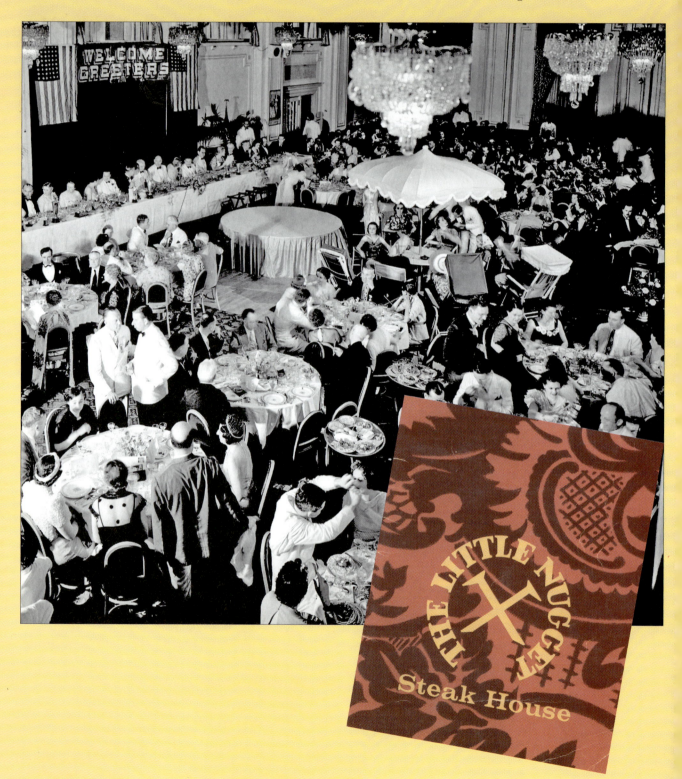

Healthy Inspired Proactive Kids Project

Helping children with nutrition issues has been one of many focuses of the Junior League volunteers since its inception in 1901. With an estimate that nearly one-third of adolescents in the United States are overweight or at risk of becoming overweight, Junior Leagues across the country are working to bring kids the important tools and information about living and eating healthly in today's society through their Kids in the kitchen program.

Since 2003, H.I.P. (Healthy, Inspired & Proactive) Kids has been the Signature Project of the Junior League of Omaha (JLO). To date $90,000 has been donated to the program. The purpose of the project is to create a community that encourages, promotes and provides healthy eating and activity choices for children. The project partners with Club Possible, a collaboration of the local chapters of Boys and Girls Club, Camp Fire, Girl Scouts and YMCA to provide consistent education to youth on nutrition and physical fitness. This project includes the following components: Ready Set Grow! (a gardening kids club project) and Foodtastics! which is focused on educating families on healthy eating choices.

"Teaching children the value of nutrition and healthy lifestyles is critical and the Junior League of Omaha is committed to encouraging kids to be healthy, inspired and proactive through our signature project H.I.P. Kids" said Junior League of Omaha Past President Karen Nelsen.

In April 2006 the Junior League of Omaha hosted a Kids in the Kitchen for 100 members of Girls Inc. of Omaha at the Girls Inc. North Center. Chefs from the Metropolitan Community College Culinary Arts Institute and the Omaha Child and Chef Foundation taught girls the basics of healthy cooking, through hands on instruction. Junior League volunteers also taught the girls how to read food labels to make smart food choices and simple, fun activities for staying fit. Each girl received a gift bag with items to help them live healthy lifestyles including a jump rope, water bottle, HIP (Healthy, Inspired, Proactive) Kids cookbook and educational materials.

Wonders of the World Bars
Makes 30 bars

1/2 cup butter
1 1/4 cups graham cracker crumbs
2 cups semi-sweet chocolate chips
5 ounces butterscotch chips

3/4 cup chopped walnuts
1 cup sweetened, shredded coconut
1 (14 oz) can sweetened condensed milk

Preheat oven to 350 degrees, 325 for a glass dish. In a 9x13-inch baking dish, melt the butter in the oven. Remove from oven and layer in the following order: graham cracker crumbs, chocolate chips, butterscotch chips, walnuts and coconut. Press down evenly. Pour milk evenly over the top. Bake 25 - 30 minutes or until lightly browned. Cool and cut into bars. Best when refrigerated.

Hot donuts at Woolworths in the 1940s.
- From the William Wentworth collection at the Douglas County Historical Society

210

Banana Bars

Serves 12

1 cup butter, cubed
1/2 cup water
2 cups flour
2 eggs
1 1/2 cups sugar
1/2 cup brown sugar, packed
1/2 cup buttermilk
1 teaspoon vanilla
1 teaspoon baking soda

1 cup bananas, mashed

FROSTING
8 ounces cream cheese, softened
1/2 cup butter
1 teaspoon vanilla
3 1/2 cups powdered sugar
1 cup chopped pecans

Preheat oven to 350 degrees. In a saucepan, bring butter and water to boil, remove from heat and cool slightly. In a large bowl, combine the flour, eggs, sugars, buttermilk, vanilla, baking soda and bananas. Beat until well-blended. Slowly add the butter mixture and mix well. Pour into greased a 9x13-inch pan. Bake for 30 - 40 minutes or until a tester comes out clean. Allow to cool.

For the frosting, beat cream cheese and 1/2 cup butter until fluffy. Beat in vanilla. Gradually add powdered sugar. Spread over bars and sprinkle with pecans.

Fresh Raspberry Brownies
Created by Randi Caniglia and submitted by Caniglia's Venice Inn

Serves 15

1 cup butter, softened
1 1/4 cups sugar
1/2 cup brown sugar, packed
4 eggs
1/2 cup cocoa
1 Tablespoon brandy
1 teaspoon vanilla
1/4 teaspoon salt

1 1/4 cups flour, sifted
1 pint fresh raspberries

GLAZE
4 ounces chocolate chips
2 Tablespoons brandy
2 teaspoons hot water
powdered sugar for dusting

Pre-heat oven to 325 degrees. Grease a 9x13-inch baking pan. In a mixing bowl, beat butter and sugars until fluffy. Add eggs, 1 at a time, and beat well after each. Stir in cocoa, brandy, vanilla and salt. Gently mix in sifted flour until just combined. Pour into pan and place raspberries on top of batter. Bake 30 - 40 minutes until tester comes out clean. Cool completely.

For the glaze, in a double boiler, melt chocolate chips, brandy and hot water over simmering water until smooth. Cool a little. Cut brownies into 3-inch bars, dust with powdered sugar and drizzle with the glaze. Rest 30 minutes before serving. !O!!

Butterscotch Pecan Bars
Serves 16

4 Tablespoons butter, melted and cooled
1 cup dark brown sugar, packed
1 egg, beaten
1 teaspoon vanilla

1 cup flour
1/4 teaspoon salt
1 teaspoon baking powder
1 cup chopped pecans

Preheat oven to 350 degrees. In a bowl, cream together the butter and sugar. Add egg and vanilla. In a separate bowl, combine flour, salt and baking powder. Stir into the wet ingredients. Fold in pecans. Pour the batter into a greased 8x8-inch pan. Bake for 20 minutes. Cool in the pan and cut into squares.

Buttermilk Brownies
Serves 20

2 cups flour, less 2 Tablespoons
2 cups sugar
1/2 teaspoon salt
1/2 cup butter
1 cup water
1/4 cup cocoa
1/2 cup shortening
1/2 cup buttermilk
2 eggs
1 teaspoon baking soda
1 teaspoon vanilla

FROSTING
1/2 cup butter
1/4 cup cocoa
1/3 cup buttermilk
2 cups powdered sugar
1 teaspoon vanilla

Preheat oven to 400 degrees. Spray jelly roll pan with cooking spray. In a large bowl, combine flour, sugar and salt and set aside. In a saucepan, bring to a high simmer, butter, water, cocoa and shortening. Pour this mixture over the dry ingredients. In a medium bowl, whisk together buttermilk, eggs, soda and vanilla. Add to other ingredients and blend. Pour into the pan and bake for 20 minutes.

For the frosting, in a saucepan, bring butter, cocoa and buttermilk to a high simmer. Add powdered sugar. Add more, if needed, until desired consistency is reached. Add vanilla. Frost brownies while warm. Sprinkle with nuts if desired.

Sunny Glazed Apple Squares
Serves 10

1 cup shortening
2 1/2 cups flour
1/2 teaspoon salt
2 eggs, separated
milk
1 1/2 cups raisin bran
8 tart apples, peeled and sliced
1 cup sugar
1 Tablespoon cinnamon

GLAZE
1 1/2 cups powdered sugar
3 Tablespoons water
1/2 teaspoon vanilla

Preheat oven to 350 degrees. In a large bowl, cut shortening into flour and salt. In a separate bowl, beat egg yolks with enough milk to make 2/3 cup. Reserve whites. Add to flour mixture and mix well. Divide dough in half. Roll first half to fit a 9x15-inch jellyroll pan. Sprinkle the raisin bran on top of dough and add the apples. Mix sugar and cinnamon and sprinkle over apples. Roll out the other half of the dough and place on top of the apples. Seal edges. Slightly beat egg whites and spread over the top crust. Bake for 1 hour.

Just before the Apple Squares finish baking, make a glaze with the powdered sugar, water and vanilla. When fully baked, remove from oven and drizzle glaze over the hot bars. Cut into squares.

Chocolate Peanut Butter Bars
Serves 16

1/2 cup sugar
1/4 cup butter
1/4 cup chunky peanut butter
1 egg, beaten
1 teaspoon vanilla

1/2 cup flour
1/2 teaspoon baking powder
1/4 teaspoon salt
8 ounces chocolate chips

Preheat oven to 350 degrees. In a large bowl, blend sugar, the butter and peanut butter. Add egg and vanilla, mixing until smooth. Stir in flour, baking powder, and salt. Fold in the chocolate chips. Place batter in a greased 8x8-inch baking pan. Bake for 20 - 25 minutes until set. Cool before cutting into squares.

An Original Ingredient

Girls (Club) Incorporated

When asked about JLO's contributions to Omaha, Past President Jeanne Salerno notes that the relationship with the Girls Club of Omaha was not only powerful, but significant. "It was one of the first financial commitments we made that was larger than our volunteer commitment," said Jeanne. In 1979, the JLO passed a $60,000 three-year commitment to the Girls Club. Even after a name change from Girls Club to Girls Inc, the League has continued to support the mission through additional funding and volunteer hours. In 1990, the JLO created and facilitated career development and leadership workshops, sponsored several Community Grant Awards and includes the girls in the current HIP Kids Project.

Very Rich Everything Bars
Makes 16 bars

2/3 cup butter
1 cup brown sugar, packed
1/4 light corn syrup
1/4 cup crunchy peanut butter
1 teaspoon vanilla
4 cups quick-cooking oats

TOPPING
2 cups semi-sweet chocolate chips
2 cups butterscotch chips
2/3 cup crunchy peanut butter
1 cup unsalted dry roasted peanuts,
    chopped

Preheat oven to 375 degrees. Grease a 9x9-inch pan. In a saucepan, melt the butter, brown sugar and corn syrup over medium heat. Stir in peanut butter and the vanilla. Sir in the oats. Press mixture into the bottom of the pan. Bake for 15 minutes, until done.

For the topping, melt chocolate and butterscotch chips together in the microwave. Stir in the peanut butter and the nuts. Spread the topping over the warm bars. Allow bars to cool on a rack, then refrigerate. Once chilled, cut into bars.

Party Nut Bars
Makes 36 bars

3 cups flour
1 1/2 cups sugar
1 teaspoon salt
1 cup butter
1 (12 oz) can mixed party nuts:
    cashews, pecans, almonds and
    peanuts

1/2 cup light corn syrup
2 Tablespoons butter
1 Tablespoon water
1 cup butterscotch chips

Preheat oven to 350 degrees. In a bowl, combine flour, sugar and salt. Cut butter into flour mixture and combine with fingers. Press into a 9x13-inch pan. Bake for 12 minutes. Cool. Evenly sprinkle nuts over cooled crust. In a small saucepan, combine corn syrup, 2 Tablespoons butter, water and butterscotch chips. Melt together over low heat, then pour over nuts. Bake an additional 12 minutes. Cool completely and cut into bars.

Chocolate Fig Pecan Bars
Makes 32 bars

2 cups flour
3/4 cup sugar, divided
10 Tablespoons butter
8 ounces dried calimyrna figs, stemmed and chopped
3/4 cup pecans, chopped

2/3 cup semi-sweet or 60% cocoa chocolate pieces
3 eggs
3/4 cup light corn syrup
1 teaspoon vanilla

Preheat oven to 350 degrees. Lightly grease a 9x13-inch pan. In a large bowl, stir together flour and 1/4 cup sugar. Cut the butter into the dry ingredients with two knives until the mixture resembles course crumbs. Press into the bottom of the pan. Bake for 15 minutes until the edges begin to brown. Remove from oven, then sprinkle figs, pecans and chocolate pieces over the crust. Lightly beat eggs, gradually beat in remaining sugar, corn syrup and vanilla until blended. Pour over crust. Return to oven for 20 - 30 minutes or until filling is firm around edges and slightly soft at the center.

Chocolate Oatmeal Carmelitos
Makes 24 bars

2 cups flour
2 cups quick-cooking oats
1 1/2 cups brown sugar, packed
1 teaspoon baking soda
1/2 teaspoon salt
1 cup butter, melted

1 (14 oz) package individually wrapped caramels, unwrapped
1/2 cup evaporated milk
2 cups semisweet chocolate chips
1/2 cup M & Ms Candy

Preheat oven to 350 degrees. Grease a 9x13-inch baking pan. In a medium bowl, stir together the flour, oats, brown sugar, baking soda and salt. Stir in the butter and press half of the mixture into the bottom of the pan. Bake for ten minutes. While the crust is baking, prepare the caramels. In a saucepan, melt the caramels and evaporated milk over medium-low heat, stirring frequently until smooth. Set aside. Remove the crust from the oven and sprinkle with chocolate chips and M & Ms. Drizzle the caramel mixture over top. Crumble the remaining oat mixture evenly over the top and pat down lightly. Bake for an additional 15 - 20 minutes or until the top is golden. Cool then cut into bars.

Peanutilicious Caramel Candy

Serves 12

BOTTOM LAYER
1 1/2 cups milk chocolate chips
1/3 cup butterscotch chips
1/4 cup creamy peanut butter

CARAMEL LAYER
1 (14 oz) package individually wrapped
    caramels, unwrapped
1/4 cup heavy cream

NOUGAT LAYER
1/4 cup butter
1 cup sugar
1/4 cup evaporated milk
1 1/2 cups marshmallow creme
1/4 cup peanut butter
1 teaspoon vanilla
1 1/2 cups salted peanuts, chopped

TOP LAYER
1 cup milk chocolate chips
1/4 cup butterscotch chips
1/4 cup creamy peanut butter

Lightly grease a 9x13-inch pan. Set aside. For the bottom layer, in a small saucepan, combine chocolate chips, butterscotch chips and peanut butter. Stir over low heat until melted and smooth. Spread into the pan and refrigerate until set.

For the nougat layer, in a saucepan, melt butter over medium-high heat. Add sugar and milk. Bring to a high simmer, for 4 to 5 minutes, stirring constantly. Remove from heat and stir in marshmallow creme, peanut butter and vanilla. Add chopped peanuts. Spread over the bottom layer and refrigerate until set.

For the caramel layer, in a saucepan, combine caramels and cream. Stir over low heat until smooth. Spread over the nougat layer. Refrigerate until set.

For the top layer, in a saucepan, combine chocolate chips, butterscotch chips and peanut butter. Stir over low heat until melted and smooth. Pour over the caramel layer and refrigerate for at least 1 hour. Cut into 1 inch squares and store in the refrigerator.

Nut Brittle

Serves 24

1 cup salted dry roasted peanuts
1 cup shelled pistachios
1 cup pecan halves
1 cup sugar

1 cup unsalted butter
1/3 cup light corn syrup
2 teaspoons honey

In a saucepan, combine nuts, sugar, butter, corn syrup and honey, over medium-high heat. Stir mixture constantly with a wooden spoon until it turns a walnut color and thickens, about 10 - 12 minutes. Quickly pour onto a silpat or buttered, foil-lined baking sheet and spread the brittle to an even thickness, about 1/3-inch, with the back of a spoon. Cool for three to four minutes. Score the brittle with a sharp knife into about 24 (2- inch) squares. When the brittle cools completely, snap along the scored marks.

Wheatfield's Pumpkin Swirl Bars

Serves 12

PUMPKIN MIXTURE
1/2 cup sugar
1/2 cup brown sugar, packed
1 teaspoon baking powder
1 teaspoon baking soda
2 teaspoons ground cloves
1 teaspoon allspice
2 teaspoons nutmeg
1 teaspoon cinnamon
2 teaspoons salt
1 1/4 cups flour
1/2 cup vegetable oil

3 eggs
5 ounces sweetened condensed milk
3 1/2 cups pumpkin

CREAM CHEESE SWIRL
12 ounces cream cheese, softened
1 1/2 cups sugar
2 eggs
1/2 cup sour cream
1 teaspoon vanilla
dash of salt

Preheat oven to 350 degrees. Grease and flour a 9x13-inch baking pan. In a large mixing bowl, combine the sugar, brown sugar, baking powder, baking soda, cloves, allspice, nutmeg, cinnamon, salt and flour. In a separate bowl, stir together the oil, eggs milk and pumpkin. Add the wet ingredients into the dry ingredients and mix well.

For the cream cheese swirl, in a mixing bowl, whip together cream cheese and sugar. Blend in the eggs, sour cream, vanilla and salt. Dollop the cream cheese mixture into the pumpkin batter and gently swirl the batters together, just enough to create a marbled appearance. Bake for 40 - 50 minutes. ¡O!¡

Great Mimi's Gingerbread Boys

Makes 4 dozen cookies

5 1/2 cups flour
1 Tablespoon baking soda
2 teaspoons salt
3/4 teaspoon ground ginger
1 teaspoon cinnamon
1 cup shortening

1 cup sugar
1 egg, beaten
1/2 teaspoon vanilla
1 cup dark molasses
1/2 cup brewed strong coffee

In a large bowl, sift together flour, soda, salt, ginger and cinnamon. In another bowl, cream shortening, adding sugar gradually. Beat until fluffy then add egg and vanilla. Stir in molasses and coffee. Add the sifted dry ingredients to the butter mixture. Mix well. Chill for 2 hours. Preheat oven to 400 degrees. Roll out the dough, 1/4-inch thick on a lightly floured board. Cut with a cookie cutter. Bake on greased sheets for 8 - 10 minutes.

This recipe makes a bunch of lovely gingerbread men. Before baking, place currants for the eyes and cinnamon imperials for the buttons. They may also be frosted.

Best Molasses Cookies
Makes 4 dozen cookies

3/4 cup butter, melted and cooled
2 cups sugar
1/2 cup blackstrap molasses
2 eggs
3 1/2 cups flour
4 teaspoons baking powder

1 teaspoon ground cloves
1 teaspoon ground ginger
1 teaspoon cinnamon
1 teaspoon salt
1/2 cup sugar, for coating

In a bowl, combine butter, sugar, molasses and eggs. Beat until fluffy. In a separate bowl, combine flour, baking powder, cloves, ginger, cinnamon and salt. Add dry ingredients to wet ingredients, mixing on low speed, until combined. Refrigerate the dough for 1 hour. Preheat oven to 350 degrees. Form a ball with 1 Tablespoon of dough and roll in 1/2 cup sugar. Place on cookie sheet and bake for 10 minutes. Cool on a wire rack.

Chocolate Caramel Candy Cookies
Makes 4 dozen cookies

1 cup sugar
1 cup brown sugar, packed
1 cup butter
2 teaspoons vanilla
2 eggs
2 1/2 cups flour

3/4 cup cocoa
1 teaspoon baking soda
1 (9 oz) package Rolo chocolate
   caramels, unwrapped
1/4 cup sugar, for coating

Preheat oven to 375 degrees. In a large bowl, beat together sugars and butter until fluffy. Add vanilla and eggs and mix well. Gradually add flour, cocoa and baking soda to mixture. Blend well. With floured hands, shape 1 Tablespoon cookie dough around each caramel candy, covering completely. Roll dough in sugar, covering completely. Bake for 7 minutes, until set and slightly cracked. Cool two minutes and remove to wire racks.

Best served when warm.

Christmas Biscotti

Makes 3 dozen cookies

1/4 cup olive oil
3/4 cup sugar
2 teaspoons vanilla
1 teaspoon almond extract
2 medium eggs

1 3/4 cups flour
1/4 teaspoon salt
1 teaspoon baking powder
3/4 cup dried cranberries
1 1/2 cups shelled pistachios

Preheat the oven to 300 degrees. In a large bowl, mix oil and sugar together until well blended. Add the vanilla and almond extract. Beat in the eggs. In a separate bowl, combine the flour, salt and baking powder. Gradually add the dry ingredients into the egg mixture. Fold in cranberries and pistachios. The dough will be very stiff.

Divide the dough in half and form two logs, 12x3-inches, on a parchment lined cookie sheet. The dough will be very sticky. Keep a bowl of cool water nearby and dip hands to keep the dough from sticking as you form the logs. Bake for 35 minutes, until the logs are light brown. Remove from oven and place on a cooling rack. Reduce the oven temperature to 275 degrees. After cooling 10 minutes, use a serrated knife to cut the logs into diagonal 1-inch slices. Turn the slices flat on the parchment and return to the oven for 12 - 18 minutes or until the exposed side becomes dry. Place on a rack to cool completely. Store in a cool and dry place.

Snickerdoodle Biscotti

Makes 2 1/2 dozen cookies

1/4 cup butter
1 cup sugar
3 eggs
1 teaspoon vanilla
2 3/4 cups flour

1 teaspoon baking powder
3/4 cup cinnamon chips
1/2 cup sugar
1 teaspoon cinnamon

Preheat oven to 350 degrees. In a large bowl, cream together butter and sugar until fluffy. Add eggs and vanilla. Mix in flour and baking powder and stir in cinnamon chips. Turn out the dough onto a floured surface and knead 8 to 10 times. Divide the dough in half and roll into logs. Flatten to 1 inch and place on greased baking sheets. Combine 1/2 cup sugar with cinnamon and sprinkle each loaf. Bake for 20 minutes or until tester comes out clean. Remove from the oven and cool slightly. Cut the loaves into 1/2-inch slices. Place the slices, cut-side up, back on the baking sheet and return to the hot oven. Turn off oven. Leave the biscotti in the oven overnight until cooled. Store in tightly covered container.

Cinnamon chips are a small baking chip found with the chocolate chips. They are most often seen around the holidays.

Humidity may significantly affect the baking time required to dry the sliced biscotti. Adjust the second baking time as needed until no longer chewy. You may need to turn the slices over to fully dry.

Lemon Biscotti with Sour Lemon Drizzle

Makes 2 1/2 dozen cookies

1/4 cup butter, softened
1 cup sugar
3 eggs
1 Tablespoon lemon rind, grated
2 Tablespoons lemon juice, divided

3 teaspoons lemon extract, divided
2 3/4 cups flour
1 Tablespoon baking powder
2/3 cup powdered sugar

Preheat oven to 350 degrees. In a large bowl, cream together butter and sugar until fluffy. Add eggs, lemon rind, 1 Tablespoon lemon juice and 1 1/2 teaspoons lemon extract. Mix in flour and baking powder. Turn out the dough onto to a floured surface and knead 8 to 10 times. Divide the dough in half and roll into logs. Flatten to 1 inch and place on greased baking sheets. Bake for 20 minutes or until tester comes out clean. Remove from the oven and cool slightly. Cut the loaves into 1/2-inch slices. Place the slices, cut-side up, back on the baking sheet and return to the hot oven. Turn off oven. Leave the biscotti in the oven overnight until cooled. For the glaze, in a small bowl, combine 1 Tablespoon lemon juice and 1 1/2 teaspoons lemon extract with the powdered sugar. Drizzle over the top of the cooled biscotti. Store in tightly covered container.

Walnut Lace Cookies

Makes 6 dozen cookies

1/2 cup unsalted butter
1/2 cup brown sugar, packed
1/3 cup light corn syrup
1/2 teaspoon salt
1 cup chopped walnuts

1/2 cup flour
1/2 cup old fashioned oats
1 teaspoon vanilla extract

Preheat oven to 350 degrees. Grease 2 baking sheets. In a medium saucepan, combine butter, brown sugar, corn syrup and salt. Bring to a boil over medium-high heat, stirring constantly. Remove from heat and stir in the walnuts, flour, oats and vanilla. Cool slightly. Drop mixture by level teaspoonfuls onto prepared sheets, spacing 3 inches apart. Bake 6 to 7 minutes until golden. Cool 2 minutes on sheets then transfer to wire racks to cool. Do not overlap cookies.

These cookies are best when made on a cool, dry day. When baked, these cookies spread quite a bit forming lacy wafers.

Applesauce Jumbles

Makes 5 dozen cookies

2 3/4 cups flour
1 1/2 cups brown sugar, packed
1 teaspoon salt
1/2 teaspoon baking soda
3/4 cup applesauce
1/2 cup shortening
2 eggs
1 teaspoon cinnamon
1 teaspoon vanilla

1 cup chocolate chips
1 cup chopped walnuts

BROWNED BUTTER GLAZE
1/3 cup butter
2 cups powdered sugar
1/2 teaspoon vanilla
2 - 4 Tablespoons hot water

Preheat oven to 350 degrees. Lightly grease cookie sheets. In a large bowl, combine flour, brown sugar, salt, soda, applesauce, shortening, eggs, cinnamon and vanilla. Stir until ingredients are creamy and completely mixed. Fold in chocolate chips and nuts. Drop level Tablespoons, 2 inches apart, onto cookie sheets. Bake 10 minutes. Cool on a wire rack.

For the Browned Butter Glaze, in a saucepan, melt butter over low heat until golden brown. Remove from heat. Blend in powdered sugar, vanilla and enough hot water to reach desired consistency. Spread warm glaze quickly over cooled cookies.

The glaze sets quickly so it is important that the cookies are cool and the glaze spread quickly.

Pistachio Lemon Cookies

Makes 4 - 5 dozen cookies

3/4 cup butter, softened
1 cup sugar, divided
1 egg
1 Tablespoon lemon zest
1 1/2 Tablespoons lemon juice

2 cups flour
1/2 teaspoon baking soda
1/4 teaspoon salt
1 cup pistachios, chopped

In a bowl, cream together butter and 3/4 cup of sugar until fluffy. Beat in egg. Add lemon zest and lemon juice. In a separate bowl, sift together flour, baking soda and salt. Blend into butter mixture. Stir until thoroughly combined. Wrap dough in plastic wrap and chill for 1 hour. Preheat oven to 350 degrees. In a small bowl, combine pistachios and remaining 1/4 cup sugar. Shape dough into 1-inch balls. Press balls into pistachio-sugar mix, turning to coat. Place on an ungreased cookie sheet and bake 10 - 12 minutes until lightly brown.

Northrup Jones Chocolate Chip Cookies

Makes 10 dozen cookies

2 1/8 cups butter or shortening, softened
1 1/8 cups brown sugar, packed
1 1/2 cups sugar
4 eggs, beaten
1/4 cup hot water
4 1/2 cups flour

1 Tablespoon baking soda
1 Tablespoon vanilla
1 (12 oz) package chocolate chips
1/2 pound chopped nuts, pecans or
walnuts

Preheat oven to 375 degrees. In a bowl, cream together butter and sugars. Add eggs, then hot water. In a separate bowl, combine flour and soda. Add in batches to the wet ingredients. Beat in the vanilla. Fold in the chips and nuts. Drop onto greased cookie sheets. Bake for 10 - 12 minutes. |O!|

Chris' Cookies

Makes 4 - 5 dozen

2 1/2 cups old fashioned oats
1 cup unsalted butter
2 eggs
1 cup sugar
1 cup brown sugar, packed
1 teaspoon vanilla
1 teaspoon baking powder

1 teaspoon baking soda
1/2 teaspoon salt
2 cups flour
1 (12 oz) package peanut butter chips
1 (12 oz) package semi-sweet chocolate
chips

Preheat oven to 375 degrees. Place oatmeal in a food processor and process until well ground. Set aside. In a bowl, beat together butter, eggs, and sugars until fluffy. Add vanilla, baking powder, baking soda and salt. Add ground oatmeal, then flour. Stir in peanut butter and chocolate chips. The batter will be thick. Drop by rounded teaspoons onto ungreased cookie sheets. Bake for 8 - 10 minutes. Remove from oven and let cool on cookie sheets a few minutes before removing to wire racks.

These are wonderful treats frozen. Slightly underbake and put them in freezer bags.

LOCAL RESOURCE GUIDE

Absolutely Fresh Seafood, 1218 South 119th Street Omaha, NE 68144 (402)827-4376 and 1727 Leavenworth Street, Omaha, NE 68102 (402)345-5057
- Largest selection of seafood in the Midwest

Aki Oriental Foods and Gifts, 4425 South 84th Street, Omaha, NE 68127, (402) 339-2671
- Asian food specialties

Ferd's Bake Shop, 1620 Vinton Street, Omaha, NE 68108 (402) 341-6204
- Kolaches and beautiful breads and rolls

Jacobo's Grocery, 4621 South 24th Street, Omaha, NE 68107 (402) 733-9009
- Latin grocery with meats and bakery

Marino's Grocery, 1716 South 13th Street, Omaha, NE 68108, (402) 341-5217
- Italian specialty items, meats and cheeses

Mediterranean Foods, Inc., 3025 South 83rd Plaza, Omaha, NE 68124 (South of Center) (402) 390-0120
- Oils, vinegars, bulk spices, olives, cheeses and pantry items

Omaha Farmer's Market, Saturdays, May through October, 11th and Jackson Streets 8 a.m. until 12:30 p.m. and Wednesdays, June through September, 11th and Howard Streets, 3 until 7 p.m. www.omahafarmersmarket.com
- Fresh produce, meats and flowers

New Asian Food Mart, 4615 South 26th Street, Omaha, NE 68107 (402) 731-6300

PHG (Premium Home and Garden), 16050 Wright Plaza Omaha, NE 68130 (402) 330-6900
www.PremiumHG.com
- A wide variety of wines, liquors, craft beers, gourmet tools and foods, cutlery and culinary accessories, and home accessories. Sioux Z Wow Marinade in stock.

Plum Creek Farms, Dean and Amy Dvorak Burchard, NE (402) 696-4535 or dvorak23@alltel.net
All About Chicken: freshest chicken and eggs

Stoysich House of Sausage, 2532 South 24th Street, Omaha, NE 68108 (402) 341-7260
- Large sausage selection, cheeses, deli, mustards, sauces

Thunderbird Salad Dressing, available at HyVee grocery stores or by calling (402) 614-FOOD or going to www.v-cuisine.com

Whole Foods Market, 10020 Regency Circle, Omaha, NE 68114 (402) 393-1200
- The world's largest retailer of natural and organic foods, with a wide selection of international foods

Wild Oats Natural Marketplace, 7801 Dodge Street Omaha, NE 68114 (402) 397-5047 and Village Pointe Shopping Center, 225 North 170th Street, Omaha, NE 68118 (402) 289-2205
- Natural and organic food center

Wohlner's Grocery, 5205 Leavenworth Street, Omaha, NE 68106 (402) 551-6875
- Fine meats and wines

WEB

www.clubsauce.com	Find Demi Glace Gold, for Johnny's Short Ribs
www.epicurious.com	Recipes, menus, cooking dictionary, shopping and more
www.maytagdairyfarms.com	For Maytag Blue Cheese or 1-800-247-2458
www.omahasteaks.com	The name says it all.
www.penzys.com	Penzy Spices, traditional spices and unique spice blends
www.plantersseed.com	The Planters Seed and Spice Company, garden seeds, plants and bulk spices
www.siouxzwow.com	Order our favorite gourmet marinade, Sioux Z Wow

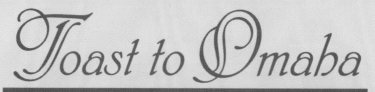

Toast to Omaha
Monthly Menu Suggestions

January - Winter Pre-game Dinner
Southwest Salsa Salad 75
Tex-Mex Sloppy Joes 125
Baked Sweet Potato Fries 92
Very Rich Everything Bars 214

February - A Romantic Dinner at Home
Caramelized Leek and Goat Cheese Crostini 30
Blackstone Hotel's Caesar Salad Maitre d'Governor 72
Lobster Corn Chowder 51
Cracked Pepper Crusted New York Strip with Whiskey Cream Sauce 122
Roasted Vidalia Onion Tarts 93
Chocolate Pistachio Phyllo Rolls 192

March - Company's Coming
Smokey Cheese Pear Appetizer 19
Spring Strawberry Spinach Salad 64
Pecan Crusted Tilapia 170
Mushroom Pilaf 95
French Bread with Garlic Aioli 181
Black Russian Cake 195

April - A Taste of Asia
Vietnamese Shrimp Rolls 21
Mandarin Spinach Salad 63
Slow Roasted Pork Roast with Hoisin 149
Thai Pepper's Fresh Mango Pie 188

May - Ladies Luncheon Shower
Parmesan Peppercorn Dip 15
Raspberry Lemonade 40
Savory Chilled Chicken Salad 73
Blueberry-Lemon Scones 104
Wonders of the World Bars 210

June - Backyard Summer Cookout after a Baseball Game
Champions Run Hummus Dip 14
Colorful Pepper Tomato Salsa 18
Beer Margaritas 41
Summer Salad 65
Chipotle Honey Lime Grilled Chicken 159
Baked Potatoes on the Grill 91
Buttermilk Brownies 212

July - Picnic at Jazz on the Green or Shakespeare on the Green

Italian Marinated Cheese 13
Chilled Herb Asparagus 87
Scrumptious Cornbread Salad 62
Tuscan Tortellini Salad 66
Caribbean Jerk Chicken 162
Chris' Cookies 222

August - Brunch Buffet on the Boat

Green Salad with Hilltop House Roquefort Dressing 78
Roasted Apricot Chicken 165
Asparagus-Prosciutto Rolls 82
Layered Mashed Potatoes and Mushrooms 91
Mother's Coffee Cake 102

September - Football Tailgate Party

Snappy Kickin' Guacamole 12
Mini Maytag Blue Cheese Burgers 35
Vivace's Tomato Bisque 48
Royal Deli Salad and Dressing 64
South of the Border Grilled Corn on the Cob 83
Butterscotch Pecan Bars 212

October - Pumpkin Carving Party

Apple Brickle Dip 202
Pumpkin Dip 203
Buffalo Chicken Dip 23
Upstream Brewing Company's Smoked Gouda Beer Soup 59
Grilled Honey Mustard Maple Pork Chops 150
Carrot Ring 93
Nebraska Fresh Crop Apple Cake 196

November - Home for the Holidays Family Feast

Jolly Holiday Spread 18
Curried Pumpkin Soup 49
Apple and Brie Chicken Breasts with Cider Sauce 166
Grilled Ham Steaks 156
Brandied Cranberries 142
Roasted Green Beans 84
Sweet Potatoes in Orange Cups 88
Bourbon Chocolate Pecan Pie 191

December - Holiday Open House Party

Cosmopolitan Cocktails 42
Festive Feta Dip 16
Marinated Shrimp and Pepper 20
Classic Crab Fondue 23
Spin Art Dip 24
Brie with Bourbon Walnut Sauce 25
Crunchy Pork Bites 34
Nut Brittle 216

PANTRY ITEMS

REFRIGERATOR	FREEZER	PRODUCE	DRY GOODS
Eggs	Ice	White potatoes	All-purpose flour
Butter or margarine	Vegetables	Sweet potatoes	Whole wheat flour (Keep in freezer for longer shelf life)
Milk	Ground beef	Onions	
Buttermilk	Whole chicken	Red onions	
Whipping cream	Boneless chicken breasts	Green onion	Cake flour
Sour cream	Ground turkey	Shallot	Cornmeal
Cream cheese	Boneless pork chops	Garlic	Cornmeal muffin mix
Mild cheese	Link and/or bulk sausage	Ginger root	Granulated sugar
Sharp cheese	Bacon	Sweet peppers	Confectioner's sugar
Mozzarella	Breads and rolls	Hot peppers	Brown sugar
Parmesan cheese	Prebaked pizza shells	Fresh mushrooms	Baking soda
Romano cheese	Fresh breadcrumbs	Dried mushrooms	Baking powder
Feta cheese	Bread cubes	Lettuce	Yeast (Keep in freezer for longer shelf life)
Blue or Roquefort cheese	Puff pastry	Cucumbers	
Cottage cheese	Phyllo dough	Tomatoes	Cornstarch
Plain yogurt	Flour tortillas	Carrots	Unsweetened cocoa
Mayonnaise	Corn tortillas	Celery	Unsweetened chocolate
Yellow mustard	Pierogies	Avocados	Semi or bitter sweet chocolate
Dijon mustard	Stuffed pasta	Tomatillos	
Worcestershire sauce	Hors d'ouevres	Apples	German chocolate
Steak sauce	Beef stock	Oranges	Biscuit mix
Horseradish	Chicken stock	Lemons	Minute tapioca
Minced garlic	Fish stock	Limes	Raisins
Ketchup	Non-dairy topping	Parsley	Dried cranberries
Pickle relish	Walnuts	Cilantro	Vegetable shortening
Hot pepper pickles	Pecans	Bananas	Oatmeal
Green olives	Almonds		Cereal
Ripe olives	Peanuts		Crackers
Kalamata olives	Ice cream or frozen yogurt		Dried breadcrumbs
Assorted pickles	Sherbert		Panko flakes (Japanese breadcrumbs)
Pesto sauce	Frozen fruits		Coconut flakes
Salsa			Pasta (such as):
Salsa verde			Penne or ziti
Jellies or jams			Spaghetti
Apple butter			Angel hair
Refrigerator biscuits			Fettuccini
Bacon (For longer shelf life, store in freezer)			Linguini
			Ditalini
Fat back (For longer shelf life, store in freezer)			Lasagna
			Orzo
Pancetta and/or prosciutto (For longer shelf life, store in freezer)			Elbows
			Egg noodles
			Long grain rice
			Brown rice
			Wild rice
			Arborio rice
			Barley
			Kidney beans
			Great Northern beans
			Lentils
			Split peas
			Onion soup mix
			Dried corn

PANTRY ITEMS

CANNED / BOTTLED

- Whole tomatoes
- Tomato paste
- Tomato puree
- Tomato sauce
- Crushed tomatoes
- Chicken broth
- Condensed cream of mushroom soup
- Canned fruits
- Mandarin oranges
- Lemon juice
- Lime juice
- Pie fillings
- Worcestershire sauce
- Soy sauce
- Liquid smoke
- Dijon mustard
- Barbeque sauce
- Enchilada sauce
- Tuna
- Anchovies
- Anchovy paste
- Green beans
- Asparagus
- Chick peas
- Kidney beans
- Navy beans
- Refried beans
- Creamed corn
- Whole kernel corn
- Evaporated milk
- Sweetened condensed milk
- Coconut milk
- Peanut butter
- Canned chiles
- Chipotle chiles in adobo sauce
- Assorted pickles
- Olives
- Capers
- Artichoke hearts
- Water chestnuts
- Chopped pimentos
- Hoisin sauce
- Fish sauce
- Oyster sauce
- Garlic chili sauce

CANNED / BOTTLED

- Sioux-Z-Wow Marinade (see resource guide)
- Salsa
- Light corn syrup
- Dark corn syrup
- Molasses
- Pure maple syrup
- Pancake syrup
- Honey
- Pure vanilla
- Almond flavoring
- Bouillon
- Hot sauce
- Grated cheese

VINEGAR / OIL

- Extra-Virgin olive oil
- Canola oil
- Peanut oil
- Sesame oil
- Grapeseed oil
- Chili oil
- Olive oil spray
- Cooking oil spray
- Red wine vinegar
- Balsamic vinegar
- Rice vinegar
- Malt vinegar
- White distilled vinegar
- Cider vinegar

SPIRITS

- Dry red wine
- Dry white wine
- Port wine
- Vermouth
- Brandy or Cognac
- Dry sherry
- Gin
- Rum
- Vodka
- Scotch
- Bourbon
- Tequila
- Assorted liqueurs
- Beer

DRIED HERBS

- Parsley
- Oregano
- Basil
- Rosemary
- Thyme
- Rubbed sage
- Marjoram
- Cilantro
- Bay leaves
- Chives
- Savory
- Tarragon
- Dill weed
- Dill seed
- Onion powder
- Minced onions
- Garlic powder
- Minced garlic

SPICES

- Peppercorns
- Coarse salt
- Iodized salt
- Seasoned salt
- Cinnamon sticks
- Ground cinnamon
- Ground and/or whole nutmeg
- Ground cloves
- Whole cloves
- Ground turmeric
- Ground allspice
- Ground ginger
- Coriander
- Cardamom
- Cream of Tartar
- Poppy seeds
- Sesame seeds
- Ground mace
- Pickling spice
- Mustard seed
- Dry mustard
- Cayenne pepper
- Celery seed
- Caraway seeds
- Fennel seeds
- Curry powder
- Ground cumin
- Ground sweet paprika
- Chili powder
- Ancho chile powder
- Chipotle chile powder
- Cajun seasoning blend
- Southwest seasoning blend
- Jerk seasoning blend
- Steak seasoning blend
- Kosher salt
- Sea salt
- Lemon Pepper

ACKNOWLEDGEMENTS

Toast to Omaha could never have been realized without the dedication and shared vision of countless individuals. Our deep gratitude goes to all those listed here and to anyone we may have inadvertently failed to mention. We thank you for your generous contributions of time, talent, energy and resources.

Tony and Valerie Abbott, owners, The French Café
Ann Marie Abboud
Kathy Alber
Jane Alesch
Alesha Alvis
Linda Matson Andersen
Janet Anderson
Sandi Anderson
Kristopher Anderzhon
Cathy Arnold
Jeff Arney
Jamie Baker
Lois Baldwin
Jennifer Bartelt
Anne Baxter
Pam Beardslee
Teresa Bednar
Marilyn Bentz
Mary Schimmel Bernstein
Jennifer Bettger
Andrea Billeter
Julie Billeter
Abby Blair
Shawna Blair
Diane Boysen
Lesley Brandt
Crystal Brislen
Jameson Bock
Paula Boggust
Anne Bothe
Dana Boyle
Kathryn Brayton
Ashley Broekemeier
Jeff Brown, executive chef, Jams
Pam Brown
Dawn Buchanan
Lori Bucholz
Danielle Bunz
Kathy Bunz
Sarah Burdick
Karen Burkley
Karen Burmood
Stephanie Bush
Jill Bydalek
Pipi Campbell Peterson

Chuck and Randi Caniglia, Caniglia's Venice Inn
Jody Carstens
Anne Carter
Kathy Cashell
Ruth Cashell
Pam Cates
Brenda Christensen
Jen Churilla
Julie Chytil
Jennifer Coco, Flatiron Café
Gil Cohen
Sue Conine
Kristy Cote
Mike Couvillion
Jessica Covi
Pam Coyle
Erin Daly
Helen Daly
Scott and Trudy Darling
Marian Davenport
Caitlin Davis
Kristi Davis
The Devonshire Club
Catherine Dick
Mary Dobleman
Lucy Dogger
Don Doty, owner, Taste Restaurant
Mary Dowd
Kelli Draper
Jeanne Dudzinski
Dorothy Due
Melissa Duffy
Deborah Duggan
Courtney Dunbar
Holly Dunning
Janet Egan
Yvette Eike
Sharon Emery
Erin Emmons
Reed Empson, chef de cuisine, M's Pub
Ron Samuelson
Ryan Eckert
JoAnne Eurich
Stephanie Ewen
Nancy Falk
Betty Feltman

Mary Jo Ferrara Klusmine
Joan Elizabeth Fink-Arney
Denise Fitzgerald
Jennifer Flanagan
Sally Foix
Lynne Foster
Robyn Freeman
Jamie Friedland
Patty Ganzer
Hector Garcia
Tony Gentile, executive chef, RoJA Mexican Grill and Margarita Bar
Kristine Gerber
Corrine Giggee
Tamara Giitter
Judy Gilliard
Phyllis Glazer
Mimi Gleason
John Gobel, Dundee Dell
Gabrielle Gomez-Tabor
Brenda Grabill
JoAnn Grabill
Kate Grabill
Gail Graeve
Melissa Grant
Lisa Gravelle
Brooke Gravett
Michele Grewcock
Claudia Grisnik, owner & chef, Taxi's Grille and Bar
Brooke Gruwell
Mary Kay Gustafson
Li Gwatkin
J.P. Haas
Susanne Haas
Laura Hale
Victoria Halgren
Denie Hall, owner, Fernando's Café and Cantina
Traci Hancock
Bea Haney
Diane Hansen

Stephanie Hansen
Cari Harris
Christine Harry
Debbie Hart
Verna Headley
Rachel Heese
Elizabeth Hendricks
Norma Hill Baker
Pam Hoesing
Leslie W. Hosford
Dave Holoch
Shannon Hoy
Tracie Hrnicek
Julie Huard
Nancy Hultquist
Rosalie Hunter
Cindy Irvine
Kristi Jacobs
Carrie Jenkins
Anne Jetter
Adeline Johnson
Mary Johnson
Kim Johnson
Jeanie Jones
Jennifer Joseph
Debbi Josephson
Lisa Kaplan
Nina Kay, Thai Pepper
Sally Kawa, Johnny's Cafe
Kerry Keelan Dineen, Spintrific Web Design
Carol Keller
Charlie Keller, chef, Sacramento Supper Club
Anne Kelley
Kara Kelley
Matthew Kellie, The Tasting Room
Tracy Kempkes
Kurt Kenkel, executive chef, Blue Sushi Sake Grill
Sheri Kennedy
Janet Kiger
MaryAnn Knappenberger
Cheryl Knudsen

Amy Knuth
Rhonda Kohl
Anne Krayer
JoAnn Kratky
Pam Krecek
Wendi Kroeger
Kim Lahman
Patty Landen
Brenda Langenberg
Julie Larsen
Sheri and Randy Leaders
Debra Leif
Kristin Lewis
Sage Lewis
Julie Liakos
Sandy Linden
Julie Linquata
Kristen Long
Marietta Luellen
Jackie Lund
Julie Lyons
Jodie Mackintosh
Ann Marcotte
Kathy Martin
Leslie Mayo
Isabel McCullought
Sarah McGowan
Jan McKenzie
Scott McKenzie
Sherry McLochlin
Kathy McPherson
Nancy Meadows
Jasmin Medin
Ann Mellen
Anne Medlock
Lori Meier
James Meliney, executive chef, Vivace
Yves Menard, owner, Charlie's on the Lake
Jenny Milligan
Nancy Mitchell
Julie Mowat
Barbara Mueksch
Darlene Mueller
Erin Murnan
National Beef Cookoff Organization

- Kathy Neary
- Karen Nelsen
- Jolaine Nielsen
- Nancy Nielsen
- Christine Nikunen
- Kerri Nikunen
- Linda Nordhues
- Vicki Novak
- Julie Oberlies
- Sherri Olson
- Ginny Lee
- Beth Ochsner
- Carla Ohm
- Sheryl Orlich
- Claire Ossino
- Lisa Owen
- Susan Pape
- Jennifer Pansing
- Mary Patterson
- Dana Patterson
- Angela Patterson
- Laraine Peck
- Beth Pedersen
- Janice Pehrson
- Jennifer Peterson
- Carol Pfannenstiel
- Brandi Popovich
- Ron Popp, Wheatfields Catering Company
- Patty Powles
- Nancy Prauner
- Jean Prendergast
- Francie Prier
- Kolleen Quinn
- Mary Lynn Reiser
- Buffy Ricceri
- Julia Rhodes
- Kyle Robino
- Mike Robino
- Karen Rohweder
- Mary Ruff
- Lisa Russell
- Gabrielle Ryan
- Kay Sandoz
- Angie Schendt
- Cheryl Schendt
- Roy Schendt
- Deb Schmadeke
- Heidi Schneiderman
- Jenny Schulte
- Meghan Shannon
- Jenny Shaw
- Jacklyn Sherrod
- Joan Shields
- Kathy Shonsey
- Shelley Siemers
- Kim Simon
- Julie Skradski
- Robin Skutt
- Carol Smith
- Jeff Snow, Catering Creations
- Peggy Sokol
- Patricia Solko
- Beatrice Sommer
- Columbo Lodge Sons of Italy
- Terri Sortino
- Victoria Stamm
- Mary Lee Steinfeldt
- Christine Stevens
- Libby Stiles
- Karen Stillwagon
- Christine Stokes
- Allen Stoneking
- Joan Streett
- Kathleen Strott
- Kelley Stuckey
- Nessie Swedlund
- Julie Takechi
- Sheila Tanner-Lincoln
- Erika Teutsch
- Sybil Thailing Olson
- Robyn Thelander
- Megan Thom
- Judy Thomas
- Amy Thomas
- Mac Thompson, owner & chef, Taxi's Grille and Bar
- Marilyn Thompson
- Sara Thompson
- Andrea Tonniges, Sweet Magnolias
- Wendy Townley
- Sue Trout
- Maureen Turner
- Rosalie Tynan
- John Ursick, executive chef, Stokes Grill and Bar
- Chris Vogt
- Krista Volzke
- Laura Wakefield
- Vicki Wampler
- Sharon Warga
- Joy Watanabe
- Lois Waterman
- Mary Watson
- Sandy Watson
- Lauren Watson
- Anne Thorne Weaver
- Tam Webb
- Kathy Wells
- Jackie Werner
- Richard White
- Nancy Whitted
- Jeanine Williams
- Kim Williams
- Andrea Wilson
- Stacy Wilson
- Mary Wilson
- Josephine Wilson, chef, Champions Club
- Norma Yin, owner, Hiro
- Brian Younglove, executive chef, The French Cafe
- Jennifer Zatechka
- Susan Zeilinger
- Linda Zimmerman

Also thank you to the following individuals who provided information, stories, photographs and memorabilia for the restaurant sections.

- Linda Matson Andersen
- Mary Bernstein
- Joanne Ferguson Cavanaugh, Omaha Public Library
- John Covi, Son's of Italy
- Scott and Trudy Darling
- Paul Goebel
- Bill Gonzalez, Durham Western
- Heritage Museum
- The Gorat Family
- Mary Johnson
- Bill and Anita Kratville
- Mary Landen
- Tony "Tange"
- Marcuccio
- Lou Marcuzzo
- Harold Norman
- Gary Rosenberg, Douglas County Historical Society
- Joe Villella
- Ann Walding-Phillips, Omaha World-Herald

Thank you to the following restaurants who provided recipes.

INDEX

A

All-Star Spaghetti with Meat Sauce	139
Absolutely Fresh Seafood	223
Aki Oriental Food and Gifts	223

ALMONDS
Cold Cucumber Soup with Almonds, Tomatoes and Chives	58
Crispy Asian Salad	68
Magi Bread	104
Mother's Coffee Cake	102
Sweet Almond Cake	105

APPLE
Apple and Brie Chicken with Cider Sauce	166
Apple Brickle Dip	202
Apple Pecan Spice Cake	103
Apple Rhubarb Crisp	189
Applesauce Jumbles	221
Autumn Butternut Squash Soup	49
Maui's Best Caramel Apple Martini	43
M's Pub Cream of Caramelized Onion and Apple Soup with Brie	54
Mulligatawny Soup	52
Nebraska's Fresh Crop Apple Cake	196
Summer Salad	65
Sunny Glazed Apple Squares	213
Apple and Brie Chicken with Cider Sauce	166
Apple Brickle Dip	202
Apple Pecan Spice Cake	103
Apple Rhubarb Crisp	189
Applesauce Jumbles	221
Apricot-Mustard Glazed Sausage Links	111

ARTICHOKE
Hunter's Wild Rice Chicken Salad	68
Layered Artichoke Pepper Cheese Torte	16
Spinach Artichoke Supreme	94
SpinArt Dip	24
Asian Chicken Lettuce Wraps, Larb Gai	30
Asian Stir-Fried Chicken Slaw	70

ASPARAGUS
Asparagus Mushroom Chowder	50
Asparagus Prosciutto Rolls	82
Chilled Herb Asparagus	87
Crab, Shrimp and Asparagus Bake	109
Marinated Asparagus	94
Roasted Asparagus with Wild Mushrooms	82
Asparagus Mushroom Chowder	50
Asparagus Prosciutto Rolls	82
Autumn Butternut Squash Soup	49
Avgolemono, Greek Chicken and Rice Soup	53

AVOCADO
Avocado Mango Salsa	13
Crab Cakes with Avocado Tartar Sauce	176
Crunchy Chicken Wild Rice Salad	67
Fresh Tuna Salad with Avocado	63
Tasty Chicken and Tabbouleh Salad with Avocado	69
Avocado Mango Salsa	13

B

B & G Drive-in	130

BACON
Bacon, Mushroom and Egg Breakfast Bake	108
Baked Bean Medley	95
BLT Bites	20
Brussels Sprouts with Peppered Bacon	84
Scrumptious Cornbread Salad	62
Sweet and Spicy Bacon	111
Upstream Brewing Company Smoked Gouda Beer Soup	59
Zesty Cobb Salad	61
Bacon, Mushroom and Egg Breakfast Bake	108
Baguette Bread	184
Baked Bean Medley	95
Baked Heartland Apple Pork Chops	154
Baked Potatoes on the Grill	91
Baked Sweet Potato Fries	92
Balsamic Maple Chicken	163
Banana Bars	211

BANANAS
Banana Bars	211
Branana Muffins	179
Bangkok Pork with Peanut Sauce	148
Barbecued Salmon	173

BEANS
Baked Bean Medley	95
Black Bean and Corn Salsa	11
Fiesta Slaw	78
Herb Bean Soup	56
Southwest Salsa Salad	75
Becker, C.F.	206
Beef Tenderloin Fillets with Stilton Portabello Sauce	121

BEEF, GROUND
All-Star Spaghetti with Meat Sauce	139
Bistro Steak Soup	57
Dundee Dell Meatloaf	133
Eight Layer Casserole	133
Hilltop House Hamburger Steak	126
Mini Maytag Blue Cheese Burgers	35
Savory Vegetable Hamburger Soup	57
Sons of Italy Meatballs	124
Tex Mex Sloppy Joes	125
Wedding Meatballs	125
Wow Southwestern Tacos	126

BEEF, RIB
Johnny's Cafe Syrah Braised Short Ribs of Beef	127

BEEF, STEAK
Beef Tenderloin Fillets with Stilton Portabello Sauce	121

Blazin' Colorado Steaks 122
Cracked Pepper Crusted New York Strip with
Whiskey Cream Sauce 122
Grilled Espresso Steaks 123
Grilled Santa Maria Tri-Tips 121
Grilled Skirt Steak with Watercress Sauce 118
Johnny's Cafe Cajun Blackened
Strip Sirloin Steaks 123
Johnny's Cafe Frisco Marinade 117
Spicy Grilled Flank Steak 118
Steak House Salad 65
Wild West Beef and Smoked Gouda Grits 127
Beer Margaritas 41
Best Ever Coconut Pound Cake, The 198
Best Molasses Cookies 218

BEVERAGES
Beer Margaritas 41
Chocolate Martini 42
Cosmopolitan 42
Cranberry Cooler 40
Hpnotiq Breeze Martini 42
Mango Splash 43
Maui's Best Caramel Apple Martini 43
Midnight Coffee Express 43
Pineapple Tea 40
Raspberry Lemonade 40
Rum Coolers 44
Scooter's Junior League Morning Rush 41
Vodka Slushies 44
Watermelon Lemonade with Kiwi Splash 41
White Sangria 44
Bishop's Buffet 194
Bishop's Buffet Chocolate Pie 194
Bistro Steak Soup 57
Black Bread 184
Black Russian Cake 195
Blackstone Hotel 2, Front Cover, 119, 120
Blackstone Hotel Caesar Salad, Maitre d-Governor 72
Blackstone Hotel Crumb Coffee Cake 103
Blackstone Hotel Original Schimmel Cheesecake 205
Blazin' Colorado Steaks 122
BLT Bites 20
Blue Mussels 31

BLUEBERRIES
Blueberry-Lemon Scones 104
Triple Berry Bread 180
Blueberry-Lemon Scones 104
Bohemian Cafe, The 145
Bolamperti, Richard 201
Bourbon-Glazed Grilled Pork Chops 149
Brandeis 46
Bravo Potatoes 90

BREADS
Baguette Bread 184
Black Bread 184
Branana Muffins 179
Cheddar Bread 183
Coconut Bread 180
French Bread with Garlic Aioli 181

Gingerbread Muffins with Lemon Curd 178
Gruyére Bread Ring 182
Magi Bread 104
Paris Puffins 183
Pepper Herb Cheese Bread 181
Pumpkin Loaves with Caramel Glaze 179
Triple Berry Bread 180
Wheatfield's Ron's Cornbread 182

BRIE
Apple and Brie Chicken with Cider Sauce 166
Brie with Bourbon Walnut Sauce 25
M's Pub Cream of Caramelized Onion and
Apple Soup with Brie 54
Brie with Bourbon Walnut Sauce 25
Brine for Meat 153

BRUSCHETTA
Bruschetta Chicken 165
Caramelized Leek and Goat Cheese Crostini 30
Roasted Tri-color Pepper Bruschetta 28
Tasting Room Bruschetta 26
Tomato Tapenade Bruschetta 27
Brussels Sprouts with Peppered Bacon 84
Buda, Al 201
Buffalo Chicken Dip 23
Buffet, Warren 168
Buttermilk Brownies 212
Butterscotch Pecan Bars 212

C

CABBAGE
Asian Stir-Fried Chicken Slaw 70
Fiesta Slaw 78
French Café Shrimp Spring Rolls
with Sweet Chile Dipping Sauce, The 21
Mini Eggrolls with Zowie Dipping Sauce 33
RoJA Shrimp Alambres with Jicama Mandarin
Slaw and Ancho Chili Tartar Sauce 175
Taxi's Cabbage and Bleu Cheese Soup 48
Calumet Restaurant 5
Caniglia Tortellini Soup 136
Caniglia, Al 134
Caniglia, Chuck 134
Caniglia, Cirino 134
Caniglia, Eli 134, 136
Caniglia, Giovanna Franco 134
Caniglia, Jerry 134
Caniglia, Lou 134
Caniglia, Ross 134
Caniglia, Sebastiano "Yano" 134
Caniglia's 134, 135, 136
Cantoni, Louie 89
Cantoni's Grill 89
Caramelized Leek and Goat Cheese Crostini 30
Caramelized Onion Dip 15
Caramelized Sweet Onion Soup
with Goat Cheese Croutons 50
Caribbean Halibut with Vegetables 172
Caribbean Jerk Chicken 162
Carrot Cake 200

Carrot Ring 93
Cascio, Al 157
Cascio, Larry 157
Cascio's 157
Catering Creations Jalapeno
and Shrimp Stuffed Tomatoes 32
Catering Creations Stuffed Mushrooms 33

CAULIFLOWER
Herbed Roasted Cauliflower 85
Parmesan Crusted Cauliflower 86
Cave, The 38
Cha-Cha Cheesy Chicken Enchilada Dip 24
Champagne Mustard Chicken 160
Champions Run Hummus 14
Charlie's on the Lake Seafood Enchiladas 133
Cheddar Bread 183
Cheesy Dill Zucchini Bake 107

CHICKEN
Apple and Brie Chicken with Cider Sauce 166
Asian Chicken Lettuce Wraps, "Larb Gai" 30
Asian Stir-Fried Chicken Slaw 70
Avgolemono, Greek Chicken and Rice Soup 53
Balsamic Maple Chicken 163
Bruschetta Chicken 165
Buffalo Chicken Dip 23
Caribbean Jerk Chicken 162
Cha-Cha Cheesy Chicken Enchilada Dip 24
Champagne Mustard Chicken 160
Chicken Chutney Pasta Salad 73
Chicken Cheese Strudel in Puff Pastry 108
Chicken Fried Rice Skillet 96
Chicken Mushroom Lasagna 142
Chicken on the Ritz 166
Chicken Tortilla Soup 55
Chipotle Honey Lime Grilled Chicken 159
Crunchy Chicken Wild Rice Salad 67
Curried Chicken in Pastry Shells 110
Game Day Gumbo 54
Garlic and Honey Glazed Chicken Pizza 162
Greek Chicken with Capers, Raisins and Feta 164
Grilled Savory Barbeque Chicken 159
Hector's Enchiladas Guadalajara 131
Hunter's Wild Rice Chicken Salad 68
Italian Artichoke Tomato Chicken 163
Juiciest Ever Roasted Chicken
with Crispy Vegetables 164
Kaleidoscope Chicken Salad 71
Macadamia Nut Chicken Salad 74
Omaha Country Club Grilled Chicken
with Vegetable and Goat Cheese Tart 62
Orange Mushroom Peppered Chicken 160
Penne Alfio 138
Pepper Cheese Chicken Pinwheels 109
Picnic Parmesan Crusted Chicken Breastss 167
Roasted Apricot Chicken 165
Savory Chilled Chicken Salad 73
Smoked Chicken Chipotle Chowder 52
Southwest Salsa Salad 75

Spicy Asian Grilled Chicken 161
Sweet and Spicy Chicken Wings 29
Tandoori-Spiced Grilled Chicken
with Mint Yogurt Sauce 158
Tasty Chicken and Tabbouleh Salad
with Avocado 69
Teriyaki Beer Grilled Chicken 158
Thai Chicken Satay with Peanut Sauce
and Cucumber Relish 28
White Cheddar Chicken Chili 53
Wild Rice Chicken Casserole 107
Zesty Cobb Salad 61
Zingy Chicken Enchiladas 132
Chicken and Chutney Pasta Salad 73
Chicken Cheese Strudel in Puff Pastry 108
Chicken Fried Rice Skillet 96
Chicken Mushroom Lasagna 142
Chicken on the Ritz 166
Chicken Tortilla Soup 55
Chilled Herb Asparagus 87

CHOCOLATE
Bishop's Buffet Chocolate Pie 194
Black Russian Cake 195
Bourbon Chocolate Pecan Pie 191
Buttermilk Brownies 212
Caniglia's Venice Inn Fresh Raspberry Brownies 211
Chocolate Caramel Candy Cookies 218
Chocolate Chip Cheesecake 205
Chocolate Citrus Zucchini Cake 195
Chocolate Fig Pecan Bars 215
Chocolate Martini 42
Chocolate Oatmeal Cake 198
Chocolate Oatmeal Caramelitos 215
Chocolate Peanut Butter Bars 213
Chocolate Pistachio Phyllo Rolls 192
Chris' Cookies 222
Mint Chocolate Candy Cake 199
Northrup Jones Chocolate Chip Cookies 222
Peanutilicious Caramel Candy 216
Sweet Magnolia's Banana Chocolate Chip
Espresso Muffins 178
Very Rich Everything Bars 214
White Chocolate Bread Pudding 193
Wonders of the World Bars 210
Chocolate Caramel Candy Cookies 218
Chocolate Chip Cheesecake 205
Chocolate Citrus Zucchini Cake 195
Chocolate Fig Pecan Bars 215
Chocolate Martini 42
Chocolate Oatmeal Cake 198
Chocolate Oatmeal Caramelitos 215
Chocolate Peanut Butter Bars 213
Chocolate Pistachio Phyllo Rolls 192
Chorizo Breakfast Burritos
with Tomatillo Avocado Sauce 112
Chris' Cookies 222
Christmas Biscotti 219
Cinnamon Cake 200

Classic Crab Fondue 23

COCONUT
Best Ever Coconut Pound Cake, The 198
Coconut Bread 180
Coconut Cake with Caramel Rum Sauce 196
Magi Bread 104
Snappy Coconut-Crusted Chicken with Zowee
   Mustard Sauce 161
Coconut Bread 180
Coconut Cake with Caramel Rum Sauce 196

COFFEE
Extravagant Espresso Cream 204
Midnight Coffee Express 43
Mocha Ice Cream Cake 203
Scooter's Junior League Morning Rush 41
Sweet Magnolia's Banana Chocolate Chip
   Espresso Muffins 176
Cold Cantaloupe Soup 58
Cold Cucumber Soup with Almonds,
   Tomatoes and Chives 58
Colorful Curried Potatoes 89
Colorful Pepper Tomato Salsa 18

CORN
French Café Nebraska Sweet Corn Puree, The 83
Husker Harvest 96
Lobster Corn Chowder 51
Scrumptious Cornbread Salad 62
South of the Border Grilled Corn on the Cob 83
Cosmopolitan 42

CRAB
Classic Crab Fondue 23
Crab Cakes with Avocado Tartar Sauce 176
Crab Stuffed Flounder Rolls 171
Crab, Shrimp and Asparagus Bake 109
Curried Crab Salad Crostini 32
Flatiron Café Shitake Crab and Havarti Gratin 97
Sensational Stuffed Red Snapper 169
Wonton Cups 37
Crab Cakes with Avocado Tartar Sauce 176
Crab Stuffed Flounder Rolls 171
Crab, Shrimp and Asparagus Bake 109
Cracked Pepper Crusted New York Strip
   with Whisky Cream Sauce 122

CRANBERRIES
Brandied Cranberries 142
Christmas Biscotti 219
Nantucket Cranberry Pie 191
Cranberry Cooler 40
Creamy Spinach Salad 76
Crème Brûlé French Toast 105
Creole Dipping Sauce for Crudités 14
Crispy Asian Salad 68
Crunchy Chicken Wild Rice Salad 67
Crunchy Pork Bites 34

CUCUMBER
Cold Cucumber Soup
   with Almonds, Tomatoes and Chives 58
Greek Village Salad 67

Curried Chicken in Pastry Shells 110
Curried Crab Salad Crostini 32
Curried Pork Chops 150
Curried Pumpkin Soup 49

D

DATES
Magi Bread 104
Manchego Cheese and Smoked Walnut
   Stuffed Dates 31
Dijon Fish Fillet 176
Dixon's Café 48

DRESSING
Creamy Spinach Salad 76
Greek Village Salad 67
Hilltop House Roquefort Dressing 78
Hilltop House Russian Dressing 79
Royal Deli Salad and Dressing 64
Southwest Salsa Salad 75
Thai Pork Spring Salad 70
Thousand Island Dressing 120
Dundee Dell Meatloaf 133

E

Eggplant Caponata 10

EGGS
Bacon, Mushroom and Egg Breakfast Bake 108
Cheesy Dill Zucchini Bake 107
Chorizo Breakfast Burritos with Tomatillo
   Avocado Sauce 112
Crab, Shrimp and Asparagus Bake 109
English Muffin Breakfast Strata 113
Scottish Eggs 34
Eight Layer Casserole 133
Empress Gardens 4
English Muffin Breakfast Strata 113
Exotic Butter Lettuce Salad 74
Explosive Pork Corkscrew Pasta
   with Habanero Pesto 137
Extraordinary Oatmeal Cake 197
Extravagant Espresso Cream 204

F

Ferd's Bake Shop 223
Fernando's Pico de Gallo 10
Festive Feta Dip 16

FETA CHEESE
Festive Feta Dip 16
Greek Village Salad 67
Six Layer Bombay Cheese Spread 17
Fettuccini Carbonara 139
Fiesta Slaw 78
Fisher, Harold "Skee" 9
Flatiron Café Shitake Crab and Havarti Gratin 97
Foley, Patrick J. 9
Foley, Tom and Michelle 130
Fontenelle Hotel, The 208
Forty Niner, The 39

Fountain Room, The	150
French Bread with Garlic Aioli	181
French Café Dijon Herb Encrusted Rack of Lamb	
Adorned with Sage Whipped Blue Potato, The	128
French Café Nebraska Sweet Corn Puree, The	83
French Café Shrimp Spring Rolls with Sweet Chile	
Dipping Sauce, The	21
French Café, The	83
Fresh Herbed Potato Cakes	87
Fresh Raspberry Brownies	211
Fresh Tuna Salad with Avocado	63
Fruit Spinach Salad	72

G

Gainsforth, Gayle	130
Game Day Gumbo	54
Garlic and Honey Glazed Chicken Pizza	162
Gas Lamp, The	170
Gingerbread Muffins with Lemon Curd	178
Goebel, Paul	201
Golden Toque	201
Gorat, Louis and Nettie	168
Gorat, Pal and Shirley	168
Gorat's Steak House	168
Gorgonzola and Fresh Thyme Pasta	140
Great Mimi's Gingerbread Boys	217
Greek Chicken with Capers, Raisins and Feta	164
Greek Village Salad	67

GREEN BEANS

Mediterranean Green Beans	85
Roasted Green Beans	84
Grilled Espresso Steaks	123
Grilled Ham Steaks	156
Grilled Honey Mustard Maple Pork Chops	150
Grilled Red Onions	92
Grilled Santa Maria Tri-Tips	121
Grilled Savory Barbeque Chicken	159
Grilled Skirt Steak with Watercress Sauce	118
Gruyére Bread Ring	182

H

Ham and Cheese Chowder	56
Hansen, Alfred and Mabel	186
Harkert, Walter E.	47
Harket House	47
Hasselback Potatoes	90
Have, Lionel	62
Hawaiian Macadamia Sole	170
Hector's Enchiladas Guadalajara	131
Henshaw Hotel	90
Herb Bean Soup	56
Herb Crusted Pork Tenderloin	147
Herbed Roasted Cauliflower	85
Hilltop House Bavarian Mint Dessert	187
Hilltop House Hamburger Steak	126
Hilltop House Restaurant	186
Hilltop House Roquefort Dressing	78
Hilltop House Russian Dressing	79

Hiro Don Katsu (Pork Filet)	152
Hosman's Drive Inn	98
Hpnotiq Breeze Martini	42
Hunter's Wild Rice Chicken Salad	68
Husker Harvest	96

I

Incontro, Joe	201
Island Fish Bake	172
Italian Artichoke Tomato Chicken	163
Italian Gardens, The	11
Italian Marinated Cheese	13
Italian Sausage Vegetable Soup	55

J

Jack Holmes Ground Cow	125
Jacobo's Grocery	223
Jam's Red Chili Macaroni and Cheese	138
Joe Tess Place	67
Johnny's Cafe	116, 117
Johnny's Cafe Cajun Blackened	
Strip Sirloin Steaks	123
Johnny's Cafe Frisco Marinade	117
Johnny's Cafe Short Rib Seasoning	127
Johnny's Cafe Syrah Braised Short Ribs of Beef	127
Jolly Holiday Spread	18
Jones, Wilbur	101
Juiciest Ever Roasted Chicken	
with Crispy Potatoes	164

K

Kaleidoscope Chicken Salad	71
Kaufmann, Henry	100
Kaufmann's Pastry Shoppe	100
Kenny's Steak House	121
Krunch Kahlua Pecan Pie	192
Kulakofsky, Reuben	120

L

La Buvette's Terrine of Frog Legs	
with Sturgeon Caviar and Oven Dried Tomato	129
La Casa	139

LAMB

French Café Dijon Herb Encrusted Rack of Lamb	
Adorned with Sage Whipped Blue Potato, The	128
Layered Artichoke Pepper Cheese Torte	16
Layered Mashed Potatoes and Mushrooms	91
Le Café de Paris	11

LEMON

Lemon Biscotti with Sour Lemon Drizzle	220
Pistachio Lemon Cookies	221
Lemon Biscotti with Sour Lemon Drizzle	220
Liber, Ann and Josef	145
Lobster Corn Chowder	51
Loose-Meat Sandwich	130
Lorello, Ross	148
Ludwick, Lori	130

M

Macadamia Nut Chicken Salad	74
Magi Bread	104
Manchego Cheese and Smoked Walnut Stuffed Dates	31
Mandarin Spinach Salad	63

MANGO
Avocado Mango Salsa	13
Mango Splash	43
Salmon with Strawberry Mango Salsa	174
Spring Greens and Mango Salad	61
Thai Pepper's Fresh Mango Pie	188

Mango Splash	43
Marinated Asparagus	94
Marinated Citrus-Mushroom Salad	77
Marinated Shrimp and Peppers	20
Marino's Grocery	223
Matson, Raymond and Mildred	186
Maui's Best Caramel Apple Martini	43
Maytag Dairy Farms	223
Mediterranean Foods, Inc.	223
Mediterranean Green Beans	85
Merry-Go-Round Restaurant	98
Midnight Coffee Express	43
Mini Eggrolls with Zowie Dipping Sauce	33
Mini Grilled Cheese and Tomato Sandwiches	36
Mini Maytag Bleu Cheese Burgers	35
Mint Chocolate Candy Cake	199
Miso Glazed Salmon	173
Mocha Ice Cream Cake	203
Moroccan Stle Red Snapper	169
Mother's Coffee Cake	102
M's Pub Cream of Caramelized Onion and Apple Soup with Brie	54
Mulligatawny Soup	52

MUSHROOM
Bacon, Mushroom and Egg Breakfast Bake	108
Catering Creations' Stuffed Mushrooms	33
Curried Pumpkin Soup	49
Flatiron Café Shitake Crab and Havarti Gratin	97
Layered Mashed Potatoes and Mushrooms	91
Marinated Citrus-Mushroom Salad	77

Mushroom Pilaf	95
Portabello Polynesian	26
Roasted Asparagus with Wild Mushrooms	82
Mushroom Pilaf	95

N

Nantucket Cranberry Pie	191
Nebraska's Fresh Crop Apple Cake	196
New Asian Food Mart	223
Nicolini, Pete	90
Northrup Jones	101
Northrup Jones Chocolate Chip Cookies	222
Northrup Jones Date Nut Drop Cookies	101
Northrup, A.D.	101
Nut Brittle	216

O

O'Brien, Thomas J.	90
Omaha Athletic Club	8
Omaha Country Club Baked Tomatoes and Rigatoni with Garlic	144
Omaha Country Club Grilled Chicken with Vegetable and Goat Cheese Tart	62
Omaha Steaks	223

ONION
Caramelized Onion Dip	15
Caramelized Sweet Onion Soup with Goat Cheese Croutons	50
Grilled Red Onions	92
M's Pub Cream of Caramelized Onion and Apple Soup with Brie	56
Roasted Vidalia Onion Tarts	93
Onion Jam	143

Open Face Peach Pie	190

ORANGE
Cranberry Cooler	40
Mandarin Spinach Salad	63
Marinated Citrus-Mushroom Salad	77
Orange Mushroom Peppered Chicken	160
Sweet Potatoes in Orange Cups	88
Vodka Slushies	44
White Sangria	44

Orange Mushroom Peppered Chicken	156
Overnight Mashed Potato Casserole	89

P

Pan Sautéed Asian Cod	171
Paris Puffins	183
Parmesan Crusted Cauliflower	86
Parmesan Peppercorn Dip	15
Party Nut Bars	214

PASTA
All-Star Spaghetti with Meat Sauce	139
Chicken Mushroom Lasagna	142
Explosive Pork Corkscrew Pasta with Habanero Pesto	137
Fettuccini Carbonara	139
Gorgonzola and Fresh Thyme Pasta	140
Jam's Red Chili Macaroni and Cheese	138
Omaha Country Club Baked Tomatoes and Rigatoni with Garlic	144
Pasta with Lemon Parmesan Cream Sauce	140
Peanutty Asian Noodle Salad	71
Penne Alfio	138
Pesto Bow Tie Pasta with Peppers	137
Shrimp Pasta	144
Taste Pesto	143
Tomato Prosciutto Pasta	141
Tortellini Primavera	141
Tuscan Tortellini Salad	66
Vietnamese Shrimp Rolls	21

Pasta with Lemon Parmesan Cream Sauce	140

PEACHES
Open Face Peach Pie ... 190
Peanutilicious Caramel Candy ... 216

PEANUTS
Asian Chicken Lettuce Wraps, "Larb Gai" ... 30
Peanutty Asian Noodle Salad ... 71
Thai Chicken Satay with Peanut Sauce
   and Cucumber Relish ... 28
Peanutty Asian Noodle Salad ... 71
Pecan Crusted Tilapia ... 170
Pecan, Caramel and Sour Cream Coffee Cake ... 102

PECANS
Apple Pecan Spice Cake ... 103
Bourbon Chocolate Pecan Pie ... 191
Butterscotch Pecan Bars ... 212
Crab Stuffed Flounder Rolls ... 171
Jolly Holiday Spread ... 18
Krunch Kahlua Pecan Pie ... 192
Nut Brittle ... 216
Party Nut Bars ... 214
Pecan Crusted Tilapia ... 170
Pecan, Caramel and Sour Cream Coffee Cake ... 102
Savory Chilled Chicken Salad ... 74
Simply Elegant Sundaes ... 202
Sugar Plum Cake ... 197
Penne Alfio ... 138
Penzy Spices ... 223
Peony Park ... 204
Pepper Cheese Chicken Pinwheels ... 109
Pepper Herb Cheese Bread ... 181
Peppered Tuna Spread ... 17

PESTO
Explosive Pork Corkscrew Pasta
   with Habanero Pesto ... 137
Pesto Bow Tie Pasta with Peppers ... 137
Taste Pesto ... 143
Pesto Bow Tie Pasta with Peppers ... 137
PHG - Premium Home and Garden ... 223
Piccolo, Tony and Grace Caniglia ... 134
Picnic Parmesan Crusted Chicken Breastss ... 167
Pineapple Tea ... 40
Pistachio Lemon Cookies ... 221
Planters Seed and Spice Company ... 223
Plum Creek Farms ... 223
Pork Chops with Parmesan Sage Cornbread Crust ... 147
Pork Piccata ... 153

PORK, CHOPS
Baked Heartland Apple Pork Chops ... 154
Bangkok Pork with Peanut Sauce ... 148
Bourbon-Glazed Grilled Pork Chops ... 149
Curried Pork Chops ... 150
Grilled Honey Mustard Maple Pork Chops ... 150
Pork Chops with Parmesan Sage
   Cornbread Crust ... 147
Slow Cooked Tangy Pork Chops ... 155

PORK, GROUND
Crunchy Pork Bites ... 34

PORK, HAM
Grilled Ham Steaks ... 156
Ham and Cheese Chowder ... 56
Herb Bean Soup ... 56
Royal Deli Salad and Dressing ... 64

PORK, LOIN
Asian Marinade for Pork Tenderloin ... 155
Explosive Pork Corkscrew Pasta
   with Habanero Pesto ... 137
Herb Crusted Pork Tenderloin ... 147
Hiro Don Katsu (Pork Filet) ... 152
Pork Piccata ... 153
Prosciutto Pork Tenderloin Medallions ... 151
Roasted Pork Tenderloin ... 151
Seared Pork Tenderloin
   with Gorgonzola Cream Sauce ... 148
Slow Roasted Pork Roast with Hoisin ... 149
Sweet and Savory Pork ... 154
Thai Pork Spring Salad ... 70
Portabello Polynesian ... 26

POTATOES
Colorful Curried Potatoes ... 89
Baked Potatoes on the Grill ... 91
Bravo Potatoes ... 90
Fresh Herbed Potato Cakes ... 87
Hasselback Potatoes ... 90
Layered Mashed Potatoes and Mushrooms ... 91
Overnight Mashed Potato Casserole ... 89
Potatoes O'Brien ... 90
Ranch Potato Salad ... 77
Sweet Potato Salad ... 76
Upstream Brewing Company
   Smoked Gouda Beer Soup ... 59
Potatoes O'Brien ... 90
Prosciutto Pork Tenderloin Medallions ... 151

PUMPKIN
Curried Pumpkin Soup ... 49
Pumpkin Dip ... 203
Pumpkin Loaves with Caramel Glaze ... 179
Wheatfield's Pumpkin Swirl Bars ... 217

Q R

Quick Carrot Slaw ... 75
Ranch Potato Salad ... 77
Raspberry Lemonade ... 40
Red, White and Green Summer Sandwich ... 131
Reed, Charles ... 206
Reed's Ice Cream ... 206
Reuben Sandwich ... 120

RHUBARB
Apple Rhubarb Crisp ... 189
Rhubarb Pudding ... 189
Sumptuous Strawberry Rhubarb Pie ... 190
Rhubarb Pudding ... 189

RICE
Avgolemono, Greek Chicken and Rice Soup ... 53
Chicken Fried Rice Skillet ... 96
Mulligatawny Soup ... 52

Wild Rice Chicken Casserole	107
Roasted Apricot Chicken	165
Roasted Asparagus with Wild Mushrooms	82
Roasted Green Beans	84
Roasted Pork Tenderloin	151
Roasted Red Pepper Dip	11
Roasted Tri-color Pepper Bruschetta	28
Roasted Vidalia Onion Tarts	93
RoJA Shrimp Alambres with Jicama Mandarin Slaw and Ancho Chili Tartar Sauce	175
Roman Caesar Salad with Seasoned Croutons	66
Ross' Steak House	148
Royal Deli Salad and Dressing	64
Rum Coolers	44

S

SALMON

Barbecued Salmon	173
Miso Glazed Salmon	173
Salmon Cucumber Toasts	22
Salmon with Strawberry Mango Salsa	174

SALSA

Avocado Mango Salsa	13
Black Bean and Corn Salsa	11
Colorful Pepper Tomato Salsa	18
Fernando's Pico de Gallo	10
Stokes Roasted Tomato Salsa	12
Tomatillo Triangles	27
Sam Comento's Steak House	156
Sam Nisi's Spare Time Cafe	146

SANDWICHES

Mini Grilled Cheese and Tomato Sandwiches	36
Red, White and Green Summer Sandwich	131

SAUSAGE

Apricot-Mustard Glazed Sausage Links	111
Brunch Baskets	110
Catering Creations' Stuffed Mushrooms	33
Chorizo Breakfast Burritos with Tomatillo Avocado Sauce	112
English Muffin Breakfast Strata	113
Game Day Gumbo	54
Italian Sausage Vegetable Soup	55
Mini Eggrolls with Zowie Dipping Sauce	33
Scottish Eggs	34
Sautéed Kale with Sun-Dried Tomatoes	86
Savory Chilled Chicken Salad	73
Savory Grilled Fruit Sundaes	202
Savory Vegetable Hamburger Soup	57
Schimmel, Bernard	120
Schimmel, Charles	119
Scooter's Junior League Morning Rush	41
Scottish Eggs	34
Scrumptious Cornbread Salad	62

SEAFOOD

Blue Mussels	31
Caribbean Halibut with Vegetables	172
Charlie's on the Lake Seafood Enchiladas	133
Crab Stuffed Flounder Rolls	171
Dijon Fish Fillet	176
Fresh Tuna Salad with Avocado	63
Hawaiian Macadamia Sole	170
Island Fish Bake	172
Lobster Corn Chowder	51
Moroccan Style Red Snapper	169
Pan Sautéed Asian Cod	171
Pecan Crusted Tilapia	170
Peppered Tuna Spread	17
Sensational Stuffed Red Snapper	169
Wonton Cups	37
Seared Pork Tenderloin with Gorgonzola Cream	148
Sensational Stuffed Red Snapper	169

SHRIMP

Catering Creations Jalapeno and Shrimp Stuffed Tomatoes	32
Charlie's on the Lake Seafood Enchiladas	133
French Café Shrimp Spring Rolls with Sweet Chile Dipping Sauce, The	21
Marinated Shrimp and Peppers	20
RoJA Shrimp Alambres with Jicama Mandarin Slaw and Ancho Chili Tartar Sauce	175
Shrimp Pasta	144
Snappy Coconut Crusted Shrimp with Zowee Mustard Sauce	161
Vietnamese Shrimp Rolls	21
Shrimp Pasta	144
Sibilia, Chef Rinaldo "Reno"	8, 90
Sidewalk Café	59
Simple Single Pie Crust	188
Simply Elegant Sundaes	202
Sioux Z Wow Marinade	33, 161, 223
Six Layer Bombay Cheese Spread	17
Skier's French Toast	106
Slow Cooked Tangy Pork Chops	155
Slow Roasted Pork Roast with Hoisin	149
Smith, Art	9
Smoked Chicken Chipotle Chowder	52
Smokey Barbecued Turkey Burgers	167
Smokey Cheese Pear Appetizer	19
Smokey Chipotle Meatballs	35
Snappy Coconut Crusted Shrimp with Zowee Mustard Sauce	161
Snappy Kickin' Guacamole	12
Snickerdoodle Biscotti	219
Snider, Fern	120
Sons of Italy	124
Sons of Italy Meatballs	124
South of the Border Grilled Corn on the Cob	83
Southwest Salsa Salad	75
Spicy Asian Grilled Chicken	161
Spicy Grilled Flank Steak	118
Spicy Spinach Spinners	22

SPINACH

Chicken Cheese Strudel in Puff Pastry	108

Creamy Spinach Salad	76
Fruit Spinach Salad	72
Mandarin Spinach Salad	63
Spicy Spinach Spinners	22
SpinArt Dip	24
Spinach Artichoke Supreme	94
Spring Strawberry Spinach Salad	64
Tortellini Spinach Soup	51
Spring Greens and Mango Salad	61
Spring Strawberry Spinach Salad	64
Steak House Salad	65
Stokes Roasted Tomato Salsa	12
Stoysich House of Sausage	223

STRAWBERRIES

Salmon with Strawberry Mango Salsa	174
Spring Strawberry Spinach Salad	64
Sumptuous Strawberry Rhubarb Pie	190
Stuffed Orange French Toast	106
Sugar and Spice Sweet Potatoes	88
Sugar Plum Cake	197
Summer Salad	65
Sumptuous Strawberry Rhubarb Pie	190
Sunny Glazed Apple Squares	213
Swedish Cream	204
Sweet Almond Cake	105
Sweet and Savory Pork	154
Sweet and Spicy Bacon	111
Sweet and Spicy Chicken Wings	29
Sweet Magnolia's Banana Chocolate Chip Espresso Muffins	178
Sweet Potato Salad	76

SWEET POTATOES (YAMS)

Baked Sweet Potato Fries	92
Sugar and Spice Sweet Potatoes	88
Sweet Potato Salad	76
Sweet Potatoes in Orange Cups	88
Sweet Potatoes in Orange Cups	88

T

Tandoori-Spiced Grilled Chicken with Mint Yogurt Sauce	158
Taste Pesto	143
Tasting Room Bruschetta	26
Tasty Chicken and Tabbouleh Salad with Avocado	69
Taxi's Cabbage and Bleu Cheese Soup	48
Teriyaki Beer Grilled Chicken	158
Tex Mex Sloppy Joes	125
Thai Chicken Satay with Peanut Sauce and Cucumber Relish	28
Thai Pepper's Fresh Mango Pie	188
Thai Pork Spring Salad	70
Thousand Island Dressing	120
Thunderbird Salad	80
Tomatillo Triangles	27
Tomato Prosciutto Pasta	141
Tomato Tapenade Bruschetta	27
Tomato-Basil Couscous Salad	69

Tortellini Primavera	141
Tortellini Spinach Soup	51
Triple Berry Bread	180
Turco, Lou	201

TURKEY, GROUND

Smokey Barbecued Turkey Burgers	167
Smokey Chipotle Meatballs	35
Tuscan Tortellini Salad	66

U V

Upstream Brewing Company's Smoked Gouda Beer Soup	59
Very Rich Everything Bars	214
Vietnamese Shrimp Rolls	21
Villamonte, Luis	80
Villella, Joe	201
Vivace's Tomato Bisque	48
Vodka Slushies	44

W

| Walnut Lace Cookies | 220 |

WALNUTS

Brie with Bourbon Walnut Sauce	25
Crunchy Pork Bites	34
Extraordinary Oatmeal Cake	197
Manchego Cheese and Smoked Walnut Stuffed Dates	31
Walnut Lace Cookies	220
Wonders of the World Bars	210
Warm Curried Carrot Dip	25
Watermelon-Lemonade with Kiwi Splash	41
Wedding Meatballs	125
Wheatfield's Pumpkin Swirl Bars	217
Wheatfield's Ron's Cornbread	182
White Cheddar Chicken Chili	53
White Chocolate Bread Pudding	193
White Sangria	44
Whole Foods Market	223
Wild Oats Natural Marketplace	223
Wild Rice Chicken Casserole	107
Wild West Beef and Smoked Gouda Grits	127
Wine Cake	199
Wohlner's Grocery	223
Wonders of the World Bars	210
Wonton Cups	37
Woolworths	210
Wow Southwestern Tacos	126

X Y Z

| Zesty Cobb Salad | 61 |
| Zingy Chicken Enchiladas | 132 |

ZUCCHINI

Cheesy Dill Zucchini Bake	107
Chocolate Citrus Zucchini Cake	195
Zucchini Boats	97
Zucchini Oven Crisps	29
Zucchini Boats	97
Zucchini Oven Crisps	29

Yes, I want additional copies of *Toast to Omaha*!

Please send _____ copies of Toast to Omaha at $24.95 each $ _____

Plus $5 postage and handling per book $ _____

Nebraska Residents add 7% sales tax $ _____

Total $ _____

Name _____

Address _____

City _____ State _____ Zip _____

Phone _____ email _____

Payment Method

_____ My check is enclosed (Make payable to Junior League of Omaha)

VISA MasterCard Card # _____ EXP. Date _____

Card verification number on the back of your card _____

Mail to: Junior League of Omaha Attn: Cookbook

608 N. 108th Court • Omaha, NE 68154-1761 • (402) 493-8818

Yes, I want additional copies of *Toast to Omaha*!

Please send _____ copies of Toast to Omaha at $24.95 each $ _____

Plus $5 postage and handling per book $ _____

Nebraska Residents add 7% sales tax $ _____

Total $ _____

Name _____

Address _____

City _____ State _____ Zip _____

Phone _____ email _____

Payment Method

_____ My check is enclosed (Make payable to Junior League of Omaha)

VISA MasterCard Card # _____ EXP. Date _____

Card verification number on the back of your card _____

Mail to: Junior League of Omaha Attn: Cookbook

608 N. 108th Court • Omaha, NE 68154-1761 • (402) 493-8818